ALL POLITICS IS LOCAL

ALL POLITICS IS LOCAL

Why Progressives Must Fight for the States

MEAGHAN WINTER

New York

Bold Type Books
116 East 16th Street, 8th Floor New York, NY 10003
www.boldtypebooks.org
@BoldTypeBooks

Printed in the United States of America

First Edition: October 2019

Published by Bold Type Books, an imprint of Perseus Books, LLC, a subsidiary of Hachette Book Group, Inc. Bold Type Books is a co-publishing venture of the Type Media Center and Perseus Books.

Print book interior design by Jeff Williams.

Library of Congress Control Number: 2019937120

ISBNs: 978-1-56858-838-4 (hardcover); 978-1-56858-837-7 (ebook)

LSC-C

10 9 8 7 6 5 4 3 2 1

For Milko

CONTENTS

INTRODUCTION

ON FEBRUARY 20, 2018, SIX DAYS AFTER SEVENTEEN people were shot and killed at Marjory Stoneman Douglas High School in Parkland, Florida, Representative Kionne McGhee, a Democrat from Miami, stood on the floor of the Florida House of Representatives. Looking on from the gallery above were Parkland students who had traveled over four hundred miles by bus to Tallahassee with the hope of persuading their state lawmakers to pass gun reforms.

McGhee asked the assembly to vote on a bill that would have banned assault weapons and high-capacity magazines. Representative Carlos Guillermo Smith—of Orlando, where a gunman had killed forty-nine and wounded another fifty-three people in the Pulse nightclub in 2016—had sponsored the bill, whose chances would expire unless the House bent its usual protocol and acted right at that moment.

"The shooting at Parkland demands extraordinary action," McGhee told the assembly.

He was trying a technical procedural maneuver, one that might have worked in an alternate reality without partisan politics. But everyone who understood what it meant that Republicans held a supermajority in the Florida assembly knew what would come next.

Richard Corcoran, the Republican Speaker of the House, interrupted McGhee. A few minutes later, the House voted on party lines, 71 to 36, not to consider the assault weapons ban.

In the gallery, students began to cry. On Twitter, student leader Emma Gonzáles wrote, "The anger that I feel right now is indescribable."[1]

Something unusual was happening. With their eloquence, temerity, and rage, the Parkland students had seized national attention. Major news networks and papers dispatched reporters to cover their calls for change. That week in February, even before knowing that hundreds of thousands of students nationwide would soon walk out of their schools and through the streets, the American public paid attention to what was happening in Tallahassee.

And yet from another vantage, the scene in the Florida capitol that day was not all that unusual. In statehouses, it is not uncommon to watch someone sit before a panel of elected officials, hold up a placard of a dead child—killed by opioids or lack of insurance or a gun—and plead for the passage of a bill that will inevitably not move out of committee because it does not fit within the political calculus of the assembly's leadership. In those hearing rooms, ordinary people often share in breathtaking impotence. Three weeks before the Parkland students arrived in Tallahassee, for example, the Florida Senate Judiciary Committee discussed the Rule of Law Adherence Act, which would have required all local government officials—explicitly including employees of the state university system—to turn over information about immigrants to federal immigration officials. The bill was similar to those shopped around the country by the American Legislative Exchange Committee (ALEC), an organization that since the 1970s has written experimental conservative state legislation. ALEC's corporate members include Geo Group, the largest provider of detention services for Immigration and Customs Enforcement (ICE) and a major donor to Florida Republicans and Donald Trump's presidential campaign. In 2016, the federal government decided to stop contracting with private prisons because a Department of Justice investigation had found they were unsafe, but after Trump's inauguration, in early 2017, Geo Group received $774 million worth of contracts to run federal prisons.[2]

On January 30, 2018, the day that the Florida immigration bill was considered in Tallahassee, so many people showed up that the hearing room reached capacity. Muslim students and Latino farmworkers and their teenage children who had traveled hours to testify against the bill weren't allowed in the packed room. Expressionless, they watched the proceedings on a television mounted in a hallway as Florida senator Aaron Bean stood at a podium and said his bill "means criminals will be kept off the streets." The bill did not advance, in what counts as a victory, in part because in 2011 immigrant rights groups staged weeks-long protests in Tallahassee to oppose a bill modeled after Arizona's 2010 law that allowed police officers to ask for immigration papers if they suspected someone was undocumented. The Florida legislature didn't pass a new aggressive anti-immigrant law until 2019, when it gave the state the power to sue local law enforcement that refused to detain people according to orders from federal immigration agencies.

The next day, January 31, Floridians concerned about sea level rise arrived in Tallahassee by the busload to ask their legislators to pass a raft of proactive climate-related reforms. Many were college students or recent graduates who had grown up along the coast and understood that the window of opportunity for stalling climate change was closing; during their lifetimes, they told me, their hometowns would be radically altered, if not sunken. By the end of the legislative session that March, none of the bills they wanted were passed, even though just ten years ago it was all but mandatory for both Democrats and Republicans in Florida to at least make overtures about the need for proactive environmental laws.

Similar scenes play out in hearing rooms across the country, usually unrecognized by the American public. Beneath the tumult of the Trump presidency, state lawmakers have largely kept to their course. As ALEC's own website explained in 2017, "State legislatures around the country have made significant progress passing bills on issues such as immigration, policing and healthcare, even as Republicans in Congress and President Trump have struggled to make similar progress at the federal level." After decades of state-based campaigns coordinated by libertarian and Republican operatives and disinvestment in the states by Democrats and progressives, right-wing politicians have swept control of statehouses across the country. The consequences of those divergent strategies are glaring today. Democrats hit a rock bottom in November 2016, when Republicans won control of either the state legislature or the governorship, or both, in forty-four states. In twenty-five of those states, like Florida, Republicans had hit the trifecta—governorship, House, and Senate. Democrats, meanwhile, had a trifecta in six coastal states. The significance of those numbers leaps out at you when you look at a map from 2009, when Democrats dominated or shared control of many states that ten years later would become blood red.[3]

For years, it has been an open secret in political circles that Democrats and progressive interest groups have prioritized federal candidates and policy at the expense of the states. The liberal political establishments—party officials, interest group and union leaders, donors and consultants—have for the most part under-resourced state-based efforts since at least the 1970s, with repercussions that have only recently been obvious to the general public. "Conservatives have traditionally had this view that they want to build and invest and focus at the state level where progressives and Democrats have really centralized and tried to build their power in Washington, DC. And I think that that theory has had negative implications for and negative consequences for Democrats and progressives across the country," said Nick Rathod, then director of the progressive organization State Innovation Exchange.[4]

The moment I grasped the severity of the power imbalance in statehouses was on a Thursday afternoon in May 2016, when I was in Jefferson City, Missouri. I was there to report on how outmatched abortion rights advocates were, but I saw all around me that the problem extended far beyond reproductive rights. In the last days of the legislative session, capitol buildings become places of frenetic energy, with lawmakers, aides, and lobbyists stalking hallways and staying awake through the night to pass or reject final bills. That Thursday, I was weighing whether to go to the capitol basement for a meeting about the Senate holding a Planned Parenthood CEO in contempt or go upstairs to listen to the House debate a bill that would have made all abortion illegal without an exception for the life of a woman. That week the assembly was also debating (and ultimately passed) what would be the first stand-your-ground gun law to take effect since Trayvon Martin was killed in 2012. I wondered whether I should watch that debate instead. As I hovered in the gray limestone hallway trying to decide which way to go, I ran into the lone ACLU lobbyist, who tracked five hundred bills related to at least a dozen issues. She told me the assembly was on the verge of passing a voter ID law, and she couldn't believe a controversial move to suppress voting rights in an election year wasn't getting any attention outside the statehouse. Now in the situation that progressive advocates in red-state capitol buildings routinely find themselves, pulled between multiple urgent priorities, I eventually rushed upstairs to watch the House debate.[5]

Some days later, when I was on my way home, several liberal blogs and news sites publicized a moment in that debate. Representative Tila Hubrecht, a trained nurse representing District 151, a southeastern parcel of the state, had said that conceiving a child during rape could be a "silver lining" from God. On the internet, Hubrecht was excoriated.[6] I realized I had heard her comment in real time and had barely registered the line. Out of context, Hubrecht could be laughed off or criticized for being one particularly absurd lawmaker, but if you had watched just a sampling of the hearings, debates, or demonstrations in Jefferson City that year, you would know that her remarks matched the tenor of dozens of other comments and the overall ethos of the assembly, which passed, by a margin of 110 to 37, the baldly unconstitutional bill she was advocating for.

Dismissing Hubrecht as a lone wacko didn't get at the heart of the issue. Each of the bills that made their way to assembly floors that spring were bellwethers of how much political sway the lawmakers who sponsored them held and which voting blocs the state's political leadership feared. In assemblies across the country, legislators were debating bills that ten years earlier might have seemed too far out of bounds to ever make it to the floor. In statehouses and administrations, the conservative movement was deploying, and succeeding with, its death-by-a-thousand-cuts strategy to whittle away at industry regulations, civil rights protections, and the social safety net. Meanwhile, because they had less power in statehouses, Democrats and progressives were not enacting solutions to the problems they prioritized. After Republicans won hundreds more state legislative seats in 2010, groups like Americans for Prosperity, ALEC, and National Right to Life had more success with their bills. Between 2011 and 2018, while the national media tracked federal politics to the exclusion of so much else, state governments passed over four hundred abortion restrictions. In 2016 alone, seventy-seven bills that would have restricted voting rights were introduced or carried over in twenty-eight states. In 2015, Wisconsin's governor Scott Walker signed a "right to work" law, making his state the twenty-fifth in the nation to prohibit unions from requiring dues from their members, which in effect drains unions of their resources and power. That year in North Carolina, after four years of slashing public education budgets by hundreds of millions of dollars, the state legislature passed a law that restricted food assistance to unemployed adults and required all employers to verify employees' immigration status, plus another law that prohibited the removal of Confederate monuments. Those bills are just a few of thousands, many almost identical, each a manifestation of the extremism that had become ordinary, with national implications.

During the summer of 2015, meanwhile, the Clinton presidential campaign joined together with the Democratic National Committee and thirty-two Democratic state parties with the expressed goal of rallying to "rebuild our party from the ground up." The joint effort raised some $60 million. But a Hillary Victory Fund staffer was depositing money in the state party coffers, only to send most of it back to national campaigns working to elect

Clinton. Only about 1 percent of the money raised went to the state parties, prompting one state party leader to call the arrangement "one-sided."[7] After that election, Democrats hit their rock bottom. This example is not an indictment only of Clinton and her staff; it is essentially forty years of the liberal establishment's priorities distilled.

Those priorities made sense for a long time. On the national stage, Democrats held control of the House of Representatives for forty-two years. Investing in national lobbying made sense for left-leaning groups. Besides, from before the Civil War, notions about the sovereignty of the states had been wound up with justifications for racial oppression.[8] For contemporaries of the civil rights movement and those born in subsequent generations, grainy footage of southern governors refusing to allow integration and permitting white police officers to beat with batons and set dogs on black protesters reinforced the idea that state officials were hell-bent on impeding progress, whereas the federal government—albeit reluctantly and inadequately—intervened to ensure a measure of justice. Trying to pioneer civil rights reforms via Mississippi's or Alabama's statehouse would have been absurd. Besides, the whole point of the movement was securing civil rights for everyone in the country, not just a lucky few. That basic premise stuck. The baby boomers who have steered the Democratic Party and left-leaning interest groups for years came of age under the assumption that the federal government is the most meaningful venue for social and political reforms.

In recent years, we have seen those assumptions unravel. As Rich Templin, legislative and political director of the Florida AFL-CIO,[9] told me, "The state level is everything. Everything that has a negative impact on people's lives happens on the state level." While that reality, minus some exceptions, is evident to anyone who has spent time tracking just about any issue from labor to energy to guns, for decades that idea failed to gain much traction among Democratic Party operatives, the directors of left-leaning foundations and interest groups, and liberal donors. At the same time, the interest groups affiliated with the left deemphasized local organizing, choosing instead to defend and expand their policy goals through advocacy and litigation. To a certain extent, that has begun to change. In the Trump era, new activists and organizers have lent might to local progressive efforts. During the high-stakes 2018 midterm elections, Democrats gained trifectas in six states, flipped six legislative chambers, and broke Republican supermajorities in four more. Those gains, while meaningful, still did not reverse the effects of 2010, when seven hundred Republican state legislators were elected, or all of the previous years when libertarians and conservatives invested in their networks in capitals like Jefferson City and Tallahassee. Republicans continue to have outsize power on the state level across the country—and that little-understood power continues to build on itself, as we will see in coming pages.

We are on a precipice. It remains unwritten whether the newfound activism on the left and reinvigoration within the Democratic Party will sustain itself. There is a difference between winning an election cycle or two and executing a long-term, proactive political strategy. The Democratic gains in 2018, including on the state level, were largely considered a reaction against Trump. "This moment has radicalized liberals and electoralized the radicals," Maurice Mitchell, director of the New York Working Families Party, summarized.[10] That change was significant. But we can't miss that the backlash against Trump, though often awe-inspiring, was nonetheless largely reactionary. For decades, the pattern has held that progressive groups have raised more money and attracted more members during eras when their missions have been threatened, as during George W. Bush's presidency, than when they have secured wins. No matter how loud or organized they have been in the past couple of years, Democrats and progressives are still conforming to that historic pattern; they are more politically energized when they are obviously losing. Meanwhile, for decades, Republicans and their allies have been proactive, staking out long-term goals that have tilted the power dynamic to their advantage. Many crucial Republican victories that changed national politics were first won on the state level. Now, as the winner-take-all 2020 elections approach, progressive funders, strategists, and activists will have to decide whether they will get out of defensive mode and make that constant, yearlong, proactive and persistent work in the states a priority for the long term.

To advance a proactive agenda, Democrats have to win in the states. Defeating Trump in 2020 might be most Democrats' ultimate goal. The 2020 presidential election is, of course, a profoundly high-stakes contest. However, Democrats and progressives cannot focus on that race, and other federal races, to the exclusion of down-ballot races and state-level policy work, or they will damn themselves to the same long-term power imbalances that led to their nationwide rock bottom in November 2016. The coming chapters of this book will illustrate why. One important reason is that statehouses are venues where lawmakers can propose ideas, set the terms of debate, and push the nation in a progressive direction.

Former Supreme Court justice Louis Brandeis wrote, "It is one of the happy incidents of the federal system that a single courageous State may, if its citizens choose, serve as a laboratory."[11] State-based campaigns for progressive reforms have worked, throughout history and within the last year. Some northern states abolished slavery eighty years before the Civil War. Wisconsin passed unemployment insurance as a model for the nation. In the 1960s, California set a higher emissions standard for vehicles. Overlooking what is happening in the states also means missing proof that victories like those are possible. In the 2018 midterms, voters in three red states—Utah, Nebraska, and Idaho—expanded Medicaid to cover more low-income workers. Washington passed a bill enshrining net neutrality in the state.

The scope and the importance of what is happening in state governments across the country are underreported, even though it is impossible to understand our political landscape without accounting for who is in power in places like Tallahassee and Little Rock and St. Paul—and who is organizing nearby. National political battles are now waged in the states. And they will be for the foreseeable future. Right-wing strategists have explicitly chosen to pursue their goals on the state level. Until recently, everyone else has largely failed to respond, for reasons that this book will explore. In those same statehouses, lawmakers hammer out the details of state budgets that literally lay out what our culture values. In recent years, in the competition for airtime, though, those proposals, like dozens of others that rolled through obscure state committees, championed by unknown lawmakers, were no match for thousands of people protesting the "Muslim ban" at airports across the country, or the *Today* show's Matt Lauer being accused of sexual harassment and assault, or Kim Jong-un boasting about his nuclear weapons, or Stormy Daniels saying she had been paid off for staying silent about an affair with President Trump, or any of the dozens of other urgent or salacious national stories that also needed to be reported. Social media algorithms and editors have been proven to privilege what is splashy, and opinions are easier to produce than detailed reports on pension funds or redistricting commissions.[12] Attention is recursive; people pay attention because everyone is paying attention. When you have never heard of a public service commission, you don't care who its members are, even if their decisions bear directly on climate change, and in turn your mortgage and insurance rates, and the fate of your city. Locked in trances of controversy, readers may not know how much they are missing as they scroll.

In the rare instance that local bills spark national discussion, those bills are usually described in isolation, as one-offs. Outrage momentarily ripples across television screens and social media, but the public doesn't necessarily see how those bills fit into a far-reaching, long-term national agenda. In recent years there has been much discussion of how race, gender, class, and other identities "intersect." Likewise, issues like guns or labor protections or clean energy that may seem separate are in fact entangled, not only in individuals' lives but in policy and political calculations. That is true on the federal stage—as in Trump's racial taunts facilitating a tax code that benefits billionaires—but also in less obvious maneuvers in the states. It is impossible to understand why, for instance, Wisconsin gave the Taiwanese manufacturer Foxconn, which produces iPhones, $4 billion worth of tax breaks and permission to ignore environmental rules unless you also understand not only corporate lobbying but also how expertly Governor Scott Walker broke the local unions and how local gun rights and antiabortion organizations turn out conservative voters to every election.[13]

There is almost no one with the necessary platform to describe how hundreds of seemingly disparate—and often ostensibly random or insignificant—bills are specifically designed, along with hundreds of others, to consolidate power for Republican lawmakers and their patrons. In recent years, giant hedge funds have acquired local newspapers struggling after the financial crisis and the explosion of online media. Investment funds have bought legacy papers like the *Denver Post* and shrunk their staffs, leaving fewer reporters to cover more terrain. Between 2004 and 2014, just as the right's coordinated campaigns in the states accelerated, local newspapers lost about a third of their full-time statehouse reporters. The remaining staff doesn't have the bandwidth to capture everything that is happening, let alone present the bird's-eye context about how one bill fits into a long-term movement. "No one has the luxury to spend all day in a hearing," one former statehouse reporter in Florida told me. Meanwhile, the largest owner of local television stations in the United States is the pro-Trump giant Sinclair Media. After Sinclair buys a station, its coverage becomes more conservative and nationally focused.[14] And, finally, after years of media consolidation, six conglomerates own and control much of the news media—everything from FiveThirty Eight.com to Fox News. As they have consolidated, those conglomerates have also focused more on national news.

As a result, even if you don't go in for Fox News or conservative talk radio, you are unlikely to come across comprehensive reports on state laws unless one of those laws is challenged and makes its way to a federal court—or someone in that state is running in a close race for a federal position. Popular podcasts produced with political junkies in mind are no better on this front. On those shows, week after week, DC- or New York–based journalists often engage in circular self-righteous glee or concerned analysis about the Trump administration's various misdeeds, or they speculate about congressional races as if discussing a fantasy football league.

And that is exactly the point. Right-wing strategists have chosen to implement their policies on the state level because almost no one is paying attention. "Since we are greatly outnumbered," Charles Koch told a roomful of his libertarian allies as they wrote their plans, they would have to exploit their "superior technology" "to create winning strategies" that they would deploy with stealth.[15] On the other hand, a longtime progressive strategist told me that because his group's policies tend to be more popular, "Our side almost always benefits from shining a light."

★ ★ ★

The stakes were already high, and manifold. On June 27, 2018, the stakes became much higher. Justice Anthony Kennedy retired from the Supreme Court, giving President Trump a second nominee to the highest court. Kennedy had long been considered a swing justice; lawyers arguing cases concerning abortion and voting rights and other issues tailored their arguments in the hopes of appealing to him. With Trump's nominee, Justice Brett Kavanaugh, confirmed and serving on the Supreme Court, conservatives have a majority, all but guaranteeing that the court will give states more leeway in writing their own laws about a wide range of issues, from emissions standards to public school funding to contraception access to voting rights. As of April 2019, the Trump administration had installed thirty-seven federal circuit court judges and fifty-three district court judges, record numbers. "One of the most significant accomplishments in President Donald Trump's first year will serve Americans for decades to come, yet it has received very little fanfare," Senate majority leader Mitch McConnell and Senator Chuck Grassley wrote of the new judges in the *National Review* in 2018. Like the conservative Supreme Court justices, those federal judges will evaluate state laws that were written, lobbied for, and passed by conservative groups and lawmakers with whom they share a network of mentors and patrons.[16]

In the past, when state governments went out of bounds, national interest groups sued and relied on the courts to uphold federal laws like the Clean Water Act and precedents like *Roe v. Wade*. That was generally the left's strategy, as we will see. Now, for the foreseeable future, litigation might still work in certain circuit courts but not in others. The guardrails have shifted. If state lawmakers vote to prohibit gay couples from adopting children, for example, a gay rights group may pause before suing the state; what if the case climbs the courts and ends up creating a nationwide precedent restricting gay parental rights? By the time you are reading this book, states may have already decided to outlaw abortion within their borders. You may be tempted not to care. Those state laws may appear to be a problem only for someone else, somebody living in Missouri or Utah, but as we will see in coming chapters, seemingly disparate local laws in fact have broad national consequences.

There is no reasonable path to defending against expanding corporate and right-wing power and advancing a lasting progressive agenda that doesn't include making inroads on the state level across the country. That is true for several reasons beyond obvious policy matters. First, in thirty-one states, state legislators draw the district maps for Congress and the state legislature races. Since the 2016 elections, much more media attention has been given to those maps and why they matter. Whoever wins control of state legislatures ahead of 2020 will have their chance to redraw many maps, forcing their opponent to play on their terms for a decade.

Conservative state lawmakers have worked to undermine the will of progressive city residents in another crucial way that has gotten much less attention: Since 2010, state lawmakers have increasingly passed so-called preemption laws, which restrict towns and cities from passing laws different from those approved by state lawmakers. Many organizers have told me that they believe real change happens on the city level. That makes sense. In cities, there are fewer barriers to drawing attention to and organizing around shared problems. And yet if their allies can't wield power in statehouses, Democratic mayors and city councils can't fully represent the will of their residents or enact their own solutions to their constituents' problems. Conservative state leaders can override them. At least twenty-eight states have restricted cities from increasing their minimum wage. As of 2018, twenty-three states had prohibited local paid medical or parental leave policies. States have also preempted cities' ability to pass laws about immigrants' rights, LGBTQ protections, tax rates, gun ownership, fracking, and pesticide runoff. Several state legislatures have considered bills that would give them total veto power over all local municipalities' laws. The blueprints for these recent laws have come from ALEC. But the concept isn't new. In the antebellum South, state lawmakers took the same tack and prevented cities from passing their own laws that would change the "relationship between master and slaves," as John C. Calhoun, former vice president and early states' rights advocate, put it. Later, the tobacco industry began lobbying to write bills that would preempt local regulations on their business. Today, when cities are disproportionately black, brown, immigrant, and LGBTQ, and rural voters have outsize voting power, preemption laws once again magnify the power of conservative white Americans.[17]

Another reason that the states hold a key to long-term progressive power is that the left needs to build its bench. Barack Obama was first elected to represent a Chicago district in the Illinois Senate. Since Obama's presidential term, much has been made of the gap of leadership in the Democratic Party. Both Hillary Clinton and Bernie Sanders supporters voted for a grandparent. State governments and local advocacy and organizing groups provide training grounds for political talents. The left's long-term disinvestment in the states partially explains why for years there was a relative dearth of national leaders in their thirties, forties, and fifties. The voices of the young are especially important now as we grapple with collective social and economic dilemmas and stall on solutions to rising student debt, widening health and income disparities, and the existential threat of climate change, dangers whose consequences are and will be disproportionately felt by today's young people.

★ ★ ★

American politics is increasingly nationalized. We are all pulled in by the same controversies, even if the spin on our individual screens is different. National organizations fund campaigns and experiment with cookie-cutter legislation in far-flung local governments. In some ways, that obliterates the old maxim "all politics is local." Originally, the saying reminded politicians that voters care about the issues that affect their localities. Today, it underscores another crucial set of truths. Especially ahead of redistricting, there is no way for a political party or social movement to win long-term without building strategic power in cities and states. Republicans have expertly used gerrymandering and local laws to disempower sources of Democratic strength. And state Democratic parties and progressive social movements cannot thrive without thousands of volunteers inserting themselves into the local culture, talking to their neighbors, organizing public events, meeting with lawmakers, and showing up to vote. Local players turn essential gears of our politics, and we can't forget that again.

This book tells stories of people working on the ground in three states: Missouri, Florida, and Colorado. The fifty states and their respective legislatures are all distinctive enough that it is impossible to generalize about them. The cultures and economies of, say, Wyoming, Georgia, and New York are obviously all different. State legislatures meet on dissimilar schedules, for different durations, some annually, others biennially, adhering to a wide range of ethics laws and expectations. In 2018, state lawmakers were paid anything from nothing to $104,000. Because state legislatures are usually in session only part of the year, because capitals are often moored far from major urban centers, and because legislative pay varies so greatly between states, serving as a state lawmaker is incompatible with most people's lives. Who can work nonstop three months a year a hundred miles from home for a relatively low salary with a mortgage or rent to pay and children to raise? A 2018 *Tampa Bay Times* report found that Florida state legislators were 147 times more likely to be CEOs and 37 times more likely to be lawyers than Floridians as a whole.[18] Those lawmakers can't possibly reflect the will of all Floridians, nearly half of whom struggle to meet daily needs like housing and food. That barrier to participation extends across the states and creates a disconnect between the general public and the inner workings of legislatures. The state capitols I have visited all remind me of high schools: in the hallways, people often move in packs according to entrenched allegiances and social hierarchies all but inscrutable to anyone whose frame of reference is outside their doors. But all fifty chambers do share some important traits, not least of which is being test kitchens for legislation and politicking.

I have chosen Missouri, Colorado, and Florida because they each have something to tell us about how Democrats and progressives lost, and how they might win again—not within a single campaign cycle but over the long haul. These states are not places where it is inevitable that right-wing politicians will control the narrative and agenda. Nor are they places where a progressive movement is easy to assemble. In national elections, they have all been swing states. We will look at each state through a different lens. In Missouri, we will trace how Republicans and their allies won power by weaponizing charged cultural issues—guns, abortion, and race—to drive a wedge between longtime Democratic voters. Those issues are often discussed on the national stage, but you can't understand why Democrats lose without understanding how the politics of guns, abortion, and race play out on the state level. Next, in Colorado we will look at how and why that state became a model for progressive organizers. During the early 2000s, Colorado Democrats and their allies built a local progressive machine to supplement the flagging local Democratic Party. Colorado proves that progressives can work together and new ideas can be implemented. In particular, we will look at the new generation of activists and lawmakers. Finally, there is Florida, where we will see what Democrats are up against when politics is transactional, driven by enormous sums of corporate money. Here we will look at why Florida is won or lost by a razor's edge in national elections but Republicans have had a lock on the state government for twenty years. And we will see that the failures of the Democratic Party and progressive organizations have dire consequences for our futures.

We don't focus on those stories enough. Any news or narrative about state government that rises to the surface tends to frame the Koch brothers or the NRA as the protagonists. And no wonder tales of plots of right-wing takeovers capture the imagination. People or groups who take decisive action in pursuit of clear goals make for excellent characters. The Koch brothers' desires, for example, put them in conflict with the interests of millions (if not billions) of people. From a purely dramatic standpoint, what a perfect story. In contrast, it is difficult to tell a story about an absence. It is almost impossible to prove a negative. And yet even the most detailed understanding of the right-wing plot doesn't mean very much if we don't also understand why there hasn't been an effective effort from the left to counter or compete with the conservative movement for control of the states. Why aren't there more progressive or even centrist leaders in statehouses? Because of choices not made, money unspent, organizations not sustained, would-be leaders never elected.

★ ★ ★

Our old language is inadequate. Before we go any further, I have to acknowledge that terms I have already used—progressive, leftist, Democratic—are not synonymous. The Democratic Party is one thing. Progressives are another. Sometimes those categories slide into each other, and sometimes Democrats and progressives are each other's antagonists. The party is a legal entity, a standard bearer of a proclaimed (if shifting) plank, and so the party and its self-described members are easier to define. Everyone else—who are they? The white suburban mothers who are registered Republicans and hold rallies for background checks for gun sales? The twenty-something climate change activist who told me that he did not identify as a leftist or progressive but humanitarian? The Black Lives Matter protesters? The immigrant rights activists? The congressional candidates running for reelection, rebranding themselves as progressives even though they voted for the Keystone Pipeline and the Iraq War? Even as partisanship is apparently at all all-time high, there aren't enough words for the people I have met, for all they want and believe. That we don't have clear definitions is part of the story. "We're inventing things so much that we don't even have the vocabulary to describe what we're after," Charley Olena, advocacy director at New Era Colorado, a youth organization, told me. "On the one hand, I think it's a good sign. It does make me think that we are headed in the right direction." She told me she defaults to "progressive," acknowledging that it doesn't contain everything. In the chapters that follow, unless I am explicitly talking about a particular cause or the Democratic Party, I will do the same.

Missouri, Florida, and Colorado each offer a window into the dilemmas inherent in building political power for ordinary people—those who don't have the built-in power that comes with being a lawmaker or billionaire. And the people working on the ground from Denver to Jefferson City to Tallahassee all provide a glimpse of what can be achieved. Today, as our culture shifts before our eyes, as protest becomes routine, reflexive, for middle-class white women as well as black and immigrant youth, the open question is whether any of these mass mobilizations, these new candidates for office, will bring about concrete change. How can we be sure that the wave of energy that has rippled through the country in the past couple of years is not just a reactionary burst that will eventually fade away as people get bored or busy or disaffected? We have seen that it is possible to galvanize Americans, to move the masses into the streets, but what needs to be accomplished before the will of those people is reflected in our culture and in the law? What structural changes need to be made before the passion of "the resistance" is cemented into not only dedication but institutions that will carry the mantle when any one person burns out?

CHAPTER ONE

"YOU COULD WRITE A WHOLE BOOK ABOUT THE PROBlems with progressive funders" is a line I heard—almost verbatim—from multiple people, of different generations, in different roles, living in different states. The "funders" came in two main varieties: institutions like charitable foundations, and ultrarich individuals whose gifts were massive enough that they eclipsed many small-dollar-donations combined. (Foundations, as we will see, are the vessels the ultrarich use to hoard and dispense their fortunes at their discretion, so there is plenty of crossover between the two varieties.) The funders' role in the progressive movement is more pivotal than I had realized when I began my reporting. Critiques of how corporations and billionaires influence our politics often center on the Supreme Court's decision in *Citizens United*, which said that political spending is a form of free speech protected by the First Amendment and therefore the government cannot prevent corporations and unions from spending in political races. That ruling transformed electoral politics by prompting a meteoric increase in campaign spending by untraceable donors. Likewise, in recent years another critique that has become fashionable is that the Democratic Party has been co-opted by corporate interests, particularly Wall Street. But discussions about the parties and electoral politics only begin to scratch the surface of why state governments have become so unresponsive to the problems facing the American public and why it is so difficult to build a sustained, proactive progressive movement.

Many of the foot soldiers advocating for social change today are not explicitly working within the party structures; they are community groups, advocacy organizations, lobbying outfits, as well as political action committees. For decades now, libertarians and conservatives allied with the Republican Party have been able to rely on their own foot soldiers, whose organizations span the country, promoting their ideas and organizing political actions all year, rather than only during campaign blitzes. Their megadonors have long invested in maintaining a constant local and statewide presence, which has translated into greater influence on the state level in particular and our politics in general. Since 2010, for example, the Koch-funded Americans for Prosperity has set up offices in thirty-eight states and now claims over three million members.[1] As one progressive put it to me, "Donors on the right support the same old boring institutions year after year." Progressive funders, meanwhile, have not made the same consistent investments. More than that, progressive funders are operating according to a different set of incentives, an underrecognized distinction with major repercussions. That a relatively small number of ultrarich people pull the levers of political power in our country is not breaking news. Americans across the political spectrum disapprove of the amount of money spent on political campaigns. In the post–*Citizens United* era, when millions upon millions of anonymous dollars are being shoveled into our political system, it may seem strange to start by scrutinizing foundations and ultra-wealthy individual charitable donors, but they are often overlooked and misunderstood. To understand how Democrats lost so much ground across the states, and to understand the challenges ahead for sustaining progressive gains, we have to understand why for so long progressive groups outside the party structure weren't able to apply a constant counterpressure to Chamber of Commerce and

Americans for Prosperity lobbyists and the like. Before we travel to Missouri, Colorado, and Florida, we have to pause on "the funders," as they are called. Their incentives undergird the entire story, from coast to coast.

One example crystallizes the core of the problem. After Congress passed the Affordable Care Act (ACA, popularly known as Obamacare) in 2010, insurance companies, right-wing foundations, and Republican state lawmakers coordinated to seize their opportunity. Blue Cross Blue Shield's lobbying efforts during that time are a stunning illustration of how under-the-radar corporate advocacy happens in the states. Blue Cross Blue Shield lobbied for Congress to include in the Affordable Care Act the individual mandate—the requirement that anyone uninsured buy insurance through the marketplace the government would establish. But Blue Cross Blue Shield also simultaneously worked with ALEC to write and push state legislation that said that the Affordable Care Act was unconstitutional because of that same individual mandate. ALEC laid out those potential state bills in a 2011 guide titled *The State Legislators Guide to Repealing Obamacare*. That package of bills is just one example of a set of state laws designed to climb the courts, with the aim of whittling away at Democratic federal policy. And because in 2010 Republican operatives had enlisted corporate donors—including Blue Cross Blue Shield—to help elect a wave of Republican state lawmakers, those bills had eager sponsors from Arizona to Georgia.[2]

Where were the foundations whose grant makers proclaim all over their websites and, presumably, during their thousand-dollar-per-plate galas that they exist to help improve the lives of the most vulnerable? It would seem that those foundations should be able to mount a counteroffensive to protect health care for the working poor. The annual spending of centrist and left-leaning foundations far exceeds the annual spending of the conservative Heritage Foundation or the Scaife Family Foundation. The Gates Foundation, generally considered a centrist and exemplary institution, is far and away the largest American foundation, with an annual budget of almost $4 billion. Every year, the left-leaning

Ford Foundation, the distant second largest, spends roughly $500 million. After the ACA passed, nonprofit organizations across the country coordinated outreach efforts to educate people about how to sign up for health coverage under the new program. They did not, and perhaps legally could not, orchestrate the kind of legal and political maneuvers, or mass collective actions, that would have been necessary to keep the new insurance program intact for the long term.

Right-wing groups, meanwhile, were already mounting their opposition to the ACA through legal challenges. The Cato Institute, a libertarian think tank, had sued the federal government within hours of President Obama signing the ACA. That suit was later thrown out, but several right-wing foundations and institutes backed by billionaires like the Kochs and the Mercers kept supplying legal arguments for its dismantling. By the end of 2011, twenty-seven states had joined a lawsuit against the federal government challenging the ACA's individual mandate and its requirement that the states expand Medicaid to cover low-income Americans. The challenge wound up in the Supreme Court, which upheld the core of the ACA and the individual mandate but decided that the states should decide for themselves whether to expand Medicaid. Within a couple of years, seventeen Republican-controlled states had decided not to expand Medicaid. Roughly two and a half million people whose incomes ranged approximately from $9,000 to $12,000 per year were caught between making too much for Medicaid but too little for marketplace subsidies and so went uninsured. Those tidy numbers—seventeen states, two and half million people—do nothing to portray uncapturable anxiety and suffering. Rendering what that loss of health coverage meant for individuals and their families is for another book. The task at hand here is to consider why, when it was well documented that right-wing groups were waging a multipronged political and legal challenge to low-income workers' access to health care, more foundations did not or could not fund a defensive strategy to protect them. That failure represents a much broader pattern.[3]

As one progressive organizer (not named in these pages) summarized for me: "Foundations are full of shit." If that seems overly dismissive or cynical, consider what foundations can and cannot fund. Of all the pivotal actors in our nation's political dramas, the Internal Revenue Code may not stand out, but its importance cannot be overstated. Many structural barriers to organizing ordinary people begin there, with that tax code that divides tax-exempt nonprofit organizations into two kinds. This is crucial: 501(c)(3) organizations are known as public charities and are barred from electoral activity and restricted from certain kinds of lobbying; 501(c)(4) organizations are described as advocacy organizations and are allowed to lobby with restrictions and can do some election-related work. But those (c)(4) organizations cannot receive government grants or contracts. Foundations cannot give (c)(4) organizations funds for election or issue-related lobbying. And individual donors can't take tax exemptions for their donations to (c)(4) organizations or campaigns. That means that donors generally have more incentive to give to public charities instead of advocacy organizations. The sheer volume of grants reflects as much. In 2017, foundations, corporations, and individual donors in the United States gave out about $410 billion to charitable organizations, much more than the $6.3 billion given as political donations. That explains why foundations decided to educate Americans about how to sign up for the ACA rather than lobby or mobilize citizens in defense of it—because education fit very safely within the IRS's public charity guidelines. For reasons we will get to in a moment, most centrist or progressive-leaning foundations are still very cautious about avoiding anything that might be perceived as undue advocacy.[4]

There is, of course, no such thing as apolitical giving, or an apolitical stance. Absenting oneself is its own political choice. Ordinary people bear the brunt of political decisions made without the heft of centrist or leftist philanthropic dollars. But those dollars are rarely distributed in ways that help ordinary people build long-term political power.

Foundations vary enough that it is difficult to paint them all with the same brush. But with few exceptions, the way centrist and left-leaning foundations parcel out their grants undermines possibilities for long-term social change. First, the grants themselves are usually modest sums, with very narrow specifications. Even foundations considered forward-thinking for their commitment to civic engagement dole out only a few thousand dollars at a time. Foundation Source, which advises foundations, found that in 2016 the average grant from an affiliated foundation with an endowment larger than $10 million was roughly $21,500. For foundations with endowments less than $1 million and those with less than $10 million, the average size of a grant was roughly $6,000 and $8,900, respectively—and those were increased sums from previous years.[5] The Gill Foundation in Denver, for example, is often cited because it has given progressive Coloradans seed money. And yet—according to a database at Foundation Center, a nonprofit that tracks philanthropy—the Gill Foundation's donations to Colorado community organizations in 2015 ranged from $2,000 to $255,000 annually, with the median somewhere around $10,000, hardly enough to run a nonprofit in a major city. Likewise, the Ford Foundation is a top donor to civic engagement programs, and yet its grants typically last only a single year. At the end of those short funding cycles, nonprofit directors are asked to account for how much social change their staff has been able to create in a year, with, say, $9,000. The answer, of course, is probably not very much. Organizing people and agitating for structural change, by definition, takes a very long time, and progress isn't necessarily linear—or obvious until decades later, as the right-wing campaigns in the states prove. That long-term work is made even harder because nonprofit directors are forever fund-raising to cobble together a budget. Fund-raising has become a full-time job. Funders are perpetually hunting for "the shiny new penny," and unlike their libertarian counterparts they rarely support the same group for decades. Organizations' constant uncertainty over resources means that they can't lay ambitious plans or guarantee their staff stable jobs. The sense of scarcity also means that would-be partner organizations with similar missions end up competing for attention and credit, which sows division and threatens the possibility of broad coalitions.

Furthermore, in most cases the funding agenda is set from above, not from the people on the ground. In fact, funding specifications may complicate or run counter to the needs of an organization's members or staff. "If you wonder why a group is doing what it's doing and it doesn't make sense, they're probably doing it because of the funders," one political nonprofit staffer summarized. No one working in nonprofit or political circles can publicly criticize these foundations, or wealthy individual donors, who hold the purse strings. And because few donors are willing to fund any sort of meaningful civic engagement in the first place, nonprofit and political staffers vying for limited resources and coveted access have even more reason to keep their criticisms to themselves.

The farce of this system is laid out in foundations' financial reports. A quick glance at foundations' investments is enough to glean that their directors aren't exactly angling to reconfigure the current economic order. The Ford Foundation owns tens of millions of dollars worth of stock shares of companies like Walmart and Facebook. The Gates Foundation owns corporate bonds for the defense contractor Lockheed Martin and several major banks like Wells Fargo and Bank of America, and stock in hundreds of major companies, including a Chinese nuclear power plant. Yes, this is how the world works. Expecting rich people (or anyone) to surrender all their worldly possessions is ridiculous. But so is forgetting that these foundations serve as tax shelters, investment funds, and status symbols. Protecting their donors' ability to make tax-deductible donations—which then multiply thanks to investments in companies like Exxon—is a primary reason why foundation directors are skittish about funding programs that the IRS might deem too political. Foundations' priorities are also reflected in their executives' salaries: in 2017, the Ford Foundation, for example, paid its director of public investment $1,093,083, its director of private equity $1,111,896, and its director of hedge funds $1,077,034. While many foundations undoubtedly subsidize life-saving programs, the reality is that they also consolidate wealth and power for a small clutch of ultrarich individuals, who in turn exert tremendous influence on our nation, with barely any accountability. Self-described political operatives are often perceived as self-interested or underhanded. In contrast, powerful philanthropic donors are often publicly veiled with the gauzy status of do-gooder, even as they use their power to shape the nation according to their preferences.[6]

Foundations and individual philanthropists act with little transparency, but they often require scrupulous accounting from their grantees, another trend that indirectly has prevented community groups from flourishing and state-based coalitions from forming. Bill Gates and others have spread the idea that foundations should be run like businesses, with decisions evaluated by clearly defined metrics. In theory, it makes sense that donors should want their grantees to be accountable for spending money well. The irony is that funders' obsession with achievement means that they don't achieve as much as they could. "Human relationships are about as inefficient as they come," reflected Carol Hedges, executive director of the Colorado Fiscal Institute, and yet relationships are the cement of most kinds of work—and especially community organizing, leadership development, and other forms of civic engagement. When those kinds of human relationships—for example, growing trust between community organizers and their underserved neighbors—don't translate in a grant report, a program might seem like an "inefficient" use of resources and therefore a risk for another round of funding.

Driven by their desire to spend on programs that can prove themselves on paper, foundations often give out those small or short-term grants. "Too many in the funding community are risk-adverse," one longtime observer tells me. When the foundation doesn't want to "take the risk" of sinking money into a long-term grant, nonprofit employees—often women and people of color—absorb personal risk by working with only short-term job security, almost always for relatively low salaries. "At some point it becomes unfair to your kids," one progressive told me. Foundations also often stick with service programs that work directly with people—like soup kitchens or school programs. If grants are remitted to an education program, grantees can report back concrete numbers of teachers trained or children tutored. If similar sums are donated to a small community organization that seeks to build low-income workers' power, it is much harder to measure success in concrete terms, and the grant officers who dole out funds for foundations have a harder time justifying their decision. As a result, as David Callahan, founder of Inside Philanthropy, said, most foundation grant makers end up "thinking like a social worker instead of thinking like a Bolshevik," the very opposite of the approach taken by those doling out the Koch and Mercer fortunes.

★ ★ ★

Right-wing foundations' forefathers, meanwhile, literally modeled themselves after revolutionary Russians, as unlikely as that sounds. And their work has always been located in state and local governments. Since the 1970s, right-wing political operatives and their ultra-wealthy patrons have invested in a web of organizations, from think tanks to local groups, that work in tandem and make their presence known week after week, not only during election cycles. Republican allies do have built-in advantages when conscripting confederates for their battles on the state level. Conservatives, after all, believe that state legislators should be the officials who decide our laws; their philosophy lends itself to concentrating state legislative power. Simple geography also explains why they can more easily network with supporters. Along the roads leading to the capitol buildings in towns like Lansing, Carson City, and Des Moines are Farm Bureaus and Chambers of Commerce and churches. A capital city is rarely a state's most diverse urban center, where Democrats tend to be packed. But another major factor in the right's advantage on the state level is its funding priorities.

To this day, right-wing donors sustain three main organizations that specifically push their agenda in the states: State Policy

Network, Americans for Prosperity, and ALEC. State Policy Network describes itself as an umbrella group for local think tanks that "cultivate thriving free-market movements in every state." Americans for Prosperity was founded in 2004 by Charles and David Koch, the billionaire owners of the giant conglomerate Koch Industries, and who as of 2019 are tied for eleventh place on the *Forbes* list of the richest people in the world. Because of their major donations and leadership in organizing other donors, the Kochs all but took control of the Republican Party starting in the late 1990s. Americans for Prosperity has chapters in a majority of states, where, among its other campaigns, it advocates against expanding Medicaid. And, finally, there is ALEC, which brings together corporate leaders, political strategists, think tank wonks, lawmakers, and others to write and chart the best course for model "pro-business" legislation.[7] Of the three, ALEC is probably the best-known tentacle of what has been dubbed the Kochtopus. But, as one longtime progressive strategist says, "people make too much of ALEC," as if that one organization alone is responsible for reconfiguring the American economy and political landscape. Instead, ALEC is "one cog in a very large machine." That the machine's gears turn together, synchronized, explains why the right's megadonors and their hires are so effective.

On leftist websites and in certain corners of the press, ALEC is often painted as evil because it passes around model legislation and coordinates lawmakers and interest groups across the country, as if the coordination itself, not the content of the bills, is what is nefarious. Coordination between lawmakers and groups with similar goals, including sharing model legislation, is in fact savvy, if not imperative. The substance of ALEC's lobbying and legislation—which gives cover to coal and payday loan and pharmaceutical companies and more—is the problem, not necessarily its methods. It is also worth considering why ALEC is so useful to legislators. New state lawmakers rarely have previous experience as an elected official. But there they sit in their navy blazers, beside heavy velvet curtains: cattle farmers and nurses, community organizers and tax attorneys, tasked with deciding how to vote on hundreds of bills on wide-ranging, often arcane topics like drainage runoff and municipal bonds for highway repairs. Within the space of two hours, a lawmaker might be presented with policy proposals on everything from hunting licenses for feral hogs to hospital reimbursements for Medicaid. Because lawmakers are expected to act on a dizzying amount of minutiae, it is unsurprising that they lean on outside experts. The most experienced people working in the halls of the capitol are often lobbyists, some of whom were once lawmakers. Those lobbyists—whether from an oil company or the ACLU—understand the state's inner workings and can translate complicated issues for inexperienced or harried lawmakers. That basic reality also explains what a significant blow it was to progressive ideals when left-leaning interest groups decided to stay focused on Washington, DC.

★ ★ ★

Understanding how and why, in contrast, far-right political strategists built a durable, interlocking network that spans the nation requires looking back at the Supreme Court's unanimous 1954 decision in *Brown v. Board of Education*, which found that segregated schools were unconstitutional. Decades later, years after *Roe v. Wade* was decided, pundits and analysts would say that the ruling fanned the flames of the culture war because it was premature, the nation wasn't ready. If white parents denouncing the integration of public schools in New York City, a supposed bastion of progressivism, in 2018, is any indication, the nation is still trying, and failing, to come to grips with *Brown*. That ruling had stark, immediate results, as well as less visible, long-term consequences for the tensions between the states and the federal government. It also shaped the proactive strategy that right-wing donors and strategists now largely take for granted. At the time, the Supreme Court had previously ruled against segregation, but never in a way that so extinguished states' authority. James Buchanan, then an unknown white southerner, was alarmed by the *Brown* decision and decided to set up a center that would proliferate ideas about how federal laws robbed individuals of their rights. Years later, the Buchanan Center would help connect some of the wealthiest men in the country, including Charles Koch and Richard Scaife, a founding patron of ALEC. (ALEC, almost unbelievably, is a (c)(3) organization that is supposed to only "educate," not involve itself in partisan advocacy.) In its earlier days, the Buchanan Center's self-anointed libertarian masterminds began a campaign of making public arguments about states' rights. The same southern state legislatures that had once passed the infamous Jim Crow laws began passing laws that codified disapproval of *Brown*. Senator Harry F. Byrd claimed publicly that Virginia, which led the charge, was defying federal power so that it would better represent Virginians. In reality, the Virginia legislators who voted to reject *Brown* represented fewer people than the legislators who voted to respect the federal government's mandate. As in many states and Congress both then and today, the Virginia legislature was apportioned so that white rural voters were overrepresented. By the end of 1956, the state legislatures of eleven southern states had passed 106 measures that supported the "resistance" to *Brown*. Across the South, violence against blacks continued, and whites questioned integration.[8]

The federal government was moving in the opposite direction, albeit slowly. During Lyndon Johnson's presidency in the 1960s, the federal government funded programs with the explicit aim of mitigating poverty and increasing civic participation. Private foundations often subsidized progressive efforts, too, by bankrolling new public-interest law firms and grassroots coalitions like the Citizens Crusade Against Poverty. Johnson signed the Civil Rights Act of 1964 and the Voting Rights Act of 1965, which prohibited a variety of local laws that had made it more difficult for black Americans to vote. Liberal foundations underwrote massive campaigns to register voters. It was well understood that those developments didn't sit well with many white Americans, nor with some elected officials. All those new voters posed a direct threat to incumbent members of Congress. In 1969, the year that Nixon assumed the presidency, Congress began hearings on foundations' political involvement. The Ford Foundation, a leader in the voter registration charge, received special scrutiny.

The bitter congressional hearings sent the message that centrists and left-leaning foundations should avoid overt political work if they wanted to be left alone. That same year, Paul Weyrich, already a Republican adviser, was accidentally invited to a meeting of liberal strategists. Later, Weyrich remembered that they had a "whole panoply of liberal groups, from the think tanks to the media to the outside groups to the legal groups to the political groups." He had an epiphany—the right needed what he called the "new conservative labyrinth." From that year until today, foundations mostly went down two divergent paths: foundations that could be perceived as centrist or liberal kept neutering overt "political" activity, as required keep their tax-exempt status, whereas foundations affiliated with the right built a "conveyer belt" of right-wing political activity.[9] Those divergent tracks represented a fundamental difference in how right-wing donors viewed themselves and their role in American society. Funders on the right believed their task was to sponsor structural transformation, and they understood that to accomplish such transformation, they needed to fund that "conservative labyrinth" of institutions that would generate ideas, pursue litigation, write policy, elect politicians, and speak to the public.

That mission was about to get a major arsenal. Two months before Nixon nominated him to the Supreme Court, in 1971, Lewis Powell Jr., a director of Philip Morris, sent what would become an infamous letter to his old friend, Eugene B. Sydnor, a director of the United States Chamber of Commerce. The directive, known as the Powell Memorandum, is widely credited with changing the course of corporate involvement in American politics. At the time, public-interest attorneys were suing corporations like DuPont and Koch Industries for the dangerous effects of their products and the byproducts of their industries, a direct threat to Philip Morris. Powell urged the Chamber of Commerce to "press vigorously in all political arenas," because "the time has come—indeed, it is long overdue—for the wisdom, ingenuity and resources of American business to be marshalled against those who would destroy it."[10]

The letter was distributed among the chamber members and their colleagues, who took to heart its threats of their potential doom. Powell's language might seem hyperbolic to a modern reader, but libertarian businessmen and academics were already trading in conspiratorial thinking. The Buchanan Center in Virginia had been quietly humming along for about fifteen years by then, building a cadre of donors, thinkers, and political operatives. As Nancy MacLean reveals in her book *Democracy in Chains*, the intellectual foundation of the libertarian political machine that has installed radical-right lawmakers and enacted their laws nationwide was far more extreme that anyone outside its close circle of founders could have imagined. Its inventors rejected the labels "conservative" or "Republican." Instead, without irony, they called themselves "revolutionaries." They wanted a total upheaval. MacLean writes that in the 1970s, around the time that Charles Koch entered the fray, James Buchanan had decided his cadre's "focus must shift from *who* rules to changing *the* rules."[11] They would dismantle public employee unions, defund public schools, and chip away at Americans' trust in their government not through one-off campaigns but by altering the fundamentals of the law to benefit them.

Within a few years of Powell's Memorandum making its rounds, corporate leaders and deep-pocketed heirs who felt persecuted because of their wealth had set up a constellation of foundations that were gearing up to change the nation's legal framework. The donors and organizers technically ran separate entities but recognized the importance of cooperation and coordination. They prized making time for idea creation and relationships. Early members of Charles Koch's think tank, the Cato Institute, borrowed lessons from Vladimir Lenin, who during the Bolshevik revolution had taught the necessity of sustaining "strong and fruitful alliances." In the 1970s and '80s, several symbiotic conservative and libertarian institutions emerged. Years later, James Pierson, a scholar at the Manhattan Institute, dispelled the idea that businesses had initially ushered in the ideological shift, saying, "What we did was way too controversial for corporations."[12]

As those donors and operatives were laying the bedrock of what was fast becoming our plutocracy, a more visible scandal was unfolding: Nixon resigned. His descent presented the Republican Party with an urgent public relations problem. As Republican advisers scrambled to perform damage control, Weyrich began assembling what would become the New Right, designed to poach Catholics and Evangelicals from the Democratic Party. He brilliantly reframed antiabortion sentiments and policies as "pro-family" and made them a core part of the Republican plank.[13] As a coalition, the New Right would endorse slashing taxes and as much of the social safety net as voters would allow—but it would market itself primarily as a beacon of religious principles and conservative social values.

The strategists aligning around right-wing causes chose to focus on pressure points that would be especially damaging to the Democratic Party and progressive social movements. Early targets of the right-wing campaigns were the unions—and public-sector unions in particular, for two main reasons. First, of course, unions were the first line of defense against a range of libertarian economic proposals, from stripping away workplace protections to cutting taxes and firing teachers. Second, the Democratic Party had long relied on big unions as their primary donors and stable of volunteers. In many longtime Democratic strongholds like Michigan and New York, but in other states, too, the unions and the Democratic Party machine were (and to a certain extent still are) synonymous.

Union membership has decreased in recent years, and even the most powerful unions aren't able to deliver surefire Democratic wins as they did in their heyday. One cause is the "right to work" laws enacted in twenty-seven states. During those same years, a majority of unions turned inward and focused on negotiating with their employers rather than staying agile and pulling more workers into broader political battles.[14] To grasp the significance of unions' decline, it is essential to recognize that unions are different from volunteer groups like Indivisible. Workers join unions because they have an urgent, pragmatic stake in their work, not because of their ideology or personality. An Indivisible member, however, joins for ideological or emotional reasons that may drop in priority if she gets busy with work or family. The full scope of the unions' decline has been documented elsewhere, and later chapters will touch on how progressives on the ground sought to supplement unions' flagging influence, but for now it is important to understand that the right-wing operatives knew that gradually declawing unions was an integral part of the plan. Many of the aforementioned fund-raising problems on the left stem from local Democratic parties coming up empty when searching for replacements for the union dollars that once buoyed them.

Koch and his compatriots were too smart to push for sweeping changes from the outset, whether they aimed to defund public schools or deregulate the oil and gas industry. Instead, libertarian strategists proposed chipping away through legal minutiae specifically designed to be too boring or complicated to rouse public protest. Later, conservative legal strategists, corporate lobbyists, and state lawmakers would use the same tactics to push forward their agenda affecting a range of issues from voting rights to abortion to clean water. They deliberately pushed for incremental changes, knowing it would take years to achieve their goals. Just like declawing the unions, each of the right-wing strategists' priorities accomplished multiple goals at once. They rarely if ever pursued a policy that did not also simultaneously leverage their political power by either creating a structural advantage for themselves or disempowering their opposition. Voting and abortion and union restrictions and more all achieved immediate policy goals, but they all also began turning the entire political landscape to favor Republicans. It would take a bird's-eye view to see the ongoing structural changes, and few Americans outside the political class had that vantage.

By the 1980s, the once-radical long-term plan was in the mainstream and well on its way. Right-wing operatives had successfully unified pillars of institutional power. They had quantifiable power in the form of donations from corporations like Chase Bank, attorneys from the Catholic Church, and direct access to the president, but they also had potent cultural myths and taboos that they could wield. Kate O'Beirne, former vice president of the Heritage Foundation, said in the late 1990s, "We've largely won the battle of ideas. We are in the implementation stage now."[15]

★ ★ ★

There lies the heart of the power imbalance between the right and left. It is often said that the right has more money. Depending on who is defined as "the right" or "the left" and what money is counted, the right does in fact often have much more cash at its disposal. Republicans typically have the backing of many more corporate donors. But it is not just that the stack of cash is higher. Corporate and wealthy donors to right-wing politicians and groups have a built-in incentive to give. When those wealthy donors give to strategists and politicians who promise to rewrite the rules, they are literally making an investment. If their preferred candidate or policy advances, they will likely see material returns on money spent, whether through a tax cut or a billion-dollar contract to run power plants or private prisons. Because the rules are rewritten in their favor, their influence perpetuates itself. This may seem like an obvious point, but it deserves underscoring. If corporations act in rational self-interest—and they have a legal fiduciary duty to make decisions that benefit their shareholders—they and their leaders are going to invest in policies that protect and enrich them. Donors across the right, then, often have a shared unifying principle. They may differ on a range of social issues. Today, for instance, Americans for Prosperity opposes the Common Core education standards, whereas the Chamber of Commerce supports them. But, generally, donors on the right have reason to make long-term strategic donations to political groups that will do their bidding. Those groups, like State Policy Network, don't have to sell themselves as charmingly subversive or cutting-edge, so long as they are practical—and so long as they cut corporate taxes and business regulations.[16]

Reliance on wealthy patrons makes liberal groups especially vulnerable, and not just from critics alleging hypocrisy. Many progressives told me that they hoped that the new volunteer groups like Indivisible will reinvigorate a movement driven by citizens, not professional activists and advocates. Volunteers are freer to agitate for what they want on their own terms. And yet philanthropy is a major driver determining which organizations survive and which Americans get to steer social change. Left-leaning groups are at the mercy of their donors' mercurial or passive priorities in a way that their counterparts on the right generally are not. Centrist and left-leaning foundations, as described, often scrub any insinuation of politics from their public images, or they give relatively small sums to, say, community groups that pledge to clean a river, while also owning shares of an energy company that pollutes rivers.

Wealthy individual donors on the left, whether they are funding a political campaign or nonprofit charity, are not giving out of rational self-interest from an economic standpoint. They give out of a sense of goodwill or moral urgency or ego. If their donations are effective enough, they could be undermining the economic interests of their own families. Those donors are fulfilling an emotional or moral need. They may be especially aggrieved over a specific cause, like disparities in women's health or education. Research shows that wildly wealthy people are more economically conservative and socially liberal than Americans overall.[17] Taken together, their individual preferences and values don't track as neatly onto a long-term strategic plan. What seems most interesting or hopeful or exciting and therefore worthy of support varies by the individual and can change by the day, especially for people whose lives are not at stake in these battles.

Individual billionaire donors are free from fiduciary duties and so can bet on a bold progressive leader by, say, hurling upward of $7 million into his campaign, as San Francisco–based hedge fund manager Tom Steyer did in 2018 for Florida gubernatorial candidate Andrew Gillum. But their freedom to follow their hearts can be a detriment to their preferred causes, too. Nonprofit directors and political strategists often see no choice but to tailor themselves to donors' ephemeral desires. Consider Steyer, one very public example of an unbridled megadonor. His foundation is a major and important donor to environmental causes. Since Trump was elected, Steyer has been on a public rampage to try to have him impeached, long before the Department of Justice released the Mueller report and well after Speaker of the House Nancy Pelosi and other prominent Democrats said publicly that seeking impeachment was not their priority. Democratic leaders have reportedly asked Steyer to quiet down and put his energy elsewhere, but he hasn't listened. Regardless of how heedless his strategy is, he can barrel ahead. Meanwhile, environmental groups across the country are scrounging for dollars and could have used more of his help for lawsuits, or even gas money to get volunteers to their elected officials' town halls. "A lot of our problems are about ego," a longtime progressive lobbyist told me.

The core difference in incentives also explains why left-leaning donors have historically not invested as much in state governments. Possessing a family fortune and a sense of grandiosity doesn't typically inspire a person to spin into moral outrage over what is happening in a hearing in Topeka or Lansing. Gains in state capitals are by definition incremental, which is to say humble. Starting in the 1970s, alert progressive organizers tried time and again to pull together organizations to support their allies in statehouses. Inevitably, donors handed them just enough money so that they could start their venture but not enough for them to keep going. In 1975, just two years after ALEC was founded, progressive organizer Lee Webb started the Conference on Alternative State and Local Policies, which provided wraparound support—conferences, model legislation, background research—for left-leaning lawmakers and advocates. Despite enthusiasm from lawmakers, the organization struggled to find steady funding and faded away in the 1980s. In the 1990s, Progressive States Network, another similar endeavor, came together and then fell apart after the unions stopped giving. In 2005, Joel Rogers, a sociology and law professor at the University of Wisconsin, tried to start the American Legislative and Issue Campaign Exchange (ALICE), which he envisioned as the left's answer to ALEC, but Rogers—who by then had thirty-plus years of political experience and a MacArthur genius grant—couldn't find donors willing to support the project. He did finally start a version of ALICE, a library of model legislation and policy research for state lawmakers, but with its modest funds ALICE couldn't fully replicate and counter ALEC.[18] In 2013, Rogers founded State Innovation Exchange (SIX), which provides model bills and organizes conferences. Several progressive lawmakers told me that SIX was helpful to them. It is also worth noting that these kinds of organizations can only be very effective if their allies hold power in statehouses and governor's offices—which often relies on campaigns having the money or manpower to turn out voters.

One fund-raiser and organizer explained, "Rich people don't care about state government." Another said state policy is "not sexy to donors."[19] What liberal donors do love, I was told, is a program with a unique, special air. They also revel in what one person called "the *New York Times* version of social change," meaning elite-oriented and federal in focus. The left, then, is largely guided by the moral whims of rich people, whereas the right is guided by their rational business decisions. This difference bears out in their spending decisions, and in Americans' lives. A change may be coming, as we will see when we get to Missouri, Colorado, and Florida, where donors and political nonprofits are trying new strategies.

CHAPTER TWO

Missouri

IN ST. LOUIS IN THE FALL OF 2017, RADIO DJS ALERTED listeners—in the same campy tone they used to announce Top 40 songs and birthday shout-outs—that protesters had blocked another road. Six years earlier, on a December night, a white police officer and veteran of the war in Iraq named Jason Stockley had fired five shots into a Buick, killing Anthony Lamar Smith, a twenty-four-year-old black man. An audio recording from the moments before the shooting had captured Stockley telling his partner, "We're killing this motherfucker, don't you know." In 2016, the office of Attorney General Chris Koster, one of the last remaining Democrats to hang on to statewide office in Missouri, sued the city of St. Louis, accusing Stockley of murder and of planting the handgun he claimed to find in Smith's car.

On September 15, 2017, Circuit Court Judge Timothy Wilson acquitted Stockley. The day of the acquittal, hundreds of protesters gathered in the streets of St. Louis. By nightfall, a small group of protesters became violent, throwing bricks at police offers. Police in riot gear used tear gas and arrested more than thirty people. Two days later, police in riot gear with batons charged through the streets using tear gas, rounding up and arresting over one hundred protesters, prompting the ACLU to file a lawsuit charging that the officers had used excessive force. Every day for weeks the protests continued, people standing together, blocking traffic in the middle of major highways and main thoroughfares.

The Stockley verdict protests had grown, in part, out of the nearby Ferguson protests over the death of Michael Brown that gave birth to the Black Lives Matter movement. The Ferguson protests, and the later acquittal of police officer Darren Wilson, disrupted what had long been the status quo in St. Louis, a Democratic city in a newly bright red state. In November of 2014, under the longtime St. Louis County prosecutor, Democrat Robert McCulloch, a grand jury decided not to indict Wilson. Local Democrats' handling of that case was another tipping point. "Part of what happened is that a lot of average, everyday black folk woke up to the reality that the Democratic Party in Missouri is primarily designed to protect the labor voter," one progressive told me. "[Local Democratic Party leaders] don't care what the person says as long as they're a good, strong union vote."

The leaders of the local Democratic Party and some of the bigger unions had been locked in a symbiotic relationship for generations. Race was such a dividing force in St. Louis that the city's white and black firefighters had separate unions. The old guard union and party leaders were white Democrats accustomed to setting a centrist or culturally conservative agenda. That began to change after 2014. A diverse coalition of activists who came together during the Ferguson protests expanded their work to include electoral politics. In the next few years, that coalition recruited and generated support for unapologetically progressive candidates for the city board of aldermen, the state assembly, and other local posts—and in several cases, they won. In 2016, Bruce Franks Jr., for example, was elected to the Missouri State Assembly. Franks—whose nine-year-old brother was used as a human shield and killed in a gunfight in 1991 when Franks was six—was a lead organizer of the Stockley verdict protests, during which he was arrested several times. He told local news outlets, and crowds, that the protests were supposed to be nonviolent but disruptive.

I traveled to Missouri because it was a state where the center was not holding. Missouri represented a web of dilemmas and contradictions that Democrats nationwide were facing and will face for the foreseeable future. On one hand, the progressive activists in Missouri were a couple of years ahead of their counterparts across the country—they had erupted into the streets and then hurled themselves into winning local elections before Democrats nationwide did so after 2016. They were determined not to avert their gaze from the thorniest questions of American life. And on the other hand, for the past fifteen years, Republicans had steadily taken over the state capitol and ditched the moderate stances that had long defined Missouri politics. In 2016, Republican Eric Greitens won the governorship, and Trump took Missouri by nineteen points. In less than a generation, Missouri had gone from a Democratic stronghold on the local level, and a swing state in national elections, to a solidly red state.

Especially after 2012—when Republicans won a supermajority in the legislature, gaining the ability to override the Democratic governor's veto—the rhetoric in the capital, Jefferson City, took a sharp rightward turn. State lawmakers proposed a bill that would require Syrian refugees to live in internment camps and another that would eliminate all corporate taxes. Those bills were among the most extreme, never likely to become law, but the overwhelming majority of Missouri lawmakers endorsed right-wing policies. In 2016, for example, state lawmakers refused to expand Medicaid to cover low-income Missourians, leaving hundreds of thousands of people uninsured. The state legislature's actions that year also showed that no matter how successful St. Louis or Kansas City progressives were in winning support for their ideas in their cities, they would hit a ceiling if they didn't also grasp power on the state level. St. Louis and Kansas City progressive and labor groups had worked over years to raise the minimum wage in their respective cities from $7.70 to $10 per hour, starting in 2017. In 2018, it was supposed to increase to $11. During the 2017 legislative session, the state capped the state minimum wage at $7.70 per hour, revoking that wage increase and preempting Missouri cities from trying to raise wages again. The state legislature also kept in place laws allowing employers to discriminate against gay people. And, between 2005 and 2015, as the Republican supermajority calcified, the state gave at least $5.2 billion in tax cuts or subsidies to private businesses, and further slashed taxes for the highest individual earners.

To reestablish themselves, Missouri Democrats needed to win back rural areas, known as "outstate." The state's two major cities—Kansas City to the west and St. Louis to the east—were Democratic strongholds, along with Columbia, a college town in the center of the state, but the local party was so hollowed out that Democrats hadn't even run candidates in many rural districts in recent years. In 2016, Stephen Webber, a then thirty-three-year-old white former marine who had served in Iraq, became the new chair of the Democratic Party of Missouri. He spent a year traveling the state, visiting every county, making promises of a Democratic revival. One argument held that the Democrats' surest way forward was emphasizing "kitchen table" economic issues like jobs and wages. It made a certain sense. And yet Republicans hadn't won over Missouri on the strength of their economic policies. For one, Missourians tend to support unions, and many of its most prominent Republicans were openly antiunion. But that was exactly the problem—there wasn't much solid evidence that Missourians had voted for local Republicans on the basis of their economic planks. Instead, local Republican candidates were loudest about divisive questions like abortion and guns and "law and order," the very questions that Democrats themselves could not always agree on. Several white self-described progressives I spoke with in St. Louis expressed ambivalence over the Stockley verdict protests. Local Democrats were also divided on whether abortion rights should be included in the party platform. If they were skittish, how would white rural voters be anything but disapproving?

There it was—one of the central dilemmas at the heart of progressive politics, where moral obligation and political calculation are often at odds, embodied in the protesters linking arms in the road, in the skeptical voices of the radio interviewers in St. Louis asking questions like, "Can you really expect the police not to use pepper spray? Isn't that handcuffing the police?" The thinking—among Democrats in Missouri and in many other states—was that if Democrats further alienated white suburban and rural voters, they could very well sabotage their long-term efforts to win back the districts necessary to regaining power statewide and nationwide. Time and again, Missourians told me that a wide portion of the rural voters made their decisions based on "God, gays, and guns." Democrats needed to win statewide to further most of their agendas—like expanding Medicaid, for example—and deliver concrete benefits to disenfranchised Missourians. Plenty of Missourians were in urgent need: per capita, Missourians are likelier to live in poverty and without health insurance or enough food than Americans as a whole.

And yet if Democrats further marginalized the ascendant generation of progressive activists and the people they represented, they were hypocrites, or milquetoast obstructionists, the very kinds of "white moderate . . . more devoted to 'order' than justice" that, as Martin Luther King Jr. wrote in his *Letter from the Birmingham Jail*, were a "greater stumbling block" to his freedom than Klansmen.[1] The deeply emotional issues that roiled Missouri, and the rest of the country, were about people's fundamental rights and dignity. They were not about the fine print of some policy, the details of which could cause two reasonable people to disagree. You can't really come up with a "centrist" or "compromise" position on something like racism or reproductive rights without undermining another person's dignity. The tension was also about more than ethics. The palpable energy of the left is in the cities. Women and black voters make up the base of the party. St. Louis voters voiced their preference for leaders willing to stand up for abortion rights and gun reform. Was it even possible that Democrats would win anything statewide that would be worth betraying their core supporters and professed ideals? The electoral data suggested they wouldn't. After Missouri drew new maps that favored

Republicans in 2010, fewer than one in four legislative districts were considered competitive for both Democrats and Republicans, and a majority of districts overall were solidly Republican.[2]

That was, and remains, one of the prevailing tensions for Democrats as they try to reclaim lost ground in Missouri and nationwide. We can't understand our current political landscape, wherein rural white voters have disproportionate power, without understanding how guns and abortion were transformed into political wedges of colossal importance, creating sharp ideological lines between people who might otherwise agree. Racism, of course, is interwoven into that history. If you are just watching the national news, it is easy to underestimate what a chokehold these issues have on our politics. Battles over gun laws and abortion laws are largely fought in the states, and so only by looking to the states can we understand how they have transformed the electoral map, and what stands in the way of progress on those issues. The story of how guns and abortion shaped American politics also illustrates what it takes for a social movement to push against the current and eventually turn the tide, gathering its own cultural, political, and legal momentum.

★ ★ ★

In October 2017, I drove out of the city and through long expanses of farmland toward Mexico, Missouri, 120 miles northwest of St. Louis. Downtown Mexico has an old-fashioned town square with a pizza shop, multiple payday loan places, and a jewelry store with display windows decorated with plaques and medals for 4-H Beef Stockmanship from the Audrain County Fair. Two miles away is a strip with a Walmart Supercenter, auto shops, and an Aldi. This region was one of the nation's first longtime Democratic strongholds to turn red, foreshadowing Republican sweeps on the state level, nationwide, from 2010 to 2016. What happened here was emblematic of a larger pattern, although few noticed it at the time. On January 24, 2001, Missouri held special elections to fill a few spots in its state legislature. That week, as television cameras focused on George W. Bush ascending to the White

House, the average citizen probably didn't see the local elections as a seminal political moment. At the time, Missouri Democrats were used to controlling the whole trifecta—House, Senate, and governorship—and moderates ran the capitol in Jefferson City. Ahead of the 2001 special election, local Republican and Democratic Party leaders, recognizing what was at stake, had funneled an unprecedented $700,000 into the race for just one state Senate seat, which Republican John Cauthorn would win.

Republican strategists had one urgent reason to pour those hundreds of thousands of dollars into an otherwise unremarkable race for Missouri's mid-state District 18, a tract roughly the size of New Hampshire, covering sparsely populated farmland and small towns. Missouri's district lines would be redrawn that year, and state legislators would draw the federal congressional districts that would stand for the next ten years. The state legislative lines would also be redrawn, by a partisan panel of legislators who would likely create maps to protect incumbents. After decades of trying to win on the Democrats' board, Republicans saw their opportunity. They hired a public relations firm to focus on District 18, the one likeliest to swing red. The pollsters used what are now commonplace but were then cutting-edge polling analytics to determine that Cauthorn, then president of the Missouri Cattlemen's Association, should skip issues that would normally pull in centrist Democrats, like school funding, and instead campaign primarily on issues that would "motivate voters," like abortion and guns.[3]

The plan worked—that year and to this day. And so here I was in Missouri, driving toward Cauthorn's family farm. The day of that special election in January 2001, Democrats ceded two Senate seats—Cauthorn's and one other—thereby losing the Missouri Senate for the first time in sixty years. Local reporters wrote that the two Republican wins could foreshadow something more, but few could have predicted how quickly those two dominoes would set off the collapse of the local Democratic Party. Meanwhile, appeals about abortion and guns are still the go-to issues that reverberate across outstate Missouri.

After I turned off the paved road, the world of the Walmart Supercenter and the Aldi receded, replaced by a grid of gravel roads that divvied up gaping cattle pastures and soy fields and wooded lots. The voices on the radio turned to static. The farms out there, set deep inside those grids of white-gray gravel, were more remote than I expected. Across the horizon there was nothing but soy, roughly a foot tall, golden on the stalk and starting to curl, ready for harvest, framed by scattered trees. John Cauthorn's life is inextricable from these fields of lilting soy. He had inherited land that his family first took possession of in 1837. Missouri had only just become a state in 1821, on the condition that slavery would be legal within its borders—an offering to the slave South, as Maine was then joining the Union as a free state. So, in what was called the Missouri Compromise, Missouri became "little Dixie." From its conception, the state of Missouri was predicated on the idea that a compromise, however misguided, could seal together a fractured nation. During the Civil War, one hundred thousand Missourians fought for the Union, fifty thousand for the Confederacy. In some ways, the battle for Missouri continued long after—until just a few years ago, local and national groups continued to count it as a bellwether state. Both major political parties had reason to invest there.

I arrived at Cauthorn's house at an especially busy time—he had spent the morning harvesting soy—but he invited me into his kitchen. Under a wooden plaque with PRAY stamped in wine-colored paint, Cauthorn told me, "In my earlier years, I probably thought of myself as a Democrat, basically because everything in this county was slanted that way.

"I'm just going to be straight with you. I think God wanted me there," he said, of running for office. He ran primarily "because of the life issue," meaning his antiabortion stance. Just before he ran, he said, the Democratic governor had "twisted the arms of rural legislators" over abortion, upsetting locals. His other two primary issues were "the Second Amendment" and improving local roads, which had fallen into disrepair.

As we talked, Cauthorn kept returning to a central idea: "I truly believe we need strong state legislative bodies to understand local issues and to protect us from the federal government." He explained that his skepticism of the Democratic Party had crept up over time, beginning back during Johnson's Great Society, which sought to redress racial injustice. When the government rolled out those social programs, he said, he started fearing for his own health care and Social Security, because in his opinion funding safety nets meant "tak[ing] money away from the people that actually were supposed to get that money." Cauthorn, who inherited fertile land, believed completely in his own independence, and believed others must likewise create their own independence, too. When he began working with the Cattlemen's Association, which shares ties with the Republican Party, his drift rightward continued.

As he spoke, with a flat affect, in short, matter-of-fact sentences that carried a whole worldview within them, I considered how many factors had had to coalesce for Cauthorn to become not only a winning candidate but someone whose attitudes were well represented, if not the dominant force, in Missouri's state government. Immediately ahead of the election, the Republican Party had swooped in with pollsters and public relations firms, yes, but that one marketing decision—focus on guns and abortion—wouldn't have worked without the hidden structural advantages that Republicans had built up over time. And it wouldn't have happened if liberal groups hadn't left so much territory wide open.

When the Republican Party approached him, asking for potential candidates, Cauthorn was already a trusted community leader because he led the Cattlemen's Association. That and other farm associations, much like the Chamber of Commerce, promote "pro-business" policies, which generally translates to loosening regulations. The local associations also, by their very existence, take the first necessary step of community organizing by connecting people to those with similar practical needs and points of view. The American Farm Bureau Federation, the largest farm association, has long been a very conservative group, and along with its team of lobbyists in Washington it maintains well-established chapters in every state. The Missouri Farm Bureau, headquartered in Jefferson City, offers its members insurance, discounts on farm equipment, and much more. It also runs a political action committee and endorses Republicans up and down the ballot. Unions might once have been their left-leaning equivalent, but there are fewer unions in rural Missouri than in the cities, and many of the remaining union members now vote Republican. When Cauthorn was running for office, farm debts and foreclosures were reaching crisis points, and the local brick factory had closed. Cauthorn told me that people in the area were struggling because there was no middle class anymore. But he didn't run on economic proposals.

Sometimes Democrats and progressives frame low-income or middle-class Republicans as people who "vote against their own interests." But that assumes that people are automatons who care only about money. We are more complicated than that. We all have an interest in seeing ourselves as moral actors. As one Missouri union member who voted for antiunion Republicans in 2016 explained, "I vote my faith and morals, number one; my country and the Constitution second; and then for my union third."[4] The Republican Party struck its gold when it came upon so many Americans' deep-seated "family values"—which really meant valuing the white family, better yet the white Christian family, the protection of which conservative culture said was paramount. Almost anything could be justified if it was done to protect the sanctity of the white family. The feeling that the white Christian family was under attack, that it needed to be protected, was the nexus of disgust at abortion and same-sex marriage, fear about tighter gun laws, and distrust of people of color. That nexus proved more powerful than any talking point about taxes.

Today we might take for granted that rhetoric about abortion and guns, underpinned by race baiting, carve out a loyal base for the Republican Party, but those issues weren't always an inevitable focal point. Both guns and abortion are, from one perspective, primarily public health issues. The people who suffer most from our current policies—such as the family members of the more than twenty thousand people who commit suicide with firearms annually or the low-income women who lose their jobs or sleep in their cars because they have to drive across state lines and wait three days to have an abortion—are largely invisible to the public eye. Neither abortion nor guns were originally partisan issues. So many of the allegiances and agendas that seem permanently dyed into our politics were completely different in previous generations.

What most Americans believe about guns and abortion doesn't actually square with how effectively conservatives have weaponized them. Both issues *do* reach the core of near-primal desires and expectations. Motherhood has been idealized for millennia. Our nation was founded on the myth of the explorer, sustained on the myth of the cowboy, both of which rely on valorizing bravado and violence. And yet, if we strip away those archetypes, turn down the noise, anger, and fear, the fact is that a majority of Americans believe both in the right to own a gun and the right to have an abortion. An overwhelming majority of Americans believe that the government can restrict those rights to some extent. We disagree on which restrictions, for whom, and when. Those issues didn't become flash points by accident. Cauthorn and his neighbors' fears won the day not because Republicans happened upon them, but because of decades of strategic, long-term investments by far-reaching, powerful groups, and because, owing to dynamics still at play, there was no equivalent local presence on the left. For the most part, left-leaning groups and their donors chose not to be there.

★ ★ ★

Our current debate over guns grew out of the same history as the Missouri Compromise. Long before Darren Wilson shot Michael Brown, discussions about gun violence were inflected with fear based on race. Comprehending how and why guns became a potent political tool for right-wing politicians requires looking way back to the Civil War, when political positions on guns were almost diametrically opposite to those held today. Ahead of the war, northern abolitionists were fierce supporters of gun rights, arguing that freed blacks needed weapons to defend themselves. States like Missouri barred slaves from owning guns and codified white men's right to seize guns from slaves. Bands of white men roved southern towns looking for slaves and freedmen, whom they would assault and kill. When the war ended, black men who had fought for the Union were permitted to buy their guns from the government at a discount. The original, full-throated calls for gun control were born then. Many southern states, including Missouri, enacted laws that prohibited blacks from voting, sitting on a jury, or owning a gun. The Ku Klux Klan formed in 1866 and soon considered itself "a patrol system," bent on threatening and hurting blacks and calling for restrictions on gun ownership.

The reign of terror continued well into Reconstruction. Between the end of the Civil War and the turn of the twentieth century, white mobs lynched an estimated five thousand black men in the United States. In response, so-called Negro militias began to form. In an act of solidarity barely imaginable today, several governors from some northern and southern states planned to ship arms to black men living in the South so that they could fend off violent whites.[5] The Klan intercepted the shipments. That history laid the groundwork for the racialized debate about guns—and who can exercise their right to bear them—that was yet to come.

The National Rifle Association was born post–Civil War, too. Its founders were former Union fighters who wanted to encourage marksmanship because they had been horrified at what bad shots their soldiers were. When lawmakers first wanted to simplify the country's patchwork of local gun laws, the NRA helped. In his book *Gunfight*, legal historian Adam Winkler explains how in the early twentieth century the NRA supported three major pieces of federal legislation, which together required licenses for gun sellers, permits for concealed carry, and a cross-state licensing system, among other provisions. The NRA's president, a New York attorney, Karl T. Frederick, testified before Congress on behalf of gun restrictions, saying, "I do not believe in the general promiscuous toting of guns."[6]

The events that would turn the NRA from a sportsmen's club to a political juggernaut came one after another throughout the 1960s and '70s. Again, racial strife inspired calls for gun laws. In the mid-1960s, race riots erupted in at least one hundred American cities. In New York City's Harlem in July 1964, for example, hundreds of people took to the streets after a white police officer shot and killed a fifteen-year-old black teenager. The protests began peacefully. After a few days, police officers began using clubs, and the protesters began throwing bottles and bricks. Chaos ensued. Police officers fired into crowds. As during Reconstruction one hundred years earlier, the images of mayhem, and the way they could be construed as validating many white Americans' preconceived racist stereotypes of violent black men, shifted white Americans' opinions about whether guns should be widely available. Black-power leaders, meanwhile, were teaching black activists that firearms were a means of empowerment. In Oakland, California, the Black Panthers tasked themselves with "policing the police" and required that new recruits learn how to handle guns, which they carried openly with a commitment not to use force unless it was used against them. Their radically pro-gun stance came to a crescendo on May 2, 1967, when a group of Panthers walked into the California state capitol building with loaded shotguns and pistols in protest of proposed gun control legislation. Their stunt drew national press attention, alongside headlines about how carrying guns in public was perfectly legal. Three months later, then governor Ronald Reagan signed a law that prohibited carrying loaded firearms in public.

The next year, 1968, brought several high-profile shootings, including the murders of Martin Luther King Jr. and, two months later, Robert F. Kennedy. King's assassination would inspire riots nationwide. The nation could not ignore gun violence, and there was overwhelming bipartisan support for stricter gun laws. This was the moment when now familiar arguments for unfettered access to guns ("the Nazis banned guns and look what happened," etc.) began to ferment and rise to the surface of political debate.

Gun-rights groups began pushing hard against federal agencies' ability to regulate guns. Although Congress did pass the Gun Control Act of 1968, which limited interstate gun sales, it also weakened the act's original scope, making it far less progressive than other reforms of the era, like the Voting Rights Act and Medicare.[7]

The NRA was not yet obsessed with messaging about the Second Amendment. That turn, the decisive change, would happen in the late 1970s, after an internal war within the organization. In one camp were those who wanted the NRA to remain primarily focused on hunting and marksmanship. In the other were those who sensed the possibility of more gun restrictions and wanted to push a more proactive political agenda. The politically minded were more ideological; they wanted to spread the message that the right to bear arms was critical to an American's ability to defend himself. As Winkler lays out, the fact that the self-defense ideologues won out is important for a couple of reasons: First, it meant the NRA would push for a more aggressive set of policies. Second, gun control advocates would go on to misunderstand the emotional core of gun ownership. As Cauthorn told me when we talked about assault weapons bans, "Once you give up one thing, then the fear is that then they're going to get the next one. They're going to click away at it until they take everything away from you." Any change in the law is perceived as a threat to personal safety, and nothing less.

The 1970s was also when nothing—or not enough—came together for the gun control movement, setting the power imbalance for decades to come. As Kristin Goss, associate professor of public policy at Duke University, writes in *Disarmed*, her thorough history of what she calls the "non-movement" to restrict guns, "At least since the 1930s, America has witnessed uncoordinated bursts of activism around gun control. But these bursts of popular outrage—and often the local and state voluntary groups they have nourished or given rise to—have quickly faded into quiescence." In the 1960s and '70s, after internal debates over strategy, gun control advocates took as their goal sweeping federal legislation.

And so they zeroed in on winning over elites in DC, not the public nationwide. Goss concludes, "In a sense, then, there has been no sustained, national gun control movement in America because gun control leaders chose, perhaps unwittingly, not to have one."[8]

At first it seemed as though gun control organizations that settled in Washington, DC, in the 1970s *would* invest in state-based grassroots groups. The National Council to Ban Handguns, the most prominent of the four major gun control groups that had emerged since the 1960s, set up meetings with vocal statewide antigun activists—of which there were only about six—and planned to position itself as an umbrella organization for those local leaders, who would have a voice in governing the national group. Then, in 1976, Jimmy Carter was elected, and the National Council to Ban Handguns' leaders decided that a stricter national gun law was imminent. That same year, an attempt to pass a Massachusetts ballot initiative that would have banned handguns failed. With an opening on the federal level and little success in a liberal state, national strategists thought diverting resources to state and local advocates would be a pointless drain. At their second annual conference, the National Council to Ban Handguns' staff announced the federal-focused plan to the state-based advocates, who flipped out. One said, with clairvoyance only recognizable today, "I disagree wholeheartedly. All the national organizations that are successful—Common Cause and the ACLU—have local chapters, state associations, and a national board."[9] Handgun Control Inc., the primary gun control organization in the 1980s, didn't invest in statewide chapters, either, for many of the same reasons, primarily that local affiliates were "a very heavy lift" that required divvying up scant resources and control over strategy and messaging.

There was a logic to the federal plan: Guns were routinely carried and sold between cities and states, so local laws could hardly be considered effective. If advocates wanted to reduce gun violence, only a national solution seemed adequate. Here it is crucial to underline a key distinction between the leaders of the gun control "non-movement" and the conservative strategists from the Heritage Foundation or NRA who would huddle at Grover Norquist's Wednesday meetings in DC to coordinate their nationwide grassroots efforts. Those conservative strategists' primary goal was to build a cohesive political movement—one that encompassed electoral strategy, policy goals, and cultural and social wins. Gun control advocates' primary goal was to reduce gun violence. Solving a public health problem like gun violence is an undertaking totally different from creating a durable political infrastructure. When advocates are trying to advance a specific cause in the immediate future, they are not necessarily making decisions that benefit a broad, long-term political movement.

Instead of investing in local groups, DC-based gun control advocates focused on writing national policy proposals and pursuing litigation. They went on to lose many pivotal cases, including those against gun manufacturers whose products they alleged were defective. Winkler convincingly argues in his book that "the damage they did to the cause of gun control remains with us to this day. Gun lovers saw the suits for what they were: an effort to make the sale of guns to civilians so costly that no business would want to do it." The lawsuits handed the NRA easy propaganda it used to goad the rural voters who are overrepresented in Congress and many state legislatures. From today's perspective, in a nation where the gun rights lobby is considered invincible, where between thirty and forty thousand people are killed by guns every year and where there is no realistic expectation that Congress will take any action, it is clear that gun control advocates' obsession with lawsuits and lobbying on the federal level did not work. At the time, though, it wasn't as obvious that the federal strategy was doomed, and gun control advocates faced real dilemmas.

For a moment, in the 1990s, the federal plan was even vindicated: in 1993, President Clinton signed the Brady Bill, which banned certain assault rifles, a major victory. The bill was named for James Brady, Reagan's White House press secretary, who was shot and paralyzed during an assassination attempt of the president, and who, along with his wife Sarah, had become the nation's most visible gun control proponent. But the Democrats lost the

House the next year, in the 1994 elections, and common wisdom blamed the Brady Bill. Democrats from southern states had been purged in favor of NRA-endorsed Republicans. The gun issue seemed like it was going to damn Democrats either way they voted.

Drawing less national attention, meanwhile, gun rights enthusiasts, including the NRA, turned to the state legislatures, launching what would be a years-long pitched battle to try to pass a law allowing Missourians to carry concealed weapons. In 1994, the NRA sent a DC lobbyist to Jefferson City to shepherd a conceal-and-carry bill through committee. DC strategists wanted the local debates it was sponsoring to seem homegrown, so the NRA lobbied hardest through a group called the Missouri Legislative Issues Council. The local activists publicly disavowed any ties to the NRA, even though they were working together with the organization.[10]

The state was considered a test kitchen; if the bill worked there, it could work elsewhere. In 1999, after years of public debate, the Missouri legislature finally put a referendum on the ballot: Missourians themselves would vote on whether concealed carry would be allowed in the state. James Brady flew in to stump against concealed carry. Wayne LaPierre, then a head of the NRA, toured the state with Sue Kleceshulte, a rape survivor, who talked about how having a gun would have kept her safe. The NRA spent roughly $4 million on its campaign. Handgun Control Inc. (which later became the Brady Campaign to End Gun Violence) estimated that it was outspent ten to one.[11]

That April, the Columbine gunmen took thirteen lives, stunning a nation not yet numbed to mass shootings, and, soon after, the Missouri ballot measure was defeated. But the gun rights lobby's resources remained formidable, and the gun control movement's triumph was short-lived. Dennis Henigan, former vice president of law and policy at the Brady Campaign, explained that the NRA's energy and resources for state-based battles seemed inexhaustible: "We would win in a legislative session, but the gun lobby would be right back in there pitching in the next session. And if they lost, then they'd be right back." He explained that the gun rights groups had an "ability to mobilize these activists year after year, and it's harder to sustain that on the gun control side. It just is."

From their perspective, gun control advocates' hands were tied. "We always recognized the importance of state legislatures, but we had to be so strategic because of limited resources," Henigan said. "We could never match the NRA in terms of resources in campaigns." It was difficult for them to raise hard money, which could be given directly to candidates but couldn't be written off on a donor's taxes. Local gun control advocates did not have the patronage of the church, business groups, or any other deep-pocketed, well-organized institution willing to bankroll fledgling political groups.

Foundations were—and to a certain extent continue to be—almost entirely unwilling to fund political solutions to gun violence, in part because their boards were committed to keeping up the ruse that there is such a thing as apolitical giving. As one advocate said, "Foundations were timid. They didn't feel like going out on a limb and supporting the partner organizations to a legislative lobbying group."[12] From 1988 to 1992, years when gun violence reached an apex, charitable foundations gave only 1 percent of their violence-prevention-related grants to projects related to gun control. That left groups like the Brady Campaign scrounging for individual donations. With scant political money, the Brady Campaign and its allies entered election battles only when the winner would have an outsize influence on local or national politics, or where the race could turn into a highly publicized model for beating the NRA elsewhere.

Gun control advocates had other incentives to pursue a federal legal strategy that went for the moon. They knew the NRA was building seemingly indomitable power in Congress and statehouses. In the early 2000s, nationwide, the NRA's political arm would spend over $3 million on state races. "We felt that courts were a forum in which the NRA's pressure and political activism would not be as directly felt," Henigan explained. Plus, he said, it was somewhat easier to raise money for litigation, since those dollars could be written off as charitable donations. Big-spending political donors willing to involve themselves in divisive causes generally hold more extreme positions than the public overall; gun control strategists made their plans ambitious enough to satisfy those ideological donors, which meant pushing for sweeping restrictions, including all-out bans. Their attorneys were cloistered in big-city offices, their battles played out in inscrutable legal documents and less often in courtrooms, and so their crusade rarely gave local advocates reason to organize fund-raisers or petition drives in church basements or living rooms. Far from view, demanding enormous changes in sharp, educated tones, urban or suburban gun control advocates became easy to caricature as uptight, overreaching liberal lunatics trying to squash rural Americans' way of life.

★ ★ ★

Abortion rights would not be as precarious today—and antiabortion voters would not be as powerful a voting bloc—had a relentless social movement not coalesced the way it did almost fifty years ago. That movement is an exemplar of what it takes to move the culture and law. Missouri was an early battleground; antiabortion Missourians were determined and willing to work with what they had. On an otherwise ordinary morning in January 1973, in a farmhouse in Moberly, roughly forty miles northwest of the small city of Mexico, Therese Sander was at the breakfast table when over the radio came news that the Supreme Court had legalized abortion nationwide. Then a thirty-year-old cattle rancher and Democrat, with three young children, Sander told her husband that she couldn't believe Americans would support something so barbaric. He seemed to shrug off people's capacity for cruelty. As weeks went on, though, Sander realized: "There was a burning compulsion inside myself that I could not ignore." She sent away for materials from National Right to Life and borrowed her parents' slide projector. Then she began giving presentations in neighbors' homes, asking to be on the local radio program, and leafleting parking lots. Sander remembers, "It was a very lonely struggle for me personally to push and keep something alive at the local level."

But Sander kept going. She cofounded the local Right to Life chapter, and eventually they came up with funding for a lobbyist. When she decided to run for office, her husband told her that no one would vote for a single-issue activist like her. He was wrong. In 2002, Sander was elected to represent Missouri House District 22. In 2007, she sponsored a multiple-provisioned antiabortion bill that, when signed into law, shuttered all but one of Missouri's clinics, required patients to wait seventy-two hours between a preliminary appointment and their procedure, and gave millions of taxpayer dollars to centers that proselytize against not only abortion but also contraception.

Her success was not always inevitable. The cultural divide that separates Sander, who told me that she once fired a lobbyist for saying that an abortion ban could have an exemption for rape, and a National Abortion Rights Action League (NARAL) employee, who told me about her abortion via text message, seems so deeply etched that it is hard not to consider that divide part of the natural order. It is also difficult to imagine an American political landscape where the abortion debate doesn't immediately polarize voters. Yet the profound vitriol that most Americans associate with the debate over abortion is relatively new, an invention of political operatives, religious leaders, and legal strategists, some of whom had sincere beliefs about when life begins, and others who wanted to consolidate their own political power by exploiting how deeply the abortion question cut to Americans' core values.

The men working at the highest levels of church and state who gave us today's abortion wars took pains not to publicize the extent of their influence. Now-familiar antiabortion rhetoric first calcified into a blunt political tool for three main reasons: First, the Catholic Church built a political blockade against the burgeoning women's movement after becoming afraid of losing its flock to the sexual revolution. Second, Republican strategists later co-opted the church's "pro-family" messaging to make their conservative plank appealing to working-class and rural voters. And, finally, the attorneys who served as the architects of the antiabortion movement plotted to write state laws that would incrementally whittle away at *Roe*. The bills those antiabortion attorneys wrote became flags local Republicans could wave to signal their allegiance to the sanctity of the conservative (white) family. The opportunity to show up and support those bills, and celebrate their passage, kept local activists engaged over years, gathering momentum.

The antiabortion attorneys chose statehouses as the primary venue for their struggle because pre-*Roe* feminists first agitated to repeal abortion laws in the states. Through the 1960s, the women's liberation movement had gained traction, as thousands more women entered universities and the workforce, had better access to contraception, and were at least marginally better represented in the media, politics, and the arts. NARAL takes its original name—National Association for Repeal of Abortion Laws—from its birth in that era, when teams of feminists brought to light what had long been taboo—the dead and maimed women who had suffered botched illegal abortions.

The repeal movement gained momentum on March 18, 1970, as New York's Assembly spent five hours arguing over a bill that would legalize "abortion on demand." The bill was written by one of its only female legislators, Constance Cook, an upstate Republican who represented a rural district, and it would allow women free rein in deciding whether to have an abortion. It was the first of its kind in the nation. The Assembly passed the bill. When, later, the Senate voted, there was a tie. Moments after the votes were tallied, George M. Michaels, a Democrat from a largely Catholic central New York district, stood up. He wanted to change his vote.

"I fully appreciate that this is the termination of my political career," Michaels said.[13]

"Abortion on demand" became legal in the state of New York. And Michaels understood the political reality. He later lost his bid for reelection.

It is hard to grasp now how different the legal and political landscape was then, roughly fifty years ago. At the time, it was Catholics who tended to be Democrats, and it was Republicans who first codified the feminists' rallying cries for contraception and abortion. Likewise, many mainstream Protestant denominations—including the American Baptist Convention, the United Presbyterian Church, and the United Methodist Church—endorsed liberalizing abortion laws. That is remarkable, considering that until 1965 it was illegal for married couples to use contraception in some states.

It makes sense, though, that Republicans would be consistent in their goal to minimize government interference by repealing abortion laws. Soon after New York passed its law—which, remember, was before *Roe* legalized abortion nationwide—Republican state lawmakers in thirteen other states easily passed bills that liberalized abortion access. Those states weren't just the ones you would expect, like California, but also others like Kansas, Mississippi, and Arkansas, which today are steeped in antiabortion culture and politicking. Many early donors to Planned Parenthood, including its Kansas City branch, were wealthy white suburban women. Planned Parenthood has been in Missouri since 1932, NARAL since 1969. One of the early rationales for expanding access to family planning was to enable poor women—"indigents" and "unwed mothers"—to limit their number of children, a calculus with its own dubious morality that played into many middle- and upper-class Americans' worldviews. President Nixon expanded federal family planning programs.

That middle-class white Americans were driving the "pro-choice" movement, as it would be named, was tinder for the culture wars. Pro-choice talking points often took for granted middle-class professional aspirations and idealized a life trajectory that did not match reality for many poor or working-class Americans. For many Americans who didn't have degrees or prestigious jobs, the notion that abortion and contraception would allow a woman to pursue a higher purpose of climbing a career ladder, achieving her financial independence, and finding her own sense of self didn't mesh with their own concept of what gave them meaning and social status—marriage and children. As those talking points pinned a woman's self-actualization to accomplishments like completing college, the pro-choice worldview challenged much more than the notion that life begins at conception. A couple living in outstate Missouri might be in debt and might not have a fancy truck, but they could respect themselves and earn respect in their community because of their long marriage and brood of children, for whom they had sacrificed. The idea that an American woman could want something other than that sacrifice challenged a prestige hierarchy and set of values that had allowed many Americans to find honor and virtue in their own struggles.

At the same time, as women moved toward the workplace and contraception became normal, the Catholic Church moved its condemnations of premarital sex, contraception, and abortion to the center of its teaching—far from its position for the first chapters of American history. Until then, the Catholic Church hadn't said too much about abortion. Before the 1850s, most people took for granted that a woman could use abortifacients before "quickening," the first moment she could feel the fetus stir, which usually happens anywhere between fifteen and twenty weeks of pregnancy. Then, in the years leading up to the Comstock era, when the government would roll out a wide range of social repressions, antiabortion sentiment began to percolate, and the Catholic bishops joined in. In 1841, Bishop Kenrick of Philadelphia kicked things off by saying that two deaths were better than one murder. By the 1960s, priests were railing from the pulpit against any politicians who contradicted the church's positions on sexual morality. By then women were flooding into universities, factories, and offices, and the full weight of the church's hierarchy bore down on dissent. Catholic priests who vocally supported family planning were excommunicated.[14]

No matter how fierce the priests' denunciations of abortion, the church probably wouldn't have had such a lasting influence on state and national politics if its leaders hadn't institutionalized their opposition to the women's movement. In 1966, the Catholic Church had formed a political arm, the National Conference of Catholic Bishops, which ran an office in DC and created local branches, like the Missouri Catholic Conference, which deployed statehouse lobbyists. Much like the NRA, the bishops wanted to deflect the idea that Catholic leadership was driving the local lobbying efforts. So they also founded National Right to Life. "The idea was to create the appearance of a widespread Catholic opposition to abortion reform so that it didn't look like Catholic opposition was a top-down effort," Patricia Miller, author of *Good Catholics*, explained.[15] As an extension of the church, National Right to Life immediately had what fledgling grassroots organizations don't: a deep reserve of cash and a built-in audience of millions.

Reproductive rights groups, like the first gun control groups, were short on resources. As volunteers from truly grassroots feminist groups like NARAL Missouri met with their local representatives, hopeful that their recent strides were just the beginning, the Catholic Church flew attorneys and lobbyists to statehouses around the country to lobby and testify against abortion liberalization laws, under the banners of both the Catholic Conference and National Right to Life. The bishops anticipated the importance of having boots on the ground and set aside funds—almost $400,000 in today's dollars—to start local chapters of antiabortion groups around the country. (Meanwhile, the pro-choice counterpart, Catholics for Choice, couldn't afford to make long-distance phone calls.)[16] Most, if not all, early antiabortion groups were outgrowths of those church-funded initiatives. The bishops also invested heavily in state legislative races, targeting swing districts, and they were often successful, flipping elections across the country.

In 1973, within a few months, two very different but equally monumental events would set in motion the reconfiguring of party politics, although no one could have anticipated it at the time. The decisions made that year and soon after eventually drew the cultural-political line between voters that now seem fixed and inevitable.

First, in January, in *Roe v. Wade*, the US Supreme Court legalized abortion nationwide.

Across the country, as the news spread, people who hadn't been paying attention to the women in the streets calling for abortion on demand or the bishops yelling about damnation suddenly took notice. Trying not to despair, Missouri Catholic Conference staffers attended the National Catholic Conference's emergency meeting in DC and, like other delegates from across the country, returned home with instructions. Within a few months, with church funds, the newly minted Missouri Citizens for Life had chapters in St. Louis, Kansas City, St. Joseph, Springfield, and, of course, the capital in Jefferson City. The group occupied a church basement a few blocks from the capitol dome. Organizers traveled the state to set up more chapters. Women like Sander had somewhere to channel their dissent. The Catholic Church's lawyers wrote antiabortion bills, the first of which allowed doctors and nurses to refuse to participate in abortion procedures. Missouri lawmakers passed the bill just months after *Roe*.

Then, that summer, that second important national event: the Watergate scandal broke. Searching for a way to reestablish credibility with the American public, Paul Weyrich and his fellow Republican Party operatives settled on reframing abortion as their very own moral crusade. Together, the many right-wing organizations founded in that era became the conservative infrastructure that would dispatch candidates able to stoke the burning compulsions inside people like Therese Sander. Her certainty, her fervor, her desire for a better world, would ensure she would never give up. Her colleagues in the church's groups felt the same way and wasted no time.

The year after *Roe*, 1974, Missouri Citizens for Life handed off to state representatives a bill that would limit a woman's right to abortion in multiple ways, including by requiring that a woman receive her husband's permission to have an abortion. In Jefferson City, lobbyists for the Catholic Conference and Missouri Citizens for Life stalked the capitol hallways, waving in busloads of church ladies from outstate, distributing plastic roses to the volunteers, who were instructed to hand them to their legislators. The volunteers often looked ragtag—most were farm wives or retirees. But if they were a little frumpy or disheveled, legislators knew for sure that they weren't hired hacks. This was exactly the kind of authentic and spontaneous-seeming groundswell the bishops had hoped for.

As for the feminists, the local Women's Abortion Action Committee had stopped holding its monthly meetings. "Since the Supreme Court decision, people just aren't interested anymore," an editorialist wrote in a St. Louis paper. "They think it's settled."[17]

It was not settled. The Missouri House passed its multi-provisioned antiabortion bill 148 to 3. The Senate did the same, 27 to 5. Planned Parenthood sued the state. There was no way the average Missourian could have anticipated where this would lead—the forty-plus years of litigation, the endless culture war.

At the same time, in a stately old building in Chicago, the third crucial element of the antiabortion movement was coming together. A handful of attorneys were founding Americans United for Life Legal Defense Fund (AUL), which they conceived of as "an ACLU of the antiabortion movement," as one early member described it to me. The AUL's long-term influence on national abortion policy cannot be overstated. While Missouri farm wives were passing out plastic roses, the then-informal legal team was coming to grips with the fact that the Supreme Court was probably not going to reverse itself anytime soon. They decided to chip away at abortion rights very slowly, over decades, with local laws, like the ones recently passed in Missouri.

The AUL attorneys knew that pulling off their plan to whittle away at abortion rights would take patience—at least twenty years. First, they would pass laws that barely seemed to change the right to abortion. They started with sample bills that required minors to receive their parents' permission to have an abortion—a notion that would seem reasonable to much of the public and would make their feminist detractors look extreme. If challenged in court, those bills would force a judge to choose between parental rights and the right to an abortion, opening the possibility that the judge would weaken *Roe*. Those savvy attorneys also anticipated that voters with pro-choice sympathies wouldn't revolt if abortion restrictions were enacted piecemeal. And they were right.

Feminist political organizers, meanwhile, believed that in *Roe* they had won a resounding victory. Many feminist organizers wanted a broad woman's movement, one wherein "reproductive rights" meant much more than abortion. With a litany of other pressing concerns like rape, domestic violence, workplace harassment, equal pay, and child-care costs, they moved on to pressure Congress to pass the not-yet-obviously-doomed-to-failure Equal Rights Amendment. "After *Roe v. Wade* pro-choice feminists primarily stayed focused on the national level and really conceded—not intentionally—but conceded the states to the pro-life movement," said Alesha Doan, associate professor of women, gender, and sexuality studies at the University of Kansas.

In contrast, the Catholic Conference and National Right to Life agreed to throw their weight behind the AUL's slow, state-based legal strategy, and they had power to wield. By the late '70s, National Right to Life had some eleven million members and roughly three thousand local chapters.[18] In Missouri, the church's lawyers wrote bills, and Concerned Citizens for Life dispensed advice and materials to volunteers like Sander, who borrowed her parents' slide projector to show pictures of fetuses to her neighbors. For years, the bills they passed were struck down by courts.

But while Sander kept doggedly leafleting parking lots, and the church and the AUL attorneys kept rewriting experimental bills, their passion for saving the unborn was becoming ever more useful to the Republican Party. Ahead of the 1980 presidential election, Paul Weyrich, with his New Right team solidifying, told Reagan to bullhorn against abortion to attract Catholics but also Evangelicals and other Protestants, too. *Roe* became shorthand for conservatives' many anxieties about the idea of equality between men and women. Abortion soon signified all threats to the purity of the American family, including women's license to pursue sex, education, and careers on their own terms. The National Right to Life Political Action Committee, the first overtly political pro-life organization of its kind, formed ahead of that election, and supported Reagan. The New Right leaders helped pull their right-to-life counterparts into the overtly partisan fray—a move that would shape public policy far beyond abortion.

As Reagan took office, feminist leaders saw the writing on the wall. Feminist organizers continued to disagree about the best way forward. With so many antiabortion politicians taking office, there were compelling arguments for focusing on many fronts. The prescient NARAL and National Organization for Women organizers who wanted to channel resources to state politics were drowned out by their colleagues who preferred to make their presence felt in Washington.[19]

In state capitals, meanwhile, the drumbeat picked up. Galvanized antiabortion attorneys and strategists gathered in local Catholic Conference headquarters across the country to write model bills, carefully choosing their wording, hoping to send the legislation all the way to the Supreme Court. They would need to assist willing lawmakers in getting the bills through their assemblies. In 1990, the AUL spent $100,000 flying 125 legislators representing forty-two states to its first of many all-expenses-paid conferences, where attendees learned to "sell" antiabortion ideas. Legislators learned to call fetuses "the unborn," clinics became "abortion mills."[20] It was win-win-win for the politicians, the antiabortion attorneys, and the religious leaders, all hoping to consolidate their power.

Missouri was an early test kitchen for antiabortion legislation after *Roe* became the law of the land. In 1989, the Supreme Court gave the antiabortion movement one of its first seminal victories in *Webster v. Reproductive Health Services*, which upheld Missouri's restrictions on abortion providers and state funding for abortion, as well as a preamble the legislature added to the state constitution that said "the life of each human being begins at conception." Missouri went on to pass some of the most restrictive abortion laws in the country, with measurable consequences. In 2011, the state had four clinics that provided abortion. In 2016, one.

To fully appreciate the antiabortion movement's political feat and see why it matters for other movements, it is instructive to remember that gun control advocates were only able to rustle up a "non-movement" of mostly ill-fated sweeping federal proposals and lawsuits. Right after the Supreme Court legalized abortion nationwide, some antiabortion advocates were tempted to take a similar tack—to try to take *Roe* down in one fatal blow. But the antiabortion movement still exists and has collected several crucial legal victories in large part because its pragmatic attorneys pushed their patient, incremental, state-based strategy to the center of the movement.

Many antiabortion advocates—usually less sophisticated and kookier ones (like Missouri's Representative Rick Moon, who starred in a YouTube video in which he beheaded a chicken after talking about abortion, presumably to appeal to viewers' emotions)—continued to push for so-called personhood amendments, which would change a state's constitution to give a fertilized egg full legal rights and therefore make abortion, many fertility treatments, and some forms of contraception illegal. Now that conservatives hold a majority on the Supreme Court, state legislatures are racing to pass ever bolder abortion restrictions, including six-week bans and other laws that would effectively ban abortion. But for decades many antiabortion lawyers saw personhood-or-bust politicians like Moon as damaging to their cause: they risk exposing the movement's radical aims, and their proposed amendments are so obviously unconstitutional that a judge would strike them down anyway, setting yet another legal precedent solidifying the right to abortion. Meanwhile, a main branch of gun control advocacy called for total bans on gun ownership. One major group, after all, called itself the National Coalition to Ban Handguns. Advocates who wanted to end civilian gun ownership altogether made themselves akin to antiabortion personhood advocates. They too were pushing for measures well outside the middle ground where most Americans' opinions, and the law, are firmly planted.

The legal plan to gradually whittle away at abortion rights with narrow state laws also helped build a grassroots movement: along the way, as antiabortion activists won small battles, they were invigorated and saw a reason to keep going. Unlike supporters of gun control, who began to see the NRA as unstoppable, antiabortion advocates could tell themselves that they were inching toward their ultimate goal. Granted, this was possible at first because of the Catholic Church's largesse, and then through the backing of right-wing foundations and Republican operatives. But it wasn't just the money, or the legal victories. Because of the antiabortion legal strategy, volunteers like Sander never went months, let alone years, without having a reason to meet to write testimony, rally, make phone calls, and all the dozens of other small-seeming but hugely important tasks that day by day build up a resistance. And the many different players working up and down the chain—from activists leafleting parking lots to think tanks grooming antiabortion judges—all saw their role in a long-term strategy.

The antiabortion attorneys' watershed moment came ahead of the presidential election in 1992, when the Supreme Court ruled in *Planned Parenthood v. Casey*, a case over Pennsylvania abortion laws written in the Catholic Conference offices in Harrisburg. (At the same time that the Catholic Church was condemning abortion as a "sexual sin," the Pennsylvania diocese's lawyers were helping to cover up one thousand cases of local priests raping and molesting children.) That landmark decision kept *Roe* in name but changed its fundamental core, allowing states much more leeway in passing laws that restricted abortion. The floodgates were open. State legislators could go ahead and campaign on shutting down clinics and have a good shot of fulfilling their promises.

The decision was especially damning for the pro-choice advocates, because *Casey* was so complicated it was hard for even the legal experts to parse. Most Americans would not understand what the ruling meant. Just as happened immediately after *Roe*, pro-choice Americans would watch the nightly news or skim the paper and would believe that the right to have an abortion was safe. But it wasn't. Far from it. Pro-choice feminists had every reason to fight as hard as they had pre-*Roe*, but the illusion of security would continue to pacify everyone but the most dedicated activists. The antiabortion activists, now well organized from coast to coast, were poised to make sure that their neighbors voted into office lawmakers who would take advantage of their new permission to restrict abortion.

That summer of 1992, a month after *Casey* was decided, Bill Clinton won the Democratic nomination for president. Throughout his campaign he said that abortion should be "safe, legal, and rare." His word choice reflected his time in Arkansas, then still dense with antiabortion Democrats. The sentiment also captures many Americans' beliefs about abortion. Unlike in partisan political conversations, an overwhelming majority of Americans see the ethics of abortion in shades of gray. The idea that abortion should be rare, though, moralized. Clinton's advisers probably thought he needed that edge of judgment to secure religious voters, and maybe he did. But that kind of defensive framing, much like the complicated legal jargon in *Casey*, made it even harder for abortion rights advocates to solicit unflinching support from mainstream Americans.

Republicans had black-and-white certainty to work with: *Abortion is murder. Abortion damages women.* For anyone with a moral compass, the call to protest a genocide is louder than the temptation to stay in bed on a Saturday morning. Moral ambivalence doesn't usually motivate you to take off work and drive two hours to a badly lit hearing room. Neither does a call to action against an arcane-seeming legal statute about a medical procedure you don't really understand. As a result, the small but persistent teams of feminists who publicly demanded abortion rights came across (to use gendered descriptors) as strident, angry, or uncompromising. Many Democrats wanted little to do with them. No wonder that by 2001 John Cauthorn's pro-gun, antiabortion ads met little resistance in Audrain County.

* * *

At the same time, across the country, the Democratic Party began to lose more ground. *Citizens United* has garnered enough attention that its name has become shorthand for all that is wrong with money and power in American politics. But an earlier change in campaign finance rules had already tipped the political scales. In 2002, Congress passed the Bipartisan Campaign Reform Act. The law was intended to repair a badly broken campaign finance system. Both major political parties had been abusing loopholes, especially for what is called "soft money"—uncapped donations to political parties for "party building" activities. Many corporations and big donors supported reforms, complaining of "shakedowns" by the political parties. The McCain-Feingold Act (as the legislation is known, for its sponsors, John McCain and Russ Feingold) banned soft money. After its passage, starting in November 2002, political parties and candidates could accept only hard-money donations, which were capped and regulated. For the first time, too, federal regulations and donation caps would also apply to state and local elections. A libertarian think tank out of Colorado immediately sued for the right to keep its donors secret. The Supreme Court loosened the law, but it remained partially intact.

Democratic leaders knew that McCain-Feingold would have major consequences for their party. Republicans tended to raise more money overall, but Democrats counted on more soft money. In the '90s, when earlier versions of campaign finance reform had been floated, some Democratic senators publicly endorsed but privately discouraged the reforms. It was understood that the public disapproved of big money in elections. As McCain-Feingold was finalized, in 2002, Congressman Richard Gephardt of Missouri said publicly that McCain-Feingold would mean that Republicans would probably raise much more money than Democrats for years to come, but he and many of his colleagues endorsed it anyway.

At the time, in the early 2000s, Democrats thought endorsing McCain-Feingold would help them appear more populist—a rebranding opportunity they were eager for after Bill Clinton's relationship with ultrarich donors had helped paint an image of an elitist Democratic Party and during an era when the "latte liberal" trope was emerging. Nevertheless, as soon as McCain-Feingold passed, the Democratic National Committee's attorney, Joseph Sandler, told the *Atlantic* that the law was "a fascist monstrosity" and "a disaster for the Democrats." As predicted, in January and February of 2003—just a couple of months after the law took effect—the gulf between the two major parties' donations was already widening: Republicans raised $39.4 million, whereas

Democrats raised $9.6 million.[21] A fund-raising imbalance remains today.

The reverberations from McCain-Feingold dramatically altered our political system beyond the new desperation for hard money. The soft-money discrepancy between parties was only the most direct consequence. More importantly, the new campaign finance laws incentivized donors and political operatives to prioritize interest groups like NARAL Pro-Choice America and the National Rifle Association, which could still legally accept unlimited amounts of soft money. Interest groups became a primary vehicle for political spending. As a result, new interest groups cropped up, and those already established were poised to exert greater control. It became even more significant that conservative strategists had been coordinating their aligned interest groups like the Heritage Foundation and the Cato Institute and corporate lobbies since the 1970s. The Koch brothers' network, too, enjoyed new power. Republicans had the advantage of more donations overall, but they also had the support of that already unified network of organizations that could legally raise unlimited amounts of soft money.

That network has built-in advantages beyond extra cash: First, the right-wing network includes not only organizations whose mission is to advance conservative policies in general, but also single-issue organizations (like the NRA and National Right to Life), to the extent that those single issues serve a utilitarian function for the overall movement. In other words, Republican operatives made alliances with those single-issue groups and their leaders because those groups and their constituents were useful for winning elections. Once elections were won, Republicans could advance their economic agenda. While both major political parties lost some of their fund-raising power, Republicans had those "same old boring institutions" that their billionaires had been supporting year after year to hold together their alliances.

Left-leaning groups had no counterpart. If anything, the interest groups associated with the left represented ideas and factions that were unpopular or easily marginalized in conservative or swing districts. Whereas Republican operatives chose to ally themselves with certain causes and interest groups precisely because they would attract the voters the party needed, the Democratic coalition was essentially "everyone else," as a number of people put it to me. The "big tent" Democratic coalition is not as monolithic as the Republican Party's current base, leaving lots of room for competing narratives and priorities. The perennial complaint about the Democrats having no central message was exacerbated by that change in campaign finance laws that gave each interest group faction more fund-raising power than the party itself.

Political parties had once been mediators of the multitude of ideas championed by dozens of interest groups. The Democratic Party's loss in stature partially explains why during the Obama years the left became increasingly fractured, unable to decide on a unifying principle, although the internal fissures were not clear to the mainstream public until the debacle of the 2016 presidential election. Big spenders like Planned Parenthood, the Sierra Club, and the AFL-CIO may have staff and board members with similar politics, but each organization is tasked with advancing a specific cause. Advocating for reproductive rights or clean energy are tasks very different from building a cohesive political platform. There is often a trade-off between the long-term goals of a movement and the short-term goals of a campaign. This is further complicated by right-wing strategists' brilliant methods of carving up the Democratic base, playing on many of those same deeply etched cultural divisions that have existed for generations. You can see why a union leader whose primary goal is flipping a swing district in a culturally conservative area, say, might not consider it strategic for the local party to take a loud position on abortion or transgender rights, whereas a reproductive justice group's funding might be designated for promoting candidates because they support abortion or transgender rights. That is but one instance of how the left's many interests are often made to seem in direct competition with each other. There is an inherent tension, then, as soon as different interest groups try to come together to find a candidate or policy proposal or campaign strategy. Competing agendas on the left became more apparent—and destructive in ways that are still playing out today—after McCain-Feingold, when Democratic candidates needed interest group support more than ever because the DNC and state Democratic parties were hollowed out.

That interest groups gained so much control is also a central reason that Democrats lost states like Missouri. For decades, major interest groups like Planned Parenthood and the Sierra Club have run largely centralized offices out of DC or New York. Brand-name interest groups have had state chapters scattered across the country, but those chapters are often technically separate entities tasked with raising the bulk, if not all, of their own funds. That means that in the very places where right-wing politicians have gained the most ground, and where local battles during campaigns and legislative sessions are the fiercest, with the most at stake, local advocates often had the fewest resources. Fast forward a few years, and national interest groups' priorities are evident in their budgets, and their salaries. In 2015 (even before the "Trump bump" when the national ACLU organizations brought in $300 million in 2017), the ACLU's national (c)(3) took in $94 million and its (c)(4) $50.6 million. Its Missouri affiliates took in a combined $1.3 million. At least that was more than its Arkansas affiliate, whose annual revenue was roughly half a million dollars. Meanwhile, the total compensation for Anthony Romero, the executive director of the national ACLU, was $413,348 in 2015 and approximately $561,000 in 2018. The rough equivalence between his salary and a state affiliate's entire budget represents a larger cognitive dissonance about what is considered enough money. On one hand, it makes sense that when hiring an executive director in an expensive city, a high-profile interest group would offer a six-figure salary. On the other, nonprofit boards of directors assume that in the places where legal rights are at greatest risk, local advocates, including lawyers, will work on a shoestring. Since the 2016 election, the ACLU has announced a new program to build up organizing groups across the country. The wild discrepancy between national and state left-leaning interest group offices is the rule, however, not the exception. The people occupying the decision-making posts in those national organizations tend to have a lot in common with those in the high ranks of foundations and political parties, including their sweeping views of New York harbor and assumptions about what is worthwhile.[22]

Those interest groups have tended to defend their causes primarily by investing in federal lobbying and pursuing litigation. The courts are often the most expedient venue for squashing unjust laws and executive orders. But by definition lawyers and lobbyists are a small group of people who work behind closed doors. The privacy of their work does not lend itself to galvanizing and organizing a coalition of people to draw public attention and get out the vote. Lawyers and lobbyists are much needed, but they are not enough on their own, as we will see in coming chapters. For the last fifteen years at least, advocacy organizations based in and preoccupied with Washington, DC, and New York steered many of the left's priorities, which meant that as the local Democratic parties began to wither, their allies weren't in town to shore up support for progressive causes.

★ ★ ★

In 2000, Stacey Newman organized her first political action. When we met, in 2016, she was a Missouri state representative, but back then she was a private citizen upset by a shooting at the North Valley Jewish Community Center in Los Angeles. A gunman had opened fire on teenage camp counselors and kindergarten-age children, seriously injuring three of the children, before driving to a nearby neighborhood and killing a thirty-nine-year old mail carrier. This was four months after Columbine. Newman arranged for a bus to take families from her St. Louis synagogue to Washington, DC, for the Million Mom March in May 2000, which until 2017's Women's March reigned as the largest-ever march on Washington. The Million Mom March was sometimes dismissed as a failure for not leading to concrete reforms for gun safety, but it left in its wake thousands of activists like Newman—the very network the "non-movement" had needed. The Brady Campaign eventually absorbed the march under its umbrella, a merger marked by tensions between local activists and the national office that stymied gun reform efforts. Back in Missouri, as she got more involved, Newman had work to do: John Cauthorn was living up to his campaign promise. During his first term he had helped pass a bill that limited lawsuits against gun manufacturers, and he had proposed yet another conceal-and-carry bill.

Newman and Jeanne Kirkton, who would also later serve in the Missouri House, began improvising a two-person resistance to the gun lobby. They started showing up in Jefferson City to meet with the governor and testify against gun bills. Newman was a stay-at-home mother, and so, unlike most city dwellers, she had the freedom to travel the four-plus hours round-trip to the capital, carrying with her a binder full of information about gun violence. Newman started organizing press conferences. Their mission became all-consuming. "We didn't know what we were doing," Newman conceded. "We weren't funded by anyone, we didn't have any outside help," she told me, with a twinge of pride in her voice. "We just went and did it ourselves." They soon realized that the local bills were experiments that would indicate to the NRA whether they could go national with their proposals. "All eyes were on Missouri," Newman said. She and Kirkton were offered encouragement from the Brady Campaign but little else. "They didn't have anything!" Newman said.

It is hard to imagine someone who embodies conservatives' necessary foil of the "gun grabber" better than Newman, who could pass for a Manhattanite, and who later decided her next cause would be abortion rights. When I spoke with Cauthorn, he conveyed his complete certainty in tidy phrases wherein the thorniest issues of American history were packed. Newman delivered her equally fervent conviction with full animation, gesturing, laughing, scoffing. Because men are often assumed to be rational, and rural men deemed authentic, here it is important to be clear: John Cauthorn and his counterparts do not have a stronger grip on reality. After all, Cauthorn told me that Americans no longer work hard and that any kind of firearms regulation could end with the federal government using heat-seeking devices to search for and seize all Americans' guns. Newman's and Cauthorn's different cadences and presentations are important, though, because when Republicans chose as their primary issues guns and abortion, they had at their disposal the double-bind that makes a caricature of women no matter how they live: pro-choice advocates could be smeared as the quintessence of selfish, anti-family whores, while gun control activists emphasizing their authority as mothers were easily made out to be killjoy nags, so nervous and safety-obsessed that they wanted to clip men's God-given freedoms, the most obvious expression of their masculinity. It would have been much harder to discredit pro-choice or gun control advocates without those convenient tropes, planted in the unconscious of most Americans no matter their political affiliation.

Newman herself told me that no one in the legislature was going to be persuaded to change positions on guns or abortion during a committee hearing or floor debate. Her opinions are fixed, as are most officials'. The crucial task is getting candidates elected, which means finding solid people to run, registering tons of people to vote, and getting more registered voters to show up to the polls. But around the time she became politically involved, that laborious work was becoming less and less possible. Within the local Democratic Party, the resources for basic electoral groundwork were drying up. Republicans still had groups with a statewide presence, like Missouri Right to Life, working on the ground to leaflet parking lots.

In 2002, every Missouri House seat and seventeen of thirty-four of the Senate seats were up for grabs. The assembly had recently instituted term limits, creating a massive, simultaneous turnover. Newman was hired to work for the local Democratic Party to organize women's groups. The idea of specifically reaching out to women with different messaging was something new. She had a salary but no budget. She remembered sitting cross-legged on the floor, before the office had desks, thinking, "How do I do this? What am I supposed to do?" That year, pushing anti-abortion, pro-gun messaging in outstate districts, Missouri Republicans increased their majority in the Senate and won over the

House. “Election night was horrible, everybody was crying,” Newman remembered. That was it. Republicans had the legislature, and they haven’t given it up since.

In 2004, when John Kerry was running for president, his campaign absorbed the local party’s staff. “Again, the armies start coming in,” Newman said. “Missouri was still a battleground state.” A field team spread out. Newman described a fevered season of organizing volunteers to make thousands of targeted calls. She organized events with national celebrities in Kansas City and St. Louis. When at the end of October polls showed that Kerry would lose Missouri, the temporary team abandoned the St. Louis office and scattered to Ohio and Florida. “Always the emphasis in any election—whether it be midterm, presidential—is the top of the ticket,” Newman explained. “This was normal.” Newman considered riding along to help in Florida. “Meanwhile, you’ve got Claire [McCaskill], who is running for governor, but now she doesn’t have the presidential resources which she was counting on. So now she’s the top of the ticket. And I’ve elected to stay, because I’m thinking, ‘Well, I’ve already got my work, my network, my everything here.’” Newman added, “I’m also thinking beyond November. I’m going to be staying in this state, I care about this state.” The remaining skeleton team prioritized reaching out to solid Democratic voters to remind them to vote. They no longer had resources to contact anyone else.

“We lose, we lose, we lose,” Newman remembered. Kerry lost. McCaskill lost. Missouri Democrats again lost in the state House and Senate. The dissolution of the Kerry campaign’s St. Louis headquarters foreshadowed what Missouri would become after losing its swing status, when it was no longer a prize teetering precariously between two warring camps, meaning national strategists would stop bothering to fight there.

CHAPTER THREE

Colorado

THAT NIGHT IN NOVEMBER 2004, WHEN THE DEMOCRATS in St. Louis lost, lost, lost, the mood was just as bleak in New York and DC, where Democratic donors and strategists had gathered to watch the returns come in. As the breakdown of the numbers became clear, with states like Missouri, Colorado, and Florida voting to give George W. Bush a second term, liberal donors and political strategists who had drained at least $350 million in trying to elect John Kerry faced a reckoning.[1] The Bush years would prove to be a time of reinvention and reinvigoration, as Democratic and progressive strategists had no choice but to realize that something had to change. That era was a precursor to the surge of the resistance after Donald Trump's election in 2016. After the elections of 2000 and 2004, too, there was despair, agitation, then hope for a new way forward. Whereas the post-2016 surge of resistance was on full display, including in the streets, the 2004 age of reinvention was more secretive. It rippled through the professional political class. Many of the ideas generated then were discussed in behind-the-scenes meetings with political operatives who were trying to figure out new ways to coordinate and deploy resources.

Those new ideas mostly bent around national politics or the internet—this was the dot-com era when a burst of web ventures took off. Moveon.org began rounding up petitions, and the meeting of progressive organizers and media types called Netroots was formed. But strategists zeroed in on local and state politics, too. In the early 2000s, Colorado Democrats got tired of losing. What came next, and its results, would later become known as "the Colorado model," shorthand among progressive donors and organizers nationwide for a blueprint that is still being attempted, with various degrees of success, in at least a dozen states, including Minnesota, Georgia, and Florida. "I think it might be the single most effective electoral machinery that has ever been built in American electoral politics," said Rob Stein, founder of the Democracy Alliance, a consortium of donors, when describing the Colorado model. Arguably more important: the players that helped build that new electoral machine didn't let their attention lapse after each election cycle. They expanded their giving and strategizing so that they cultivated a generation of talented leaders, and a whole new political culture.

I traveled to Denver in 2017 and 2018 to see what made its politics different. Everyone I spoke with told me that Colorado was a great—even the best—place to work in progressive politics. On November 6, 2018, in the much-anticipated midterms, Colorado Democrats secured a trifecta—governorship, House, and Senate. That big win was cited in national postelection roundups as evidence that Democrats were turning the tides, that the "resistance" had created tangible gains. Colorado Democrats' successes, though, were more than a reaction against Trump or a lucky night or a demographic shift. The state's progressive organizations did not burst into existence after 2016. People had been working day in and day out, for years, to keep Colorado Democrats and progressives in the game. Sometimes they lost, sometimes they won. Their turning point was not 2016 but 2000. The seeds of their renewal were planted as a reaction not to Donald Trump but to George W. Bush and their local Republican lawmakers.

★ ★ ★

When a cadre of Coloradans first decided to take matters into their own hands, there was no indication that they would win. At first, their efforts were one long-shot try, and then another. Republicans had controlled the assembly since the 1960s. Sure, this was Colorado, with its frontier heritage, its live-and-let-live ethos, and its independent voters, a state with a strand of progressivism so central to its core that it was the first state in the nation where women were elected to the legislature. Coloradan women had the right to vote twenty-six years before the Nineteenth Amendment established women's suffrage nationwide. But this was the Colorado of the early 2000s, the pre-marijuana-legalization Colorado, where the governor, Bill Owens, had recently been named by the conservative magazine *National Review* "America's Best Governor" for not backing down on gun rights after the shooting at Columbine High School, as well as for not approving of Planned Parenthood, and, when he was in the state assembly back in 1992, supporting a measure that prohibited the legislature from raising taxes without the public's expressed consent. That latter measure had been a longtime dream of libertarian activists, never passed in another state despite ardent advocacy from Americans for Prosperity.[2] In Colorado, as elsewhere, the rural-urban divide was a cultural fault line.

As the 2000 elections approached, Colorado Democrats hustled like never before to overcome that fault line and win on the state level. It worked. Democrats won control of the state Senate. Then, two years later, they lost it again. That briefly held victory showed them that winning was possible. In anticipation of the 2004 elections, Alice Madden, then the minority leader in the Colorado House, talked with Al Yates, who had just stepped down from his role as president of Colorado State University. Yates knew Pat Stryker, an heiress then worth about $1.5 billion (and by 2019 about $2.6 billion). Stryker lived in Fort Collins, north of Denver, and was by all accounts a low-key, private person. She had first gotten involved in state politics by hurling the weight of her fortune to stop a ballot initiative that would have required all public-school classes to be taught in English. Madden, Yates, and Stryker set up a meeting.[3]

Democrats needed to win just one extra seat in the state Senate to reclaim control. Madden put together a PowerPoint presentation that outlined five districts she wanted Democrats to target in order to win the state House, too. That summer of 2004, Madden and Yates drove out to Fort Collins to persuade Stryker that their plan to retake the House was worth a major donation. Madden laid out what she called "a business case." When I talked with her in 2018, a time when the national press was speculating daily about the "Blue Wave" as either impending or overhyped, Madden told me that when she heard political prognosticating she always thought, "Show me the numbers, show me the turnover, where the incumbents are, what the Democratic performance is . . . literally, who lives in this district, what are their interests."

That day in 2004, nervous, feeling out of her depth, Madden presented that kind of granular information to Stryker, with Yates watching. Yates remarked that if they needed to win five swing seats, they needed to target more. Madden suggested that if Stryker gave enough, they could target seven or eight districts. "Once we got her involved," Madden told me, "it really changed the game, because when you have money it attracts money. Suddenly, we were legitimate." (The same principle is behind the name of EMILY's List, which stands for Early Money Is Like Yeast.) Madden knew a war chest was a practical necessity if they were going to challenge Republicans' long-standing hold on the state.

Around the same time, Stryker and three other ultra-wealthy Coloradans—Tim Gill, Rutt Bridges, and Jared Polis—had gotten in touch with one another, knowing that they were each dissatisfied with the status quo. Later, when they were credited with or lambasted for reshaping Colorado politics, they were known as the Gang of Four, or the Four Horsemen. When they met, each had already independently gotten involved in political or philanthropic efforts, largely out of public view. Stryker had led the push against the English-language amendment. Gill, otherwise a relatively nonpartisan patron of the arts, had put a few thousand dollars into trying to defeat Initiative Two, the statewide ballot measure that allowed for discrimination on the basis of sexual orientation and was approved by voters during the 1992 election. Until 2007, that antigay measure overrode protections already passed in cities like Denver and Boulder. Bridges had created the Bell Policy Center, which he called a think tank dedicated to the moderate voice "in an increasingly polarized landscape." The most extreme among the pet investments was probably Jared Polis's decision to spend $1 million on his 2000 campaign for a spot on the state's school board, a part-time unpaid position helping to oversee the Colorado Department of Education. After all that money, he beat his opponent by 90 out of 1.6 million votes cast. His self-funded victory foreshadowed later runs, and wins, for Congress and governor.

For Polis, the price of entry to elected office was a relative pittance. When he was in his early twenties, he had sold an online greeting card company for $430 million in stock and $350 million in cash. Tim Gill had built a software company called Quark and sold his stake in the company for half a billion dollars. Rutt Bridges was also a multimillionaire after inventing software used in the oil and gas industry. Stryker was the only one in the cohort who had become ultrarich through an inheritance.[4]

Those four represented a larger, still-accelerating change. An increasing share of philanthropic and political donors are from "the new economy," meaning tech and finance, versus "the old economy" of oil or gas extraction. Whereas the old-money crowd—Rockefeller, Koch, and the like—tend to invest in conservative causes and institutions, tech billionaires are more likely to skew to the left, at least on divisive questions like abortion, guns, LGBTQ issues, and immigration. Their views differed from the rest of Americans', too. "The rich are very different from us in their views of policy," explained David Callahan, author and founder of Inside Philanthropy, a watchdog group. "They're more economically conservative, more socially liberal and more internationalist."

Bloomberg Businessweek would later call Gill "America's Gay Corporate Warrior," after Colorado's antigay legislation inspired him to coordinate gay donors to flood pro-gay-rights local and state candidates around the country with donations, raising millions for far-flung heartland races that otherwise would have flown under the radar for people living in New York or San Francisco. They were part of an emerging Democratic donor class that would give to political groups outside the party. Between 2004 and 2008, political organizations with the 527 designation—precursors to political action committees (PACs)—raised and gave to candidates roughly $1.5 billion, most of which went to Democrats.[5]

That summer of 2004, the Gang of Four or their surrogates (Yates standing in for Stryker, Ted Trimpa, a former tobacco lobbyist, for Tim Gill), as well as fellow Democratic state lawmakers and leaders of various progressive groups like NARAL, Colorado Conservation Voters, and the AFL-CIO, met in a conference room of the Colorado Education Association, a grim, blockish building across the street from the state capitol. They talked about their singular goal. Unlike so many other ambitious megadonors and political operatives fixated on felling President George W. Bush or controlling Congress, the Coloradans kept their focus on getting more Democrats under the gold-capped capitol dome across the street.

The regular gatherings of surrogates from various organizations were soon known as the Roundtable. One attendee told me that the first rule of the Roundtable, which would come to be the primary principle of Colorado progressive politics, was "Check your shit at the door." They were determined not to succumb to the infighting that typically engulfed efforts to get left-leaning groups working together. That meant that they would not discuss the merits of any one issue or policy. Instead, they would do whatever it took to put Democrats in office, under the assumption that having more Democrats in general would be better for any one donor or organization's preferred cause, whether gay rights or labor law.

Roundtable members came to a key realization early on. Remember, this was two years after Congress passed the McCain-Feingold Act, which limited how political parties could coordinate with campaigns. But interest groups were still allowed to work together. Members of the Roundtable began to see themselves as a replacement for the Democratic Party. Newcomers were able to take the reins for a number of reasons that also explained why Colorado politics was a relatively clean affair, compared to business-as-usual in states like Florida, Missouri, or New York. First, Colorado became a state after the Civil War, so vestiges of slavery and the Jim Crow era were not as etched into its culture and laws as in states like Missouri and Florida. Because Colorado was a young state, and because Democrats had rarely been in charge, there was no Democratic machine whose gears spun on kickbacks and fear of retribution. Few if any multinational corporations were headquartered in Colorado, and so there were relatively few corporate players trying to buy influence. Oil and gas companies spent huge sums on elections and lobbying, but they were the exception. And nonprofit good-government groups like Common Cause had been located in Denver for decades by the time the Roundtable got together. Nonprofits and activists had fought for more transparency, a value that was embraced by the general public in a region proud of its libertarian ethos.[6]

While the money the Roundtable spent later became the focus of attention, the coordination between different players is what made the effort unique, Madden told me. Democrats were always going to have less money, so they needed to stretch what they had. They synchronized their plans so that they wouldn't double or triple up on radio ads or mailers or volunteers in certain areas while neglecting others. "None of this was rocket science, but nobody was doing it," which boggled their minds, she explained. She credited their success in part to the fact that many of them were relatively new if not totally green when it came to running campaigns: "It's hard to think inside the box when you've never been in the box."

Maybe the superrich donors and political junkies sharing Whole Foods cheese plates in that conference room on Colfax Avenue in downtown Denver weren't any more predisposed to being in touch with the average Coloradan's fears and dreams than longtime members of a political machine, but they had on their side the confidence of having amassed hundreds of millions of dollars before hitting middle age. Polis reflected later that "there's no reason to think [party leaders] would be good at running campaigns and making tough decisions." From the Roundtable founders' perspective, the shortsighted cronyism of the Democratic Party had stymied what could have been; the insurgent strategists wanted to use a "business mentality."[7] This, too, was part of a broader trend with philanthropy and politics. Democrats in general had become preoccupied with analytics, perhaps to the party's detriment, as many later argued. Top philanthropists were also spreading the idea that nonprofits should aspire to operate like private businesses, prioritizing efficiency as a measure of efficacy. Donors were encouraged to invest in whatever programs could prove their efficiency. The premise that a professional class and wealthy patrons, precisely because of their experience creating businesses and managing wealth, could create leaner, more efficient, and therefore more helpful nonprofit organizations was very much in the air when the Gang of Four took it upon themselves to improve Colorado's politics.

The newly assembled Colorado Roundtable zeroed in on their targeted districts, eventually spending roughly $1.5 million on state races. Republicans had no way of anticipating what was about to happen. That, Madden said, was their best advantage. The Gang of Four funded a blitz of negative ads against Republican candidates for state offices. They fought to win. That didn't mean taking the high road. They pummeled Republicans with negative ads. Madden remembered how, for example, they had unseated Bob Briggs, a well-liked representative from a district just outside Denver. He had voted against a bill that would have expanded programs for survivors of domestic violence. One of the Gang of Four's political action committees mailed out glossy ads picturing a woman with a black eye. Madden conceded later: "I mean, that was pretty intense, obviously."[8] On November 2, 2004, while national strategists watched the bottom fall out, again, Colorado Democrats celebrated winning control of the state Senate and House, to the surprise of almost everyone—including some Roundtable members. Somewhere at least, Democrats had figured out how to win.

* * *

As the Gang of Four teamed up, veteran progressive organizers and Democratic operatives in DC were trying to imagine their way out of their own dilemmas. After Al Gore lost to George W. Bush, in the high-stakes debacle over misread ballots in 2000, and then Republicans won both houses of Congress in 2002, several new ideas and organizations emerged simultaneously—and they would dovetail with what was happening on Colfax Avenue in Denver. John Podesta, former chief of staff to President Bill Clinton, made the rounds on the dinner party circuit, selling donors on the idea of a left-leaning "think tank on steroids." Back in the '90s, George Soros's Open Society Foundations had commissioned a study that made waves in DC circles. It found that liberals lagged behind conservatives in idea generation because they had no capacity to formulate a political philosophy. In other words, no one was ponying up funding for the left's political intellectuals to stand back and think big. Soros, however, was allergic to any whiff of ideological politics and rejected the idea of funding a partisan think tank. In 2003, Podesta founded the Center for American Progress, which he and his staff would model on the right's idea-generating behemoths like the Heritage Foundation.[9]

Gloria Totten, who had just served as the political director of NARAL Pro-Choice America, was then founding Progressive Majority, which sought to recruit, train, and elect progressive state and local lawmakers. While working at NARAL, Totten had witnessed firsthand the state affiliate directors quitting en masse in protest over how little support they received from the national organization. For years, progressive leaders had understood that they and their allies were failing to cultivate enough talent. Totten and others believed that because the Democratic Party had assumed responsibility for recruiting and training potential candidates, those candidates were drifting rightward along with the centrists who steered the party. Meanwhile, the candidate training programs that did exist, both within and outside the party, were modest in scope. "How are we going to change the world finding a dozen candidates at a time?" Totten remembered thinking. "So that's when I came up with this notion of doing a farm team system and switching completely from national to state and local and building a bench." Progressive Majority would specifically focus on supporting strong progressives who wanted to be elected to city councils and state legislatures. They provided "soup to nuts" support. Progressive Majority, Totten said soon after its founding, was "the first step in a long-range project to fill the pipeline with the next generation of progressive elected leaders."[10]

Around the same time, a handful of longtime and well-connected organizers started America Votes. Cofounder Cecile Richards, a former labor organizer (and soon-to-be president of Planned Parenthood) and daughter of the former governor of Texas Ann Richards, described America Votes as a "traffic cop" and intermediary for the various arms of the Democratic coalition—labor, environmental groups, pro-choice organizations, and so forth. America Votes' other cofounders included Ellen Malcolm, who had started EMILY's List, the group that endorsed and supported pro-choice female candidates; Carl Pope, executive director of the Sierra Club; Harold M. Ickes, a former Clinton administration official; and Steve Rosenthal and Andy Stern, directors of the national progressive unions AFL-CIO and Service Employees International Union, respectively. The group would work behind the scenes, and with a national focus, but its creation signaled progressive leaders' shared recognition of their side's underlying weaknesses and the need for a new, unified strategy.[11]

That these organizations came into existence around the same time was key to their survival, Totten told me later. "The progressive movement needed to move beyond single-issue organizations that were trying to do everything to multi-issue organizations that did one thing really well, or two things really well," she explained. "We were all in sync about making the case for the structure and the kind of work. We were able to make similar cases to donors about the importance of the states."

Another key player was fomenting a plan: In Washington, DC, soon after the 2004 election, Rob Stein, a former Clinton official, started a front group called Copper Beech LLC. Copper beech trees take almost a century to mature, and so Stein decided they were an apt metaphor for what he hoped would happen, should his plan work. Bush's reelection had not been his wake-up call. Instead, after almost a decade of obsessive research, he well understood how during the 1970s Lewis Powell had inspired right-wing donors and business leaders to invest steadily over generations in what Stein called a "message machine."[12] In 2003, just as Podesta, Richards, Totten, and many others were talking about the need for their respective ventures, Stein had created a PowerPoint presentation about the "the infrastructure" that held up the right-wing apparatus: anchor donors provided constant streams of money, and political operatives worked like investment bankers by dispersing that money into various organizations. Stein's central premise was that Republicans were successful because of that system. In a sense, Stein was repeating what Reagan's adviser Paul Weyrich had done many years earlier, when he caught on to the 1970s liberal establishment's coordination.

The urgency was heightened, as the Gang of Four and their allies in Colorado had discovered, because post-McCain-Feingold the Democratic Party was totally broke. Everyone understood that it would stay broke. In his book about the shifting political winds of the 2000s, *The Argument*, political journalist Matt Bai hit upon the perfect analogy after talking with Andy Rappaport. Rappaport was a venture capitalist who believed that the Democrats were grasping around for "the Thing" that would save them. The Democratic Party, Bai wrote, had become like General Motors post-globalization. As times changed, both the Democratic Party and GM's leadership took for granted their behemoth status, which blinded them to the real threat posed by new rivals. By the time both GM and the Democratic Party's leadership caught on, it was too late. "It wasn't that GM couldn't see what was happening. It was just that too much of the company's identity was bound up in its twentieth-century glory days and its disjointed bureaucracy that they had spawned," Bai wrote.[13] The problem, of course, wasn't simply that they needed to tweak their messaging; they needed a new framework altogether. Likewise, the Democratic Party kept running analytics and searching for its version of the Thing, always harking back to a basic set of New Deal positions that rang with nostalgia for an era that few living Americans had experienced.

The future of political organizing and innovation was outside of the official party structures. There, maybe, Stein and his cohort believed, was the Thing. Republican candidates already had the support of the right's infrastructure that existed outside the party. Democratic candidates had no analogous support. Progressive donors and nonparty organizations needed to kick it into gear and organize themselves toward aligned goals. Stein became evangelical. He showed his PowerPoint to some of the well-connected people he knew in Washington. Similar ideas had been discussed for years, but Stein crystallized the message and assembled audiences who were ready to listen. To billionaires, influential politicos, and the people around them, he proselytized his insights: people in different roles needed to regularly come together for strategy conversations that considered the interests of a broad movement—one that involved donors, political strategists, activists, and advocates. They needed to figure out a system that would incentivize big donors to give consistently, as the patrons of the right's many organizations did.

In 2005, Stein cofounded the Democracy Alliance, a coalition of progressive donors, with the aim of building a left-leaning infrastructure. That year, the Democracy Alliance held its first meeting for donors, in Arizona. A few months later, the Democracy Alliance had eighty members who each pledged to contribute at least $200,000 per year to the fund. The Democracy Alliance staff would divvy up those funds among the selected progressive groups.[14] Most of the groups were based in DC and national in focus. Among the exceptions was Totten's Progressive Majority, which would keep its laser focus on flipping city councils and state legislatures by finding, grooming, and electing strong candidates.

If everything jelled, they imagined, in some not-so-distant future something like this would happen: Totten's group would get progressive candidates on the ballot, America Votes would coordinate groups that drummed up energy for progressive ideals and turned out voters, the Center for American Progress would supply those groups and journalists with data that would bolster their arguments, and so forth. None of those players, no matter how strategic, could be effective in a vacuum. It didn't matter, for example, if there was a fabulous candidate for office if no one had heard of her or showed up to vote. That message, and the lesson of 2004, was received. Today, it is almost impossible to make it through a conversation about the status of the progressive movement without hearing the word "infrastructure." Foundation officers, Democratic party directors, community organizers, lobbyists, everybody brings up the need for an infrastructure—lots of organizations that are all rooted in the same place and fulfill different but synchronized roles. It may not be the most dazzling or emotionally resonant term, but "infrastructure" defines what politicos decided was missing.

One of the first people Stein talked with was Rappaport, who was intrigued. Before long, he was turned off by the prospect of the Democracy Alliance turning into a social club. He was more interested in a genuine incubator and so focused on his and his wife's investment firm, Skyline Public Works. Later, some critics would validate his premonition and say that the Democracy Alliance was mired by the same issues as the Democratic Party. Donors who gave because they wanted access to elected officials had too much say; strategies were designed to win federal elections in a handful of swing states. Yet, despite internal fissures, the Democracy Alliance kept growing. By 2008, the coalition parceled out more than $80 million to thirty-five different groups.[15] Some of those groups, like Progressive Majority, promoted local or state-based initiatives. The Democracy Alliance's underlying goal was shifting power in national politics and policy.

The Gang of Four, meanwhile, got in touch with Stein. They formed the Colorado Democracy Alliance (a totally separate entity with a borrowed name just because they liked it so much), which would focus primarily on the state. The Colorado Democracy Alliance would have paid staff that would serve as a conduit between donors and progressive groups. The affiliated groups would come together for regular roundtable meetings to coordinate strategy, just as their cadre had for the 2004 election. Stein told me that for a state's electoral machine to be effective it needed to have local staff that could serve a variety of functions, like crunching data for campaigns, registering voters, organizing different communities, and getting the word out. Soon after the Colorado Democracy Alliance formed, Stein cofounded the Committee on States, which would serve as an umbrella group for roundtables that they would start in other states, starting with North Carolina and Minnesota. Some fifteen years later, as we head into the winner-take-all 2020 elections, operatives and organizers are still assessing states' chances to swing or stay Democratic by looking at their local infrastructures. In a few states, including Missouri and Florida, progressives are trying to solidify newer infrastructures. They don't have what Colorado had—local billionaires willing to bolster statewide progressive organizations. And that makes all the difference. It is worth remembering: the Gang of Four and their counterparts nationwide may have given to the Colorado Democracy Alliance and other campaigns out of a sense of moral obligation or fear for their own civil rights rather than desire to invest in self-interested economic policies, but those corporate warriors' collective influence nonetheless harks back to Supreme Court justice Louis Brandeis's evergreen observation that "we can have democracy in this country or we can have great wealth concentrated in the hands of a few, but we can't have both."[16]

That tension, and the reality that our political system is driven by money, was also inherent in establishing and scaling up the nationally focused Democracy Alliance. Its founders wrestled with questions like: How many donors should join? What would their responsibilities be? and What should be kept secret? Trying to set protocols also unearthed a rabbit hole of questions that were at once logistical and philosophical, the same questions that progressive institutions and organizers are still trying to answer: Who should have final say in how the money was spent and the agenda set? Donors needed to be given enough control that they felt ownership and wanted to keep giving. But the whole point of the operation was to execute a strategic plan, and that would mean the staff setting clear parameters. Would Democracy Alliance staff having final veto power alienate billionaire donors used to getting their way? Eventually it was decided that the Democracy Alliance wouldn't hand out funds but instead would bring donors to biannual meetings where the donors themselves could decide which of the vetted organizations to fund.

And then, of course, there were the standard questions critics would ask of various attempts at funding the progressive movement: What about the local organizations, the people themselves? Was an initiative really a groundbreaking progressive enterprise if the purse strings were held by mostly white megadonors or political consultants who expected their grantees to stick to their proscribed program to achieve their end goal? Shouldn't the people actually involved in the day-to-day work of the movements on the ground get to make the big decisions? Nobody liked rich people from other places coming in and telling them what to do. And yet the whole point was to be coordinated, to mirror the Kochs and their Americans for Prosperity, which worked like a well-oiled machine in large part because it was hierarchical, with a chain of command. Then again, progressives didn't value those kinds of hierarchies as much as they valued equality, representation, even messiness, so who cared how the Kochs structured their groups? Well, everybody cared, because the Kochs were winning everywhere. They won because they had a plan. There were hierarchies within the progressive circles, too, and attempts to pretend otherwise were disingenuous. And so, these questions continue to loop on repeat, a yet-to-be-resolved series of dilemmas about how to reconcile progressives' need for a constant stream of huge sums of money, a well-executed ground game, and a system that creates those conditions without exiling any or all of the different cohorts needed to win.

When I talked to Stein years later, several months after the 2016 election, he wanted to emphasize a distinction that was still relevant, maybe more relevant than ever. There are electoral groups tasked with getting people elected. And there are movements, which take on pushing the culture and politics forward on causes, for example Black Lives Matter or the environmental movement. To keep progressives in the game, Stein told me, the people working in both those camps—electoral campaigns and social movements—needed to understand that there was an "honest tension" between the roles that they fulfilled. Electoral staff needed to be "disciplined, rigorous" about which candidate or policy idea could win in a particular district. Movement people, naturally, often had reasons to fervently disagree with the electoral strategists' choices, and to push back. This idea would stick with me as I talked to people around the country. It was easier to reconcile a wide range of points of view on which tactics or candidates were best when I understood that everyone had a different role. Endorsing one candidate or philosophy over another was not necessarily proof of moral fiber, ruthlessness, or wild-eyed idealism. Stein's point was that electoral and movement strategists cannot let their different vantages prevent them from working together: "We are in a fundamental transition of relationships among parties, electoral nonprofits, and movements. And there's no custodian of all wisdom on how best to do it. But particularly on the left, unless there's alignment, we will kill ourselves and the other side will win every day."

* * *

As the Colorado Democracy Alliance came into existence, another unlikely catalyst for change arrived in Denver: a group of friends graduated from the University of Colorado–Boulder.

Among them was Leslie Herod, who was Representative Herod of Denver's Eighth District when I met her in 2017; Steve Fenberg, who in 2016 was elected to the state Senate; Joe Neguse, who was elected to Congress in the 2018 midterms; and Lisa Kaufmann, chief of staff to then-Congressman Jared Polis. Back in the mid-2000s, at a glance, they weren't your average recent college graduates. They were former "student government nerds," as Fenberg put it. That alone distinguished them. Across the country, Americans ages eighteen to twenty-nine were less politically engaged and voted at lower rates than older Americans. That was especially true outside presidential elections. In 2002, a midterm election year, just 22 percent of eligible Americans under thirty had voted; in 2004, for the presidential election, 49 percent voted.[17] Their generation had grown up well after the days when NAACP organizers who led voting drives were murdered and yet before the economy collapsed and drove young people into the streets. The wars without end in Iraq and Afghanistan dragged on, under false pretenses. Their generation's relationship to politics was marked by profound disillusionment.

The group of friends from CU Boulder had already learned from experience that progress was not inevitable but possible. The inner workings of a student government hardly seem like critical details in any history, but it is exactly these kinds of unglamorous programs and experiences that put people on track to becoming local political leaders. The Farm Bureau meetings in outstate Missouri, for example, helped facilitate the careers of Republican legislators. CU Boulder student government alums—like Kamala Harris's policy adviser Sergio Gonzales—have gone on to hold influential posts at relatively young ages. No wonder. At Boulder, student leaders had a staggering amount of responsibility. Their annual budget was roughly $20 million. Student leaders themselves oversaw the full operation of student centers around campus—meaning they handled their budgets and administration.[18] For many young people, attending a four-year college means coming to a social consciousness in the realm of big ideas, sharpening ideology in the abstract, but at Boulder it also meant grappling with the same kinds of immediate dilemmas that make governing different from activism. They couldn't barrel blindly toward whatever idea they thought was morally right. Whereas student protesters could demand that the university divest from the fossil fuel industry, for example, a leader tasked with balancing the budget needed to ask whether divesting was worth reducing workers' benefits. They had to weigh real trade-offs.

Then they graduated. "We had expected these really big jobs to come our way," Herod remembered. "Quite frankly, they didn't." She laughed when recalling her friends' surprise that nobody wanted to hire them based on their college titles. The only political opportunities that seemed available were short-term jobs walking around campuses with a clipboard, soliciting donations or signatures. At Boulder their accomplishments included hammering out a plan to expand benefits for employees at the university centers under their control. Under their plan, employees' health benefits covered domestic partners, a coup for gay employees. That policy was groundbreaking—gay marriage wouldn't be legalized nationwide for twelve years—and it pressured the University of Colorado's administration to recognize civil unions in its blanket policy for other campus employees. After that, dead-end canvassing jobs weren't going to cut it. They had grown accustomed to operating in a system based on implicit trust in young people. They wanted to keep doing political work. But they didn't know how. "When it came to state-level politics," Fenberg remembered, "you really had to fight your way in. Even then, it was difficult to navigate. We didn't understand the rules. We didn't have anyone to help." They were frustrated by outside groups coming into Colorado when they wanted to swing national elections—and then leaving. They didn't want to join the Democratic Party's ranks, either. They wanted to work to change local power dynamics, to push for progressive ideals, to sustain a movement that would last. To do that, they realized, they needed to build something new themselves. "We knew that there was a need for it, because if it had already existed then we would've been a part of it," Fenberg explained.

In the summer of 2006, Neguse and Herod were working as aides in the capitol. Fenberg was going to work as a camp counselor in the mountains. Fenberg's roommate showed him a forwarded e-mail from his parents. A family foundation—Skyline Public Works—was looking to fund a youth organization. It was almost uncanny; the call for proposals described exactly what the group of friends wanted to start. They knew that they wanted their not-yet-existent organization to register young people to vote. But, so far, they had only talked about their project. Getting seed money would make it real. They applied. Fenberg was at the camp when he got the call that they were finalists for the grant. When, over a decade later, Fenberg and Herod both recounted the events, at this moment in the story their voices shifted, inflected with amazement and pride, as if they still couldn't believe their luck and what they had managed to pull off. There were over one hundred applications. They were among the very few flown to Washington, DC, to meet the funders. They originally planned on calling themselves YPAC, Young People Affecting Change, which sounded official, but then it occurred to them that it might not be legal to call themselves a PAC if they weren't really a political action committee. Herod came up with the name New Era Colorado. They went with it. Then, a few weeks later, the program officers flew to Denver. Fenberg met them for an interview in the lobby of a high-end downtown hotel and tried to present himself as a political entrepreneur, not a camp counselor.

"I barely probably had a suit to wear," Fenberg remembered. "We were a startup, we didn't really exist yet, but at the same time we have to act like we did exist, or at least . . . like we knew exactly what we would do if we got the money." Once Fenberg's performance in the hotel worked, they had one more major hurdle. The grant was a matching grant, meaning that they would get the funds only if they came up with an equal amount—$250,000—from other donors. None of them had ever raised money before. Herod had an idea of whom she could ask.

By the time the New Era cohort needed seed money, the ground in Colorado had been softened. Previously, or someplace else, it might have been all but impossible to find a single person willing to make a bet on a startup organization run by twenty-somethings who would register voters in a demographic that didn't usually vote, and starting in a nonpresidential election year. But the times and strategy had changed. Surrogates from Colorado progressive organizations were now meeting and coordinating regularly through "the table." A roundtable of (c)4 advocacy organizations (which legally could do some overtly political work) had already been established. Within a couple of years, there was also a (c)3 table (composed of organizations whose mandate needed to be education and engagement). Those groups would send surrogates to strategy meetings, constantly confer with one another, and eventually share board members. Meanwhile, through the gay political scene in Denver, Herod knew Ted Trimpa, who worked for Tim Gill. He helped arrange meetings. Herod summed up, "In came the Four Horsemen, the stalwarts of the progressive movement in Colorado . . . and they matched right away, and we're off."

★ ★ ★

When I first arrived in Denver, it didn't occur to me that New Era was groundbreaking. As I toured the offices of various political groups, I almost skipped its gray-green house on Humboldt Street. New Era was then the largest youth civic engagement outfit in the country, run by a woman still in her twenties. They were marshaling a $1.8 million budget to register tens of thousands of voters. But its mission did not awe me. I was thinking the way too many foundation officers and assigning editors think, hunting for a shiny penny that will make for an unusual story. New Era's primary mission—registering young people to vote—seemed, frankly, sort of boring, or at least not dramatic enough to carry the hope of a new politics. The importance of the outfit struck me over the course of many conversations. Numerous other people who were shaping Colorado politics had come up through New Era. By bringing young people into politics, New Era had helped build a bench. Looking at New Era provided a way to look at the successes of the infrastructure in general. There was another major reason that New Era served as model of how progressives might build power on the local level. New Era found a method for solving a riddle at the heart of all political work. Political strategists have coveted low-propensity voters' attention for decades. New Era figured out how to get young people to want to participate in elections—and in political organizing and advocacy. That is the whole game.

None of its later achievements seemed destined in 2006, when New Era set up shop in an office a mile and a half from the capitol dome. When they started it was just Fenberg, the executive director, and Carrie Jackson, the first hire, a program director. Joe Neguse was president of the board, Herod vice president, Kauffman a board member. They would register young voters and find ways to pique young people's interest in the political process. "We do year-round political engagement," Fenberg told a reporter early on. "We don't want just election cycle thinking." And they explicitly did not want to be seen as the typical political types who took jobs working for the Democratic or the Republican Party. "We wanted to rebrand politics by young people for young people and bridge the gap between social life and politics," Fenberg said. "Here's the deal," the early website explained in a no-frills black font on beige, the look of the web back then: "We know our generation is being overlooked." They posted an agenda: election reform; lowering the age to run for office; student debt; progressive environmental solutions. Their 2006 voting guides pictured drawings of men wearing blue suits and gray ties, with crossed arms, and blank gray ovals for faces. Block letters proclaimed "THEY DON'T EXPECT YOU TO VOTE. PROVE THEM WRONG."

Behind the scenes, the responsibility of keeping New Era going rested primarily on Fenberg's shoulders. "I think that's why Steve went gray a little bit early," Herod told me, laughing. Building a nonprofit at the age of twenty-two was no small thing, even if they were in Colorado, supposedly a new bastion of upstart progressivism. "It was hard, probably the hardest thing I've ever done, maybe the hardest thing I ever will do," Fenberg told me. He had to continuously fund-raise. In retrospect he considered that crucial because he was forced to learn how to raise money—a skill learned only under duress—but at the time he made a lot of cold calls that went unreturned. The Gang of Four was funding organizations, but unlike the ACLU or Common Cause, New Era wasn't a brand name and hadn't proved itself. They weren't part of the in-group yet. "It was a lot of pressure to not only raise your own salary at that age but to have other people's salaries dependent on your job performance," Fenberg said. "So, when I couldn't pay an organizer, I took that pretty seriously." Sometimes they didn't make payroll. Meanwhile, New Era's board of directors was made up of other twenty-somethings, many of them his friends. "It's not like I had a board of experts to coach me," he remembered. "The way we learned was just by making a lot of mistakes, and it was really embarrassing."

Skyline Public Works provided training and remote staff for backup. Every week, as was required, Fenberg would get on the phone with Skyline staff and the three other grantees working in different states—all twenty-somethings piloting their own organizations. Being a part of that group was more instrumental to their survival and eventual success than anything else, Fenberg said. They would report their numbers and discuss problems, a routine that was alternately a life raft and a source of stress and competition. One of the people on the line each week was Matt Singer, patching in from Missoula, Montana.

When he was nineteen, money was tight and Singer had dropped out of college. He started working the graveyard shift in the kitchen at Perkins, a diner chain, in Billings. Working as a fry cook, Singer made an observation that he would take with him when he entered politics. Two good cooks could run the Perkins kitchen themselves. But cooks kept turning over because they were paid so little, necessitating three or four less-skilled cooks per shift. If the restaurant had raised their pay just a little, spending a few more bucks per hour, the competent cooks would have stayed and kept the operation running smoothly with fewer employees, ultimately not costing the restaurant any more money. Restaurant managers, meanwhile, were paid dramatically more and could do only a couple of things around the restaurant, none of them tasks that mattered much when things got busy. Those same principles applied to the hierarchies and pay scales within and between political organizations. And that observation would echo in my ears as I talked with organizers and campaign staff across the country.

While he was working at Perkins, Singer got involved at Montana Conservation Voters, which offered him a job as a community organizer in Missoula, a university town, on the opposite side of the state. "I jumped at the opportunity," Singer said. After he got to work in Missoula, "my bosses kept saying, 'Don't worry about young people. Young people don't vote,'" he remembered. He ignored that advice, since people around his age were the only ones who returned his calls.

A couple of years later, the cohort of young people that he had helped bring together with Montana Conservation Voters started their own group, Forward Montana. One of the other founders, Kevin Furey, a twenty-one-year-old who had just returned from serving in the Army Reserve in Iraq, ran for state legislature and, with their help, won. Within a few years, with a budget of something like $1,500, the young volunteers helped secure what Singer called "lots of small victories," like making sure the state changed its sexual assault policy so that minors who reported sexual assault wouldn't be given citations for underage drinking. "I've always started with the main assumption that we should meet people where they live," Singer told me, when I asked whether they focused on city, state, or national politics. "Where they live isn't a layer of government. Where they live is a set of problems in their life that they want addressed."

At the helm of Forward Montana, Singer also secured seed money from the Rappaport family that allowed him to make the organization more ambitious. He credited them with being ahead of the curve when it came to realizing the importance of investing in groups working within their cities and states. And unlike most large-scale donors, they weren't timorous about the prospect that maybe not everything would work out perfectly. "They told us that they didn't expect that all three of the organizations that they invested in would survive two years. They were okay with that and very much came in with a venture capital mind-set," Singer said. In tech and in venture capital—Rappaport's worlds—gambles were understood as necessary. They were built into the business model. Nobody has ever invented anything by doing what was guaranteed to work. And yet in the mainstream philanthropic and political funding worlds, analytics had winnowed down what was considered worthy to all but exclude the exact kinds of experimentation needed to solve problems. Funders often demanded proof of success from their grantees. Political operatives lived and died by analytics and the polls.

When we talked, years later, Singer riffed on how funders often frame donating money as taking a risk. "Really, what you're talking about is the risk that what you're donating to isn't going to work. That's not actually risk. That isn't going to hurt anybody. An actual risky donation would be something that you give and there's some chance that it is going to explode and cause harm." The Rappaports got that, Singer said. Then, Skyline ended the program early. "They were smart," Herod reflected, in that they had decided to enter swing states to engage likely Democrats two years ahead of the presidential year, rather than parachuting in three months before Election Day.

★ ★ ★

Across the country, meanwhile, political entrepreneurs were putting the new investments to work. Week after week, Progressive Majority was also trying to pull unlikely people into the political process at the local level. Starting in Washington, Wisconsin, and Pennsylvania, and then in three additional states every year, staffers scouted for potential progressive candidates. When Progressive Majority found their own progressives, they were able to skip what had become an empty ritual of Totten trying to persuade Democratic election committees that an unflinching progressive candidate was in fact a viable possibility in one district or another. Totten saw why her argument for solid progressivism was hard for some Democrats to swallow. Common wisdom had long held that Democrats could strike a balance between the competing factions of their base and also appeal to swing voters by offering candidates who would be perceived as centrist, as if they could find a median political figure everyone would like. "It is kind of counterintuitive to say what I say, which is, 'Stand up, be bold, push bold progressive solutions to real problems that people have, and we will connect. You will connect,'" Totten explained. She and her cohort believed that strong arguments and positions would better appeal to swing or infrequent voters, an intuition that some political science data supports. There is less of a "mushy middle" in American politics than there are lots of people for whom neither of the party's platforms is satisfying because they simultaneously hold far-right and far-left views. One study found that only 26.5 percent of the 2016 electorate held right-of-center views on economic policy.[19] At least hypothetically, that should leave an opening for candidates who focus their campaigns on raising the minimum wage or expanding Medicaid.

Progressive Majority's staff chose to open offices in states where it was possible to flip control of the legislature or city councils. "It wasn't a free-for-all where anybody who wants to run is going to be supported. It was very targeted toward shifting numbers and majorities, which we did systematically," Totten explained. They found candidates and gave them wraparound training and campaign support. They ran a political action committee to fund the races in each of their chosen states. Donors got behind the idea, Totten told me later, because "it was a really simple concept." The local Democratic parties had all but stopped similar recruitment and training, she said, because "it's superhard, laborious work." Prospective candidates "don't just fall from the sky."

"Listen," Totten would tell new hires, "this is going to be just like walking into a heating and air-conditioning company and sitting down with their call slips and cold calling people for business all day long. That's this job." Between 2004 and 2010, "We flipped six state legislatures and forty-seven local governments,"

Totten told me. For a stretch, it looked like Progressive Majority was on track, and momentum around local and state elections was growing.

★ ★ ★

Losing their main benefactor gave New Era more freedom. New Era wasn't an arm of the Democratic Party. It wasn't a chapter of a giant umbrella organization with oversight from a seasoned (read: cautious and stodgy) national director. And now it wasn't an adjunct of any foundation program, either. They were in charge. To raise money, they hosted keg parties where they charged for a cup. They made T-shirts and passed out condoms with wrappers that said "Vote, F*cker." "We were our own boss. That was what made it powerful and dangerous," Fenberg remembered. "We never had to run anything up the chain of command. We were scrappy, but we were also really agile." They didn't have anyone to censor them. "It's really easy to ignore the ideas of being genuine and organic when everyone is a professional consultant. We had zero consultants. We couldn't afford one if we wanted one. We were just twenty-two-year-olds that [were] like, 'Yes, this is what seems cool on Facebook right now.'"

In the first couple of years, keeping everything together overwhelmed Fenberg. "I would see my friends at other organizations, and their job was a piece of the puzzle, not the whole puzzle," he remembered. He started thinking, "Maybe I'm not the right person for this." Not long into his tenure as executive director, he handed the board his resignation. But then, weeks later, as they began interviewing candidates to replace him, he changed his mind and went back to work.

In those early days, New Era made YouTube videos that few if any political consultants would have green-lighted. In February 2007, less than a year after they officially launched, it was time for the caucuses. New Era staff understood that many young voters had no idea what a caucus was. Even informed locals could have been thrown off that year; the caucus date was five weeks earlier than usual. New Era came up with a YouTube video called

"The Caucus Comes Early." "Essentially, it's, um, two people kind of getting it on. It's steamy and over the top but meant to be funny," a young Fenberg told the press. "At the very end you see the girl kind of rolling her eyes, and they're done. And then it says 'Beware: The Caucus Comes Early This Year.' Then it gives information on what it means to be a caucus state, when it is and [how] you should be prepared for it." A few months later, there were Boulder City Council elections, the very sort of races that make most people's eyes glaze over. Seven of the nine city council seats were open, though, providing an outsize opportunity to influence the direction of the city. Ballots for that race were sent by mail. Young people tend to move around a lot, so many of them wouldn't get their ballots. New Era created a YouTube video called "Vote Naked," with information about how to make sure residents would receive their ballots, shot so that the pictured voters, a couple, looked naked.[20]

Today, after hundreds of hours of prime-time cable news programming have been dedicated to whether the president and his attorney paid off a former porn actress to keep silent about their affair, it seems almost quaint that anyone would blush over allusions to sex in a YouTube campaign that aimed to get young adults to the polls. But the reigning local politicos did not approve. Democratic Party officials asked—or, more accurately, demanded—that Fenberg pull the caucus video. He told them that New Era wasn't under their thumb. Legally the party couldn't give directives to an organization like theirs. More than that, New Era didn't share the party's primary objective of electing Democrats. Donors who wanted to get more young people to the polls might have had the ulterior motive of securing Democratic seats—young people are much more progressive than Americans as a whole—but that wasn't New Era's mission. "Our metric was engaging young people in the political process," Fenberg said. "In some ways, we were crashing the party. In other ways, we were inheriting it because we are the next generation of people to be doing this work." But that meant sometimes being inconvenient for both Democrats and Republicans. "Young people are often welcomed into the process when it serves people's interest. When it doesn't, they're really skeptical, and so [young people are seen as] carpetbaggers and they don't deserve to vote. I think that's just something that you are going to see forever."

Their strategies weren't just more provocative; they were more effective. In 2004, about fifteen people had shown up to the Boulder caucus. In 2008, almost five hundred people showed up, and a mass of them were under thirty.[21] Everyone I spoke to who had worked at New Era told me that their program worked because young people themselves were in charge of connecting with their audience—other young people. We all know that skin-crawling embarrassment of watching someone overdoing it as they try and fail to ingratiate themselves with someone outside their demographic. Registering to vote in particular is such a nuts-and-bolts task that it takes a certain spin to make it seem like something more than a civic chore, especially for a generation raised on irony and steeped in cynicism. "We were not only allowed to but probably required to sort of push the envelope a little bit," Fenberg said. Herod, who had gone on to work at the Gill Foundation, knew it was time for her to leave the board when at meetings she started catching herself getting cautious, thinking, "I don't know if we can say that."

By the time the 2008 election season rolled around, New Era owned a bus, which roved around the city and state packed with seasonal staff and volunteers. "Right now, so many groups are doing voter registration, but after the election, they'll leave," Fenberg said at the time. "We're pretty much the only ones out there doing it year-round and not just gearing up for a general election."[22] That election was their proving ground. Ninety percent of the people they registered to vote showed up at the polls. In a state where some district races were decided by a few hundred votes, that made a major dent. The share of young people who showed up to vote in Colorado increased in 2008. Colorado went to Barack Obama; on the state level, Democrats held on to their trifecta. Meanwhile, the mass migration of young people into the state, and into Denver in particular, was just picking up. New Era was perfectly positioned—its base was growing, and national and local donors understood the need for registering voters in a swing state. They had earned their place at the Roundtable meetings. They were in business.

In Montana, a different story unfolded. In Missoula, during those same years, Singer and Forward Montana were running on a parallel track. They helped to elect progressives to the city council, organized for local LGBTQ protection ordinances, pressured John Driscoll and Jon Tester to support the Affordable Care Act, and kept increasing voter turnout. "I kept looking around and being like, 'Man, we are doing good work,'" Singer remembered. Montana, though, didn't catch the eye of national donors as often as Colorado because it wasn't in the coveted "swing state" column. Missoula wasn't home to a network of donors willing or able to shell out tens of thousands of dollars to a constellation of nonprofits. "We were raising twenty-five or thirty thousand dollars a year in small donations in Missoula from our own young membership, but without some major donors we just weren't sustainable. Every month was month to month," Singer said. "That's a terrifying way to operate." The divergent fates of Forward Montana and New Era Colorado reflect just how recursive attention and opportunity are in politics. As Singer packed up to move to another state, the New Era founders had lots of reasons to stay in Colorado. They felt themselves on the brink of a new political age, one that was possible only because of years of careful investment.

CHAPTER FOUR

Florida

ADDRESSING A PACKED OPEN-AIR STADIUM IN ORLANDO, to thunderous applause, Barack Obama told the crowd, "Florida is crying out for a change." It was the fall of 2008, and he and his recent rival, Hillary Clinton, were touring the state, together and separately, reiterating to crowds that they needed to knock on doors and tell their friends to vote. "We can't take one vote for granted," Clinton told her supporters, urging them to volunteer for Obama.[1] To win Florida, the ultimate swing state, where all eyes turn every four years, the Obama campaign showed up in full force, as it would again in 2012. Roughly sixty local field offices were propped up, and legions of temporary staffers were hired to fan across the state. Republicans had controlled the state assembly and governorship since the 1990s, and Florida voters had infamously handed George W. Bush his first term in the ballot debacle of 2000. When Florida gave Obama his decisive electoral points, for local Democrats that victorious night felt like a coup, a new beginning.

But the Obama campaign in Florida was a roughly $40 million enterprise, not an effort that could realistically be sustained every year. Once the presidency was won, almost everybody packed up.

Praised as innovative, the Obama apparatus was also mostly disposable. In the winter of 2008, meanwhile, the permanent staff of the statewide Florida Democratic Party shrank back to about ten employees tasked with organizing and keeping energized 4,800,890 registered Florida Democrats, raising funds to compete for upcoming races for governor, attorney general, and other cabinet positions, plus about 20 state Senate and all 120 state House seats, not to mention keeping tabs on the various Democratic commissions in sixty-seven counties and calling public attention to legislation rolling through the Republican-controlled assembly in Tallahassee. And Tallahassee was roughly five hundred miles away from the majority of the state's Democrats, who live in South Florida. It was a lot for a small team, to say the least. Until 2012, the DNC ran Organizing for America, an organization of volunteers who were supposed to shepherd their communities through the health care debate, but looking back, former volunteers give it mixed reviews, from "excellent" to "a disaster."

Despite Florida's outsize importance to national politics, the Florida Democratic Party was pretty much on its own for its fund-raising and organizing efforts, unless a presidential campaign was under way. When you understand the scope of what Florida Democrats need to accomplish during the nonpresidential races, it becomes very apparent why, as of 2019, they haven't held the governorship in over twenty years. The enormity of the state, which runs 832 miles from the tip of the Keys off the southern coast to Pensacola in its northwestern Panhandle, poses an incredible challenge for any kind of coordinated statewide effort, especially an underresourced one that depends on organizing ordinary people. The Democratic Party didn't have a permanent infrastructure that spanned the state, and, arguably more important, neither did unions nor other left-leaning organizations. That same void that the Gang of Four had tried to fill in Colorado still defined the political landscape in Florida.

All statewide political work in Florida was, and is, an especially Herculean task. I wanted to skip the jokes, but the Floridians I met kept bringing them up, sounding proud. "We're the weirdest state, aren't we? Come on, we are the weirdest state," one person said. "It's weird and crazy and complicated and I love it," said another. There is no unifying Floridian identity in part because there are relatively few native Floridians. Today, roughly two-thirds of Florida residents are transplants who bring with them values they learned elsewhere, whether in Toledo or Brooklyn or Havana. Unlike new Coloradans, who tend to be young, Florida transplants from other states are disproportionately old. Florida has the country's oldest electorate—and they are increasingly from midwestern states, or the conservative pockets of northeastern ones, not the liberal northern cities that used to send most snowbirds.[2] And that is one big reason Florida voters lean conservative. Those retirees are by definition well-off enough to have retired, and they are cordoned off from concerns about how well the schools are funded or whether it is possible to rent a studio apartment in Orlando while being paid the state's minimum wage. Simply because of their age, they will also face fewer consequences of climate change than younger Floridians. Because they consistently vote, and because they are packed into the largest swing state, those retirees (and often their racial resentment, desire for low taxes, and disbelief in climate change) have an outsize effect on state and national politics and policy.

Anyone trying to appeal to a majority of Floridians, to win over enough younger people to cancel out the wishes of the older Republican crowd, also needs to craft a message that will resonate across wildly different landscapes and subcultures. Gun-show billboards, Farm Bureaus, and Evangelical megachurches are part of Florida, as are manicured subdivisions and art deco hotels and gay clubs and retirement homes with golf courses and urban sprawl with *quinceañera* dress shops and TJ Maxx, Pollo Tropical, LA Fitness, and Publix with to-go windows that sell empanadas and espresso. Former governor Bob Graham called Florida a constellation of city-states, each with its own character.[3] There is another old saying—that Florida has California's problems with Alabama's legislature. (After traveling to Tallahassee, I would add New Jersey–style political corruption.) But for all its supposed absurdity, for all its exaggerated qualities, Florida reflects the defining characteristics of the nation, distilled. That means that running for statewide office in Florida is a lot like running for president. Except, if you're a Democrat, without the resources of a presidential campaign.

Still, from an outside perspective, it seemed possible if not likely that Obama's 2008 win poised Florida Democrats to take back the governorship in 2010—thereby breaking the Republican trifecta. How could the Democratic momentum not build on itself?

The 2010 elections were a monumental event in recent American politics. The results of that election transformed power dynamics across the nation for a decade, just as the 2020 state-level elections will. That year's race for governor of Florida was a competition of outsize consequence, for Floridians then and for national politics today. At first, the election didn't seem like a harbinger of what was to come nationwide. But the story of how Florida Democrats struggled to hold their party together during Obama's term crystallizes how Democrats lost states nationwide. That 2010 race demonstrates, too, that local power begets national power.

★ ★ ★

Alex Sink was Florida's chief financial officer, an elected cabinet position, when ahead of the 2010 election she made clear to party officials that she wanted to run for governor. Sink was a former statewide president of NationsBank, which later became Bank of America. Her husband, Bill McBride, had challenged Governor Jeb Bush in 2002. McBride was a partner at Holland & Knight, one of the state's largest law firms, whose clients included Fortune 500 companies. He centered his campaign on restoring public education, the reason he had decided to run. McBride lost that election, badly. It was his experience that would later inspire Sink to run.

"I'd be lying to say that we didn't understand the realities of it," said a former Florida Democratic Party staffer. The expertise that so qualified Sink for the CFO post in 2007 had a very different connotation in 2010. The Great Recession had hit Florida especially hard. In 2008 and 2009 alone, 825,000 Floridians had received foreclosure filings. In 2010, almost half of Florida homeowners owed more on their mortgage than their property was worth, and the state's unemployment rate was about 11 percent. The losses were not evenly dispersed. South Florida—which includes Miami-Dade, Broward, and Palm Beach Counties—had some of the highest foreclosure rates in the United States. It is now well documented that banks had shifted from their historic practice of "red-lining," meaning excluding minority applicants from loans, to "green-lining," meaning disproportionately giving black and Hispanic applicants lines of credit with interest rates that later dramatically increased. As a result, black and Hispanic middle- and working-class neighborhoods were ground zero of the financial crisis. Those same South Florida counties were the Democratic strongholds, home to roughly one-third of the state's registered Democrats. Those voters absolutely needed to turn out if the Democrats were going to have any shot at winning the governorship or cabinet posts. As Sink herself told me, "If you can't really rack up the votes in South Florida, as a Democrat you can't win."[4]

Maybe a former bank president was not the ideal candidate to run in the middle of the Great Recession, but another reality was that no other Democrat had won a statewide office in eight years. "If not her, then who?" as one then–Florida Democratic Party staffer put it. There were a few Democratic mayors, but they weren't well known outside their city limits. For the governor's race, that party staffer said, "There wasn't really an Option B."

There was a logic to Sink's candidacy: The Democrats needed a candidate for governor who could win statewide, and Sink already had—no small feat. She had strong credentials. She had worked her way up from bank teller to president. Her ties with the business community, including her Bank of America connections and her position on the board of the Florida Chamber of Commerce, a major lobby for corporations, were welcomed by many within the Democratic Party because those relationships would enable her to fund-raise effectively. And fund-raising was imperative. The Florida Democratic Party was trapped in the same downward trajectory as its counterparts in states like Missouri.

Howard Dean, former governor of Vermont and the chairman of the Democratic National Committee, paraphrased the circular problem: "[Democratic state parties] have no resources so they can't do a good job," and as a result, "Who would give them money?"

As chairman of the DNC, Dean had just implemented what he called the fifty-state strategy. Under his charge, from 2005 to 2008, the DNC hired staffers and trained volunteers in all fifty states, not just the ones that made strategists salivate because they were immediate toss-ups. His plan explicitly called for building infrastructure to alleviate the usual dynamic of short-term staffers crashing in and rushing out, following the tides of presidential polls. For state parties, Dean said, an extra $60,000 and a few staffers "meant everything" to people on the ground. Dean and his staff also pushed using new internet platforms to solicit small donations from thousands of Americans instead of leaning on megadonors.

The fifty-state strategy was vindicated in 2006 and 2008. But the plan was openly criticized and mocked by members of the liberal establishment and presented skeptically by national outlets like the *New York Times*. Paul Begala, a former Clinton administration aide, summarized the strategy on CNN by saying that Dean was "hiring a bunch of staff people to wander around Utah and Mississippi and pick their nose." Begala later apologized, but the gaffe showed the prevailing common wisdom.[5] After Dean stepped down from the DNC in 2008, the fifty-state strategy was abandoned. Ten years later, under Tom Perez, in the aftermath of the 2016 election, the Democratic Party would promise a return to the fifty-state strategy, offering it again as the road to redemption for the party out of power.

In Florida (and other states), meanwhile, after Democrats had lost control of the state assembly, corporations and associations saw them as a waste of money. It would be Republican leadership who would steer the committees that would decide which laws to pass and whether and how to regulate the state's industries. No Democrat, for example, would decide which energy bills would make it to the floor for a vote, so energy companies had less reason to buy their favor. "Democrats really didn't have a say at all," said Ana Cruz, former executive director of the Florida Democratic Party, and so Democratic candidates became "absolutely irrelevant." She explained the consequences: "[Local Democrats] didn't have any leverage to raise money, to even barely fund the operations of a quarter of the Democratic Party, let alone a full-fledged field operation, media operations, and everything it takes to directly contact voters in a state this size."

Losses spiraled. Because Democratic lawmakers could rarely if ever pass their own bills, they had little to show for themselves, and no strong narrative to share with voters back home. Republican lawmakers, meanwhile, could pass bills sponsored by the NRA or the real estate industry and other allies, creating a feedback loop wherein donors and lobbyists gave them more attention, spurring more wins and many stories they could share on the campaign trail.

At the same time, left-leaning donors and interest groups came to consider Florida Democrats a lost cause. Once a state was relegated to the "hopeless" column, it was hard to see how that perception would change. The scale of Florida—all those hundreds of miles and different languages and cultures—has historically put off national donors, Ana Cruz explained. When national donors are weighing where to send their money, they see that political dollars deployed in a small state like New Hampshire will likely make an appreciable difference, whereas in vast, complicated Florida their donations will amount to a drop in the bucket. Florida has its own megadonors who winter in coastal locales like Palm Beach. But the DNC and national arms of the left-leaning interest groups have courted those donors, and they have often sent their gifts toward national coffers.

Sink's respect in the business community was considered all but imperative—maybe, the Democrats hoped, she would be outspent modestly, not outrageously. Candidates for governor who want to run television and radio ads in Florida need to do so in at least seven different media markets, an expense that runs into the tens of millions of dollars. The Democratic Party had long justified taking donations from banks, the sugar and energy industries, private prison companies, and the like, rationalizing that they needed to fund themselves somehow.

Success seemed possible. Everyone expected Sink's opponent in the 2010 general election would be Republican attorney general Bill McCollum, a former congressman and a fellow cabinet member, with whom Sink had worked to set up a program to connect foreclosure defendants with pro bono attorneys.[6] Sink—and McCollum for that matter—fit the mold of many winning Florida politicians who advocated for moderate positions. The only other Democrat holding statewide office in 2010 was Senator Bill Nelson, who embodied a tempered style and politics. Imagining an alternate reality wherein a progressive candidate won by passionately declaring that she would hold corporations accountable and fight for working-class families and civil rights requires imagining an alternate Florida.

★ ★ ★

That version of Florida didn't exist for several interconnected reasons. The basic building blocks of the progressive infrastructure just weren't there. When I spoke to Sink, in 2018, she brought up ACORN and its demise to illustrate the central problem. Since 1970, the Association of Community Organizations for Reform Now (ACORN) had run local offices across the country and had registered voters and organized middle- and working-class Americans around issues like wage theft and affordable housing. ACORN led a coordinated effort to put an initiative that raised the state's hourly minimum wage from $5.15 to $6.15 on the November 2004 ballot and generated enough public support for it to pass. Their strategy and success laid the groundwork for other minimum-wage ballot initiatives, including today's Fight for Fifteen. More than that, they were proof that organizing worked in Florida.

One measure of ACORN's success was right-wing operatives' determination to shut them down. In 2010, as Sink was running for governor, one especially high-profile stunt had just been plastered across the national news. James O'Keefe and Hannah Giles dressed up as a pimp and prostitute and traveled the country visiting ACORN offices. Later, ACORN's Florida staff said the pair visited them but were turned away. In Baltimore, though, O'Keefe serendipitously filmed their conversation with ACORN staff. He then published footage that appeared to show staff abetting human trafficking. Congress held hearings and ordered an investigation. The congressional report found that ACORN had broken no law. Still, ACORN lost its federal funding. Over the next year, as the 2010 campaigns unfolded, its offices in thirty-eight states were shuttered.[7]

O'Keefe would continue to haunt progressive organizations. In 2014, he showed up at New Era Colorado's Fort Collins office, posing as a campus activist. Staff suspected something was off and alerted Fenberg, who guessed it was O'Keefe and called the police. That same year he also showed up at local Colorado Democratic Party offices. Staff at progressive organizations remain spooked to this day. When I call a political nonprofit, it is not unusual for a staff person to quiz me to ensure I am not an O'Keefe-style plant. As we will see when we return to Missouri, O'Keefe's style of propaganda has done real damage and made paranoia common sense.

The farther-reaching implications, of course, went well beyond the walls of any nonprofit. Future organizing was thwarted. In Florida, there was no group prepared to replace ACORN, which had employed one thousand staffers nationwide. Here, again, we have to count everyone who was absent: The national brand-name interest groups like Planned Parenthood and the Sierra Club had local staff in Florida, but they were cloistered within their subcultures, focused on their individual causes. As in Missouri and other states, those local chapters were largely responsible for their own funding and programming. In small conservative states that meant running on a pittance; in Florida, where some residents of Tampa or Miami Beach were willing to throw down for openly progressive causes, that meant the Palm Beach and Miami Planned Parenthood political arms, for example, were constantly in competition over the same donors. Litigation and advocacy remained the go-to line of defense against expanding right-wing power for reasons previously outlined, many of them pragmatic.

Attempts to bring Florida's many scattered, shoestring progressive groups together were still nascent. The post-2004 efforts to rebuild the progressive movement from the ground up hadn't made their way to Florida, although seeds had been planted. The New Florida Majority, a Democracy Alliance grantee that would later work with Center for American Progress, had formed in 2009. America Votes was trying to open a Florida office, but the lone staffer kept turning over. Progress Florida was operational, but it was running on a total budget of $100,000, with one full-time director who made $35,000 per year, making them essentially a voice in the wilderness.

The Florida Constitution itself discouraged collective action. Florida has been a right-to-work state since 1944. So-called right-to-work laws allow workers to skip paying union dues while enjoying union-won protections. That de-incentivizes union membership, thereby decreasing unions' collective wealth and political power. Nationwide, union membership has decreased in recent decades, especially in the private sector and in right-to-work states. In 2009 in Florida, only about 7 percent of employees were unionized. The former political director of the Florida chapter of the American Federation of State, County and Municipal Employees (AFSCME), a union that represents public sector workers, told me that they had branches in five regions of the state, but because workers feared that they would be retaliated against with firings or denied promotions, AFSCME struggled to expand membership. The Tallahassee-based chapter had the fewest members because, with antiunion Republicans in charge, state workers understood that joining the union would not make them popular with their bosses. A majority of Florida's union members belonged to the teachers' union, the biggest union in Florida and the only one with a decent statewide presence. The teachers' union was one of the Democratic Party's most stalwart allies, but that wasn't going to save anyone's candidacy. In 2013, the Thomas B. Fordham

Institute, a conservative group, and Education Reform Now, a Democratic group supportive of charter schools, published a report that ranked the nation's teachers' unions state by state, ostensibly to size up the competition. The report measured the unions' resources and membership, political involvement, scope of bargaining, state policies, and perceived influence. The Florida teachers' union's overall rank was dead last. To underline this point: the biggest and most powerful union in Florida was the least powerful of its kind in the nation.

Unions were not going to buoy Democratic candidates or campaigns. Because they struggled to raise their own funds from their few members, Florida unions often counted on donations from their richer counterparts in blue states. They focused many of their ambitions on negotiating with employers, not organizing a broader political coalition. When elections drew near, former Democratic staffers said, the teachers' union would write a check to the Democratic Party, which the party would usually use on TV ads. Party officials were often frustrated that the unions didn't organize a fuller political program that could turn out volunteers to canvas ahead of elections, or rally or testify during legislative sessions. At the time, SEIU, the service workers' union, had a strong presence in South Florida, where many of the hospital workers were unionized. Their work didn't necessarily translate into muscle for Democrats statewide.

That the progressive network on the ground in Florida was a patchwork of underfunded and sometimes mismanaged organizations and volunteer chapters had multiple long-term ripple effects beyond the outcomes of elections. There were few opportunities for young Democrats or progressives to learn the ropes of political work. During the presidential election seasons of 2008 and 2012, when the Democratic Party finally had money to hire campaign managers to buttress state efforts, a former Democratic staffer said he "struggled mightily" to find qualified people who had done any kind of related work in Florida. He couldn't poach political staff from local organizations because they didn't exist. The same dynamics that made it difficult to hire qualified staff also made it difficult to keep working in progressive politics in Florida. For people who had put in time in entry positions, there was no career ladder to speak of. A staff position at the Florida Democratic Party paid around $40,000 per year and demanded long, often stressful hours.

Who, then, was available for hire? Consultants. The consultant class called the shots in many a Florida campaign and steered candidates toward television, billboards, and canvassing firms. When a campaign bought a TV ad, the consultant who set up the deal got a kickback. That was standard. Party staffers accepted the system as the most efficient way to get the word out. "TV is king," Cruz, one such believer, told me. The whole business model, the whole system, relied on the idea that consultants had a premium on some supposed wisdom about what appealed to the residents of some tract outside Jacksonville or Fort Lauderdale.

Because they were Democrats working in Florida, their candidates almost always lost. "Sometimes I think we're the very worst people to be communicating with voters," one Florida consultant admitted to me, because their occupational hazards included speaking in ugly political language—"mobilizing constituencies"—and living in the weeds of ideas and policies that most people barely considered. But regardless of whether their advice worked and their candidate won, the same consultants were rehired to work on the next cycle's campaign. Consultants' business model was built on the belief that the competitive edge rested in making a candidate appealing or tweaking a public relations strategy instead of organizing and mobilizing supporters. (This underlying assumption was propelled by a twenty-four-hour news cycle of television pundits, whose speculation took front stage, as if it was a candidate's gaffe, and not get-out-the-vote efforts, that would decide everything.) "Consultants don't commit to field operations," Cynthia Busch, chair of the Broward Democratic Party, told me. "There's no money being made running the field operation." Though a field director might make a decent salary, "it's not the same as sending out mailers and putting ads on TV. That's big business." And so, although volunteers voiced concern, few of the leaders calling the shots within the Democratic Party had much personal incentive to question the efficacy of the consultant-driven model.

In the short term, all those factors suggested that Sink was a pragmatic choice for governor. If her campaign was going to buy TV ads and hire people to knock on doors, it would need donations. All of the dozens of people I spoke with about Florida politics told me some version of "It all comes down to money."

★ ★ ★

While Democrats' losses made it harder and harder for them to regain a foothold, Republicans had, characteristically, found multiple ways to make sure that their power perpetuated itself. In Florida, Republican assembly members were taking a sharp rightward turn. Republicans had sealed control of the state legislature in the 1990s. They hadn't won on the romanticism of their ideas. Instead, local Republicans took the advice of the chairman of the Republican National Committee, Lee Atwater. Known as "the Darth Vader of the Republican Party," he was also George H. W. Bush's former campaign manager and Jeb Bush's soon-to-be mentor.[8] For decades, the Democrats who controlled the Florida assembly had drawn district maps that kept them in power. They were an old guard lot, mostly Blue Dogs, many of whom were reluctant to vote for abortion rights or against gun rights and more than willing, for example, to take donations from the sugar industry, despite its flagrant polluting and labor abuses. Before the 1990 census, Republicans had won enough seats in the Florida House that the two parties would share control of drawing the new district maps. Atwater and his lawyer Benjamin Ginsberg hatched a plan that they would execute on the federal level and in eight southern states. For their Florida plan, they solicited the help of the chair of the state Republican Party, State Senator Tom Slade, who approached black members of the Florida assembly.

Atwater saw an opportunity in the Voting Rights Act of 1964, which required that districts be apportioned in such a way as to guarantee that voters could elect black candidates. Following

Atwater's directives, Slade made a bargain with black Democratic legislators in Florida. He proposed maps that would create new districts with strong black majorities, a practice later called "packing." If most black voters were packed into a few districts, black candidates (including those then in office) would be all but guaranteed to win safe elections. And if Florida's black voters were no longer scattered across multiple districts, as they were in the Democrat-drawn maps, more districts would be easier for Republicans to win. In Slade's plan, Republicans would surrender a few districts but lock in an advantage overall. Black legislators, meanwhile, would be guaranteed three new districts. Slade also included in their conversations the Cuban caucus, who had been estranged from the state Republican leadership, and promised them a new Cuban majority district in South Florida.[9]

There is no confusing Atwater's motive. He later described the trajectory of Republican messaging on race by explaining, "You start out in 1954 by saying, 'Nigger, nigger, nigger.' By 1968 you can't say 'nigger'—that hurts you. Backfires. So you say stuff like forced busing, states' rights and all that stuff."[10] In 1990, Atwater and Ginsberg were confident that even if their attempts at what's now called racial gerrymandering were challenged in court, they would prevail. Reagan and George H. W. Bush had nominated lots of conservative judges to the federal courts, a strong indication that the multiple arms of right-wing infrastructure were working.

Florida's white Democratic leaders tried to dissuade the black Democrats from accepting Slade's deal. Their counterproposal guaranteed only one additional black congressional seat. State Representative Darryl Reaves of Miami replied that the offer showed that the whites leading the Democratic Party still acted as though their black colleagues "had a leash around their necks."[11] The Republicans had stoked a long-simmering resentment. For years, the Democratic Party had called upon black leaders to summon voters but had made no room for them in the political hierarchy. Slade's offer to install more black officials, then, struck a chord. In a move that secured their careers but all but ended their chances of achieving anything while in office, Reaves and his cohort accepted the Republican maps. As Atwater predicted, the Democrats challenged the maps in court, and they wound up before a Republican-appointed judge, who required some changes but sanctioned a similar set of Republican-drawn maps. Black Floridians would see their representation increase from fourteen to nineteen in the state assembly and from zero to three in Congress. But Democrats haven't held power in the statehouse since.

Atwater's plan delivered immediate gains. In 1994, Republicans won enough seats to share control of the state Senate. By 1999 Florida Republicans held the trifecta—governorship, House, and Senate—for the first time since Reconstruction.

The bargain between the black Democrats and the Republicans shows the contradictions of representation. If white Democratic leaders had not blocked their black colleagues from assuming positions of power, those black assembly members might not have rebelled against the interests of the party as a coalition. And yet the presence of additional black and Hispanic elected officials in Tallahassee shows the limits of diversity of representation as an end goal. Ten years later, black citizens of Florida were proportionally represented in the Florida legislature; Hispanics were not, although they were better represented than in some states (which isn't saying much).[12] But the Democrats in Tallahassee had negligible power in determining the outcome of policy proposals. Instead, because Republicans had a supermajority, Democrats were often in the all-but-powerless situation Carlos Guillermo Smith and Kionne McGhee found themselves in as they stood on the Florida House floor in February 2018 and unsuccessfully implored their colleagues to vote on a bill that would restrict assault weapons and high-capacity magazines. Democrats could try to draw attention and steer the narrative for long-term battles. But they had little leverage.

When Jeb Bush served as governor of Florida, from 1999 to 2007, he continued the tradition of finding ways to change the political system to disempower his opponents. Bush had attracted the attention of national Republicans even during his first, failed, attempt to become governor, in 1994. He was loudly anti-gay-rights and gun reform, and he wanted to abolish the Department of Education. Impressed, Grover Norquist flew to Miami to meet him. As they talked in a restaurant in Little Havana, Norquist marveled that Jeb had internalized Reagan's ideals more completely than his father.[13] When Jeb came of age, the whole country had been steeped in Reaganite ideology, even when Democrats were in charge. The idea that work delivered salvation and that the free market delivered opportunity and even moral rectitude was buried deep in the American psyche. In 1992, Bill Clinton had run for president promising "to end welfare as we know it." In 1996, Clinton signed the Personal Responsibility and Work Opportunity Reconciliation Act, cowritten by Norquist and sponsored by Newt Gingrich, and a central component of the iconic Contract with America, which did away with New Deal–era welfare programs and instituted work and vocational training requirements for Americans receiving food or cash assistance. The US Chamber of Commerce, which pushed for the "workfare" component, called it a "reassertion of America's work ethic." At the heart of the culture that endorsed the Contract with America beat a beautiful story, if you could believe it: the United States was a place of implicit fairness and goodwill where business leaders sowed and reaped shared prosperity. It was a beautiful idea that resonated with Floridians, many of whom were Latin American immigrants seeking stability, or midwestern retirees who by definition had made enough money to relocate to a condo by the beach.

Bush chose education as one cornerstone of his agenda, a near-perfect decision. It was a classic example of Republican strategists brilliantly pushing an initiative that simultaneously advanced a policy agenda and shifted the entire political system to their advantage. They always accomplished multiple goals at once. And they repeatedly deployed that age-old strategy, "divide and conquer," by pitting various factions of the American public against each other. Antiabortion legislation, for example, divided rural from urban Democrats and so had an outsize impact on redistricting. Voting laws are about structural power. Education reform was similar. During his first term, Bush helped introduce Florida, and the nation, to the idea of "corporate school reform" when he advocated that public education funding should be diverted to tuition for charter, private, and religious schools. His proposal would be used as a blueprint nationwide. By raising doubts about public education, Bush and his allies gave teachers' unions, made up of public school teachers, another battle to fight. Diminishing their fund-raising and political power meant weakening Democrats in general. Calls for education reform also sowed division within the Democratic base, alienating unequivocal supporters of the teachers' unions from supporters of charter schools or plans to pay teachers based on their students' test scores. Just as with incremental abortion laws that required parental consent, reasonable people who didn't see the larger political schema could easily agree with Republicans. Talking about education also allowed Bush to stake out a moral high ground; inner-city parents wanted the best for their kids, and the Democratic Party, steered mostly by members of the white middle class, wasn't offering to upend the entire segregated school system. Black Democratic lawmakers in particular had reason to support policies billed as "school reform."

By pushing his model of education reform, Bush not only changed education policy but also weakened his political opponents' ability to counter him in general. It was an example of what Gloria Totten called the Republicans' "two-fer, three-fer" initiatives, which were designed to change fundamental power dynamics within the government and political system while advancing Republican policies. The left, meanwhile, had no similar strategy of focusing on political goals that would change the underlying terms of engagement. This went back to the differences in outlook and values between those marshaling funding for the right and the left. Left-leaning funders had historically not created space for idea generation and strategy setting, whereas the architects of the right understood their importance. As a result, the few left-leaning economic think tanks routinely e-mailed out policy briefs detailing the importance of unions and a higher minimum wage—the same issues that Democrats have been harping on for decades. Yes, those issues were important. But raising the minimum wage was not a true systemic change that would alter the economic landscape, and it would not dramatically magnify progressives' political power, the way that Republican priorities were chosen because they magnified their base and their leaders' power. "Our side does nothing," Totten told me. "We're good at identifying problems and not good at identifying solutions."

During his two terms as governor, Bush shifted the existing power dynamics, slowly, in unglamorous ways. He delivered on campaign pledges to defund government agencies tasked with regulating businesses. He made a series of administrative changes that Sink said might seem like "subtle little things" but in her estimation were part of a "grand scheme to lock up power at least at the state level" for Republicans and their allies: He shrank the state cabinet from seven to four members, compressing posts previously responsible for monitoring insurance, banking, and the state treasury into one position—chief financial officer. That change also meant that Bush would be the tie-breaker in any divided cabinet vote. Under Bush, Florida also abolished its Department of Labor, the agency that in most states deals with wage-theft complaints and other workplace grievances. By 2016, at least a dozen other states had dismantled their labor departments.[14]

Commuters traveling down I-95, listening to the news on their way home from work, probably weren't going to swerve off the road when they heard a quick bulletin saying that a few state agencies were merging. In immediate, practical terms, it meant that employers had more leeway to treat their workers poorly, with much less scrutiny. By 2010, well after the state labor agency closed, there were only six US Department of Labor federal workers who covered Florida, meaning each was responsible for about 1.2 million workers, in the nation's third-largest economy.[15] In the long term, by deflating state agencies and public education, Bush was also fulfilling the legacy of the libertarian Virginian strategists of the 1950s, carrying out the long-held plans of the likes of

Grover Norquist and foreshadowing what would soon happen in several other states and on the federal level.

★ ★ ★

Ahead of 2010, Republican operatives zeroed in on another way to give their allies a long-term advantage. They unrolled a surreptitious plan hatched by Chris Jankowski, a longtime strategist. One detail in Jankowski's biography would be beyond boring had it not inspired a nation-changing epiphany one night in 2009: in the '90s, Jankowski traveled to state capitals to lobby for the American Council of Life Insurers. In those far-flung towns, he saw how easy—and yet crucial—it was to capture state legislators. His employer wrote big checks to Congress and sent a few hundred dollars to state legislators, but he recommended, "For a little more money than you're spending now—but a fraction of what you're spending in D.C.—we could really have an impact in these states." The realization resurfaced that night in 2009, as David Daley describes in his book *Ratf**ked*. At the time, Democrats controlled twenty-seven state legislatures. Jankowski knew that, in many states, whichever political party controlled the legislature after the 2010 elections would be in charge of redrawing district maps. If Republicans won over more state legislatures, Democrats would be playing on the Republicans' board in both state and federal elections for ten years. Then the Republicans' advantage would build on itself so that it would be even more difficult for Democrats to come back from those losses. Winning the states in 2010 would mean winning for the long term.[16]

While Sink was preparing to run for governor, Jankowski persuaded the Republican State Leadership Committee (RSLC) to endorse his ambitious, semi-covert plot, which came to be called "Redmap." He was acting on the same logic as Atwater had a generation earlier. In early 2010, Jankowski and Ed Gillespie, head of the RSLC, traveled the country with a PowerPoint presentation detailing their plan. They met with financiers, lobbyists, trade associations, and oil tycoons. Soon, major corporations and conservative groups, including the US Chamber of Commerce, Walmart,

AT&T, and many others, were donating. Donors were told that Congress probably wasn't possible until 2012, after the district maps were drawn, but that the state legislatures were the prime goal for 2010. The plan was simple. They would target races where Democrats were vulnerable. Since that included so many races, they would focus on those where a win would increase chances that an assembly would flip and give Republicans control of the all-important map-drawing.

The money rolled in. At a fund-raiser with the Dallas Petroleum Club, Karl Rove told the crowd, "People call us a vast right-wing conspiracy, but we're really a half-assed right-wing conspiracy. Now it's time to get serious." Months before, in January 2010, the Supreme Court had issued its ruling in *Citizens United*, allowing corporations and unions to give unlimited amounts of money to persuade voters. The timing was serendipitous for Jankowski, Rove, and their compatriots, but it wasn't a total coincidence. The plaintiff in the case, Citizens United, was a conservative group that had made a movie maligning Hillary Clinton ahead of her bid for the presidency in 2008. Its legal challenge was led by James Bopp, a longtime antiabortion attorney, who had helped hone the right's strategy of pushing the envelope with local laws in the hopes that they would eventually climb the courts and inspire judges to make incremental changes to federal law. The *Citizens United* ruling was both the result and the catalyst of right-wing attorneys and political operatives' long-standing ability to work together to change the system to their benefit. That year, undisclosed donations, called "dark money," flooded political campaigns. By Labor Day of 2010, two months before Election Day, the Republican State Leadership Committee had a three-to-one funding advantage over the Democratic Legislative Campaign Committee.[17]

★ ★ ★

That spring, the race in Florida changed. First, on April 9, 2010, Rick Scott announced that he was running for the Republican nomination for governor, challenging McCollum, who had thirty years of experience in Florida politics. Scott had lived in the state for only seven years. He had never held elected office. He had come from Texas by way of Connecticut after the hospital company he founded, Columbia/HCA, was discovered to have engaged in widespread fraud under his watch. Columbia/HCA overcharged Medicaid by millions of dollars, gave doctors illegal kickbacks, and fired or threatened doctors and nurses who brought concerns to supervisors, among other forms of malfeasance. In the early 2000s, the company pleaded guilty to fourteen felonies and paid a total of $1.7 billion in fines, at the time the largest fine ever paid to the government. Scott made it out of Columbia/HCA and Texas with a fortune that in 2010 was worth about $219 million—an estimated $75 million of which he would spend on his 2010 gubernatorial race, maligning McCollum and then Sink as "Tallahassee insiders."[18]

Scott had come to something like prominence over the previous year, leading a group he called Conservatives for Patients' Rights, which ran a website and television commercials that encouraged people to go to congressional town halls to protest the Affordable Care Act. His call to action was not slapped together. Conservatives for Patients' Rights was supported by the Koch brothers. The group used the public relations firm that Kellyanne Conway worked for—the same firm that had advertised on behalf of Gingrich and Norquist's Contract with America, and that in 2009 was simultaneously working to block the Supreme Court confirmation of Sonia Sotomayor by smearing her as a "racist." After ACA town halls across the country dissolved into shouting, Scott made rounds on the national media circuit. During one CNN appearance, anchor Rick Sanchez peppered Scott with questions while smiling, incredulous, almost gleeful at how rich the irony was, how absurd it was that Scott would claim to be an honest broker of health care reform. Few appreciated the change that was occurring nationwide. Even local Republican operatives failed to see what was happening. Many of the state's power brokers and biggest corporate donors lined up behind McCollum.[19]

Just a week after Rick Scott announced his candidacy, on April 20, 2010, an oil rig exploded in the Gulf of Mexico, fifty miles off the shore of Louisiana, just west of Florida's Panhandle. Eleven men were killed. Over the next three months, an estimated two hundred million gallons of oil gushed into the Gulf, affecting sixteen thousand miles of coastline. By the end of the summer, a twenty-two-mile plume of oil had settled on the floor of the ocean.[20]

Images from the disaster played on television screens throughout the country. Though the oil rig hadn't been intentionally detonated, the explosion of the *Deepwater Horizon* rig was not really an accident in the true sense of the word. The EPA had been sanctioning British Petroleum (BP), the gas company that owned and operated the rig, for "willful violations" of safety and environmental laws for at least five years when the *Deepwater Horizon* rig exploded. The company's flouting of rules in multiple states had left at least 15 workers dead and 170 injured. US Department of Labor reports showed a pattern of BP management threatening employees who complained that equipment needed repairs or adjustments to be safe and lawful. For BP's leadership, the decision to use faulty equipment was a calculated business risk. If periodically something devastating happened—leaving a few workers dead, a town or a port contaminated, a local economy in shambles—and BP had to pay out the maximum required by law, or some fraction of that, plus lawyers' fees, they would still turn a sizable profit. In 2010, BP reported its first loss in years after paying a $6.8 billion fine, but in 2011 it was in the black again, bringing in $5.3 billion in profits. The Gulf coastal communities of Alabama, Louisiana, Mississippi, and Florida, however, lost an estimated $22.7 billion in tourism revenue as a result of the disaster. As in much of Florida, the local economy in the Panhandle depends on tourism.[21]

As the *Deepwater Horizon* news played on repeat on major news channels, headlines were just as bleak on the opposite edge of the state. Judges in South Florida set up special rooms in courthouses to accommodate the steady stream of foreclosure defendants. As Election Day approached, news broke that Bank of America had hired clerks to "robo-sign" giant piles of foreclosure documents without reading them.[22] That year, you didn't need any particular expertise in banking or the oil industry to see what had happened; private companies had used faulty apparatus to extract wealth, and nobody in the government had stopped them in time to prevent the devastation they caused across Florida. Business leaders had cheated. Government had failed. Ordinary people were suffering the consequences.

Tea Party protesters held anti-Obama rallies, waving their yellow Gadsden flags emblazoned with a snake extending its tongue and the warning DON'T TREAD ON ME. Rick Scott kept appearing on Fox News to talk about ending Obamacare. He described himself as an outsider. He promised jobs. He called upon that resonant Reaganite idea that Jeb Bush had helped cultivate: business would set society free. It goes without saying that he loudly opposed gun reform and abortion rights. At the same time, Scott departed from Jeb Bush's legacy in fateful ways, the implications of which would simmer beneath the surface of national discourse for another several years.

Scott denied that climate change was real. For decades, concern for the environment wasn't a partisan issue within the state government. "In Florida, you couldn't get elected unless you were conservation-minded. Even if you were Republican," Laura Reynolds, an environmental scientist and longtime advocate, said. If anything, it was Republicans, whose constituents often owned beachfront property, who were louder about the need for environmental protections than were Democrats, who often minimized the need for environmental laws while representing districts where polluting agriculture companies doled out major campaign contributions. Jeb Bush led a much-criticized but nonetheless high-profile effort to preserve the Everglades. Supporting land conservation was separate from supporting efforts to combat climate change—which would require a different set of industry regulations and government programs—but it was something. And Governor Charlie Crist, a centrist Republican, had spearheaded a climate change summit. There was room to critique his administration for not going far enough, but Crist recognized the problem at hand.

Scott's climate change denial fit into a larger break within the Republican Party. From the 1980s through the early 2000s, as research about climate change showed without question that it would bring calamity, many Republican lawmakers wanted to be proactive. Whether a politician assumed a realistic—which meant urgent—stance on climate change did not split down party lines. When John McCain ran for president on the Republican ticket in 2008, he had a stronger climate change record than Obama. It was not inevitable that climate change would become a divisive partisan issue. Some of the potential solutions to climate change hinged on providing market incentives to invest in new technology, right in line with traditional Republican economic values. But insiders within the fossil fuel industry had known, since the 1970s, that if the public understood that burning fossil fuels was imperiling the long-term survival of humanity, there would be an outcry to limit the scope of their business practices. Fossil fuel industry leaders designed and financed a plan to actively disseminate false information, discredit legitimate scientists, and throw climate change into doubt for the mainstream public. They began supporting politicians who would do the same. Around the time Rick Scott decided to run for office, the fossil fuel industry helped make climate change denial a central thread of Republicanism.[23]

The other fateful difference between Scott and his immediate predecessors was that whereas Jeb Bush had deliberately sought out ties with Hispanic and black organizations and argued to his Republican colleagues that they needed to strongly distance themselves from the party's long history of race-baiting, Scott made claims like, "We have over 700,000 illegal immigrants in the state. They're costing us billions of dollars, and they're taking legal residents' jobs." Scott's campaign manager was Susie Wiles, who would go on to become first a partner at Ballard Partners, the most profitable and influential lobbying firm in Tallahassee, and then cochair and communications director for Donald Trump's Florida presidential campaign. Scott also hired Tony Fabrizio, a longtime Republican pollster and strategist. Fabrizio, too, would join Trump's campaign, at the request of Paul Manafort, and in 2017 he would advise France's far-right candidate for prime minister, Marine Le Pen, who campaigned on "protecting France" from immigrants and "savage globalization." Wiles and Fabrizio cut their teeth helping Scott malign Obama and McCollum, "the desperate career politician." They were behind the scenes when Scott told Floridians that "illegal immigrants" should "go home."[24]

In the August Republican primary, Scott defeated the sitting attorney general by about 3 percentage points. He said in his victory speech, "In Tallahassee tonight, the dealmakers are crying in their cocktails."[25] Once Scott was the Republican nominee, however, the usual dealmakers rallied behind him.

That summer of 2010, a political neophyte with a shady business record still seemed like a risky bet, even one with a personal fortune to burn and his party's nomination, and even in Florida, the fraud capital of the country. None of the state's major newspapers endorsed Scott, which presumably had as much to do with his declining to meet with and answer questions from their editorial boards (the long-standing expectation of candidates) as with Columbia/HCA's many instances of fraud. Meanwhile, because the *Citizens United* ruling permitted donors to Scott's political action committee to remain anonymous, those newspapers couldn't explain to Floridians who was donating to his campaign or why. Individual donations to statewide candidates in Florida were capped at $3,000, and donors to parties had to name themselves, but not so with political action committees. The average size of a donation to Scott's PAC, Let's Get to Work, was $65,384. Let's Get to Work eventually amassed $46 million, a chunk of which came from Scott's own fortune.[26]

* * *

Florida Democratic Party leaders had choices to make. That summer and fall, in triage mode, they had to be stingy with their resources—and attention. The priority would be winning back the governor's mansion, and that meant diverting as many dollars and staffers as possible to propping up the Sink campaign. Here, again, we must attempt to count everyone who was absent, measuring all that they could not do. Those absences begin to answer the question that for another decade the pundits would ask: If Obama won

Florida twice, even after the mortgage crisis, why couldn't Florida's Democratic gubernatorial candidates win?

That year (as in many others), the Democrats did not run candidates in every race for the state House and Senate. If a Republican candidate had especially strong corporate ties or lots of early donations, the Florida Democratic Party sometimes decided to skip that race, considering it a lost cause. In some instances, party officials tried to get a candidate on the ballot but couldn't persuade anyone to run, for good reason. Campaigns were relentless, requiring soliciting funds and endorsements, walking neighborhoods and knocking on doors in ninety-degree weather, not to mention enduring public scrutiny. It was openly acknowledged that the Democratic Party would not be able to provide what the campaign would cost. And even if somehow a Democratic candidate did win, the job would provide few emotional or material rewards. New lawmakers would spend three months of the year in Tallahassee, potentially hours of travel away from home, in long hearings, unable to pass their preferred legislation. It is not hard to imagine why most people would want to spend the summer doing anything else.

When a Democrat did run for an assembly seat, party officials wrestled with how many dollars to send that candidate. If there was no chance of taking back the assembly that year (and there wasn't), then by sending relatively small sums to many little-known state candidates were they throwing away funds that, combined, could make the difference for the tight governor's race? Progressive members of the party, inspired by Howard Dean's fifty-state strategy, believed that funding state candidates, no matter how likely to win, in all districts, would inevitably help the top of the ticket, too, because those scrappy local candidates might pull in voters otherwise inclined to stay home during an off-year election. They disagreed with the "zero-sum game" line of thinking that presumed that helping one candidate meant depriving another. Still, in 2010 there were districts scattered across the state—from the northern conservative rural stretches to South Florida, home to some of the densest Democratic voting blocs in the nation—where nobody from the Democratic Party challenged the Republican candidate.

The Democratic Party's ground game—or lack thereof—in South Florida during the 2010 election was emblematic of a much larger failure. "It's insane when you think of it," said Cynthia Busch, then the field organizer for Sink's campaign in Broward County. Because there was no Broward campaign office, Busch volunteered out of a borrowed real estate office. For most of the 2010 campaign, Busch told me, there were two paid staffers who were responsible for both Palm Beach and Broward Counties—3,706 square miles of urban sprawl where a combined total of 920,767 registered Democrats lived. Two years earlier, lots of Obama volunteers had walked those neighborhoods. Many of them had tried to stay involved through Organizing for America. But in 2010, Busch remembered, "the Obama volunteers could never be mobilized because there was no staff to mobilize them."

For years, the Democratic Party, and other independent political groups, had spent their energy mobilizing voters, rather than organizing them, Busch and others told me, and that was the heart of the problem. Mobilizing meant encouraging people to show up to perform a short-term function like voting or protesting. Organizing meant getting people together, empowering them, giving them the responsibility and freedom to bring in more people, expand the agenda, take on more work. The Obama campaign had been successful because it had used organizing principles. But organizing takes time. Because money tended to flood into Florida at the last minute, a couple of months before the election, there wasn't time to build a true organization. In the late summer of 2010, the party officials decided that in the interest of speed and efficiency they would hire paid canvassers instead of working on finding volunteers. Busch told me that volunteers are better because their commitment to the cause comes through in their interactions with voters.

It is hard to imagine a paid canvasser—or anyone—capable of communicating with everyone on any given block in South Florida. Miami, for one, is a majority minority city, known, of course, as the capital of Latin America. Only about 12 percent of its population is non-Hispanic white. Miami-Dade and surrounding counties also have large Jewish communities. At a glance, the demographic makeup might seem like a windfall for Democratic coalition-building, but in fact the diversity of South Florida has been a hindrance. A majority of the people who live in Miami-Dade, and the nearby counties, hold political beliefs informed by the memory of the political climate in another country—Haiti, Trinidad, Jamaica, Cuba, Venezuela, Honduras. The diversity within and between South Florida neighborhoods presents immediate practical and also enormous philosophical challenges. All radio ads or flyers have to be run in English, Spanish, and Creole, tripling the cost. It also means that unless you literally know where people are coming from, you aren't going to be able to reach them. Cuban Americans who left their homeland seeking the right to speak their minds are unlikely to go in for rhetoric about "socialism" or "revolution," for example. That language, though, might better appeal to their children, or their Puerto Rican neighbors. For years, and through today, Democratic Party strategists tended to lump millions of people from wildly different sociopolitical backgrounds into the category "Hispanic," regardless of whether they were fifth-generation Americans or newly naturalized citizens who arrived as refugees. There is no "Hispanic community" or "immigrant community" in South Florida as much as dozens of such communities. And all those potential voters have different concerns that can keep them from participating. Many immigrants who have settled in South Florida have come from countries where political participation was dangerous. Others perceive political action as disrespectful to the country that has provided them refuge. After sacrificing everything to come to this country, some immigrants may not allow themselves to see deep flaws in the United States, because believing in its promise of opportunity and justice is the only way to make sense of their sacrifice. Still others are not citizens, sometimes because they are undocumented, sometimes because they hold visas, and sometimes because they are remaining indefinitely on green cards to hang on to their dream of someday moving back to their homeland. And then there are the most ordinary reasons that political participation is difficult: in the working-class and middle-class neighborhoods of South Florida, and Tampa and Orlando and Jacksonville, as across the nation, people are preoccupied with the daily tasks of keeping their lives together. Campaigns for social change often demand the most from people who are already at the greatest disadvantage. That is especially true in places without institutional donors willing to bolster the people's cause.

The party needed Hispanic (and West Indian and Haitian and African American) leadership to tailor messages and strategies for different pockets of the electorate, and it needed legions of black and brown volunteers who could go talk to the people most inclined to listen to them. But the consensus among Hispanic Democratic Party members was that leadership neglected Hispanics, or courted them only moments before they needed their vote. "Not many candidates, Democratic candidates, unfortunately, reached out to the Hispanic community," said Noemi McGregor, president of the Democratic Hispanic Caucus. "We have been here, but we've never been reached out [to]." Hispanic turnout was often low, so Florida Democrats had rationalized not spending limited resources targeting Hispanics voters, let alone building up Hispanic-led political programs. But that, McGregor said, created a self-fulfilling prophecy. "If you don't reach out to the Hispanic community, they're not going to vote," she said. "It is that simple."

In 2010, Democrats really needed effective ambassadors on the ground. Foreclosure signs punctured lawn after lawn across Florida. Obama's struggles to pass a watered-down health care plan dominated the news. "When you think about the fact that they didn't mobilize Democrats through a volunteer program, it was just political malpractice, because [Alex Sink] did her job, she did the persuading part," Busch said. "If you were going to motivate people to vote who were having a really hard time being motivated, sending a sort of ill-trained, paid person to those doors really wasn't going to do the trick. You needed to have a really sustained, aggressive program that really articulated to people what was at stake."

* * *

Rick Scott told voters what was at stake. He laid responsibility for the global financial crisis at Alex Sink's feet. During their televised debates and in his ads, which with his tens of millions of dollars he could run whenever he wanted, Scott accused Sink of losing a giant portion of the state's pension fund—a major issue in a state with the nation's oldest electorate. He also claimed that Sink oversaw securities fraud at Bank of America, which amounted to taking money from retirees, and that while CFO she had "funneled" $770,000 to Bank of America. In stump speeches and commercials, he charged that she was "an Obama liberal" who did "Obama math."[27]

"It was a total lie," Sink said. "We Democrats have a hard time dealing with that." The press had a hard time with that, too. Unraveling Scott's false claims required too much for a quick soundbite. Florida's pension fund *had* decreased during Sink's tenure as CFO. Investment funds depreciate when the stock market plummets, and it had in 2008. Bank of America *had* been sued for securities fraud. The very attorney who had sued Bank of America over that fraud told the *Palm Beach Post* that Sink "didn't have anything to do with it" because those decisions were made in the bank's national headquarters. Sink had overseen the commercial side of banking—a staid business uninvolved with the complex new financial products that had felled the economy. But in the narrative that Scott was spinning, those distinctions seemed beside the point. When the *Tampa Bay Times*' Politifact.com disproved some of Scott's claims about Sink, the explanation filled a two-thousand-word article full of rules about securities brokerages. Those nuanced refutations were no match for Scott on Fox News promising to create seven hundred thousand new jobs.[28]

"We were just being outstrategized and outmessaged," Sink told me. "He's a broken record, and all he says is 'Let's get to work.'" In her talking points, Sink criticized Scott's company's record of fraud, but he responded with more charges that she was responsible for Bank of America's role in the financial crisis. "He was out there repeating the same glib sound bites everywhere he went. It stuck with people. I had much better policies and much better plans, but my team was never able to come up with, 'What's Alex's soundbite going to be that's effective?' I think Democrats in general are really, really bad about that kind of messaging stuff. What are three words that the voters are going to remember that are really simply said?"

Sink's media strategist had told her that as a female candidate she needed to be reserved, advice she later doubted. Being a female candidate for an executive position came with unique perils. Professional women of her generation had fought to win respect by remaining calm and reserved no matter what. When Sink spoke about the economy, she often spoke in euphemisms. And yet it's hard to see how she could have substantively changed her 2010 message without becoming a different person. Back when the assembly was controlled by Democrats, Sink had served on the executive board of the Greater Miami Chamber of Commerce, where she ran the chamber's state affairs committee, which promoted its "pro-business" legislative agenda in the statehouse in Tallahassee. At the time (granted, twenty years earlier) the Florida Chamber had lobbied to dissuade the assembly from raising the minimum wage, or requiring employers to provide health insurance, or increasing unemployment benefits for laid-off Floridians.[29]

Sink had no beautiful idea to call upon that challenged the Republicans' beautiful idea that the free market would deliver prosperity. Later, the Florida Democratic Party commissioned a poll that found that voters weren't sure what the party stood for. The common wisdom became that voters wanted to vote for something, not against someone.

It's possible that a Democrat better able to identify with and channel the dislocation and anger shared by many Floridians that year might have won the election. It's also possible that such a candidate would have lost. Obama's promise of hope and change had fallen so far short that it is conceivable local Democrats would not have been willing to drive through Miami traffic for anyone. The Democrats that I spoke with about the 2010 race—members of both the progressive and establishment wings of the party—all told me that they thought that Alex Sink would have been a good governor. Maybe the economy wasn't everything; multiple Florida politicos also told me that they believed Sink's dodges on gay adoption and abortion rights, meant to keep Dixiecrats in her corner, hurt her chances of attracting young progressive volunteers and voters. Others told me that Sink had campaigned well but the party apparatus failed her. "We didn't have any kind of meaningful ground game going in Dade, Broward, and Palm Beach Counties," Sink told me, assessing her own shortcomings. Polling from the time generally showed that Floridians liked moderates. Theories about what could have been are always speculations.

★ ★ ★

On November 2, 2010, nationwide, Republicans won an additional 675 state legislative seats and another six governorships. Democrats ceded ground across the country, even in unanticipated places like Minnesota, North Carolina, Ohio, and Wisconsin. National news outlets focused on Congress, as Republicans won control of the House and closed in on the Senate. That night, 2,557,785 Floridians voted for Alex Sink, and 2,619,335 for Rick Scott. Sink lost by about 1 percent, roughly 60,000 votes. The margin was tiny. The weakest link was South Florida, where Democratic turnout was way down compared to 2008. In Broward and Miami-Dade Counties, only roughly 40 percent of registered Democrats showed up to vote.

The next morning, in Washington, DC, Progressive Majority's board chair came into Gloria Totten's office. Their candidates had lost all over the country. "We need to close up shop. If progressives can only win when Democrats win, then we might as well not even do this," Totten recalled him saying. She pushed back. But they had already had a difficult couple of years. "When the Bernie Madoff stuff went down, I lost six donors and $1.3 million dollars in one day, just like that. Because people said, 'I can't send the money. It's gone,'" she told me. During the financial crisis, more donors stopped giving. Relying on individual donors and foundations meant, ironically, that the fortunes of the progressive movement were tied to the wealthiest Americans' portfolios.

That same day, November 3, President Obama described the election as a "shellacking."[30] In the national news, the Republican sweeps of 2010 were largely credited to Tea Party activists, and described as a referendum on Obama, especially his handling of the financial crisis. In the background, out of immediate view, Jankowski and his colleagues took in that their plan had worked.

Totten went back to the drawing board, writing plans for how progressives could retake Florida, starting with its Senate. "I did the targeting. I did six, eight years of targeting in Florida to show [donors] the path," Totten said. After she gave the presentation, she remembered, the prospective donors responded, "It's too far away, it's too long, it's too many cycles." After so many losses in 2010, Progressive Majority started losing its traction.

Florida political organizers guessed that they had again lost the confidence of the donor class. "It's possible we're so dysfunctional that national donors don't want to give," one speculated. National donors were not necessarily buying into the idea that the most prudent course of action was dumping even more money into a place with an extra-complicated electorate and a Democratic political establishment that seemed scattershot at best. But how else would the next candidates be in a better position? If organizing and mobilizing the Democratic base in Florida, and especially South Florida, was a daunting task, it was also—and remains to this day—an imperative one. Control of the state, and control of the nation, hangs in the balance.

Progressive Majority, meanwhile, couldn't withstand the shellacking. "Then it felt like it was too hard. The numbers were so bad," Totten remembered. The 2010 state legislative losses read as a rebuke to the idea of sending money into local and state-level campaigns. Sink, meanwhile, woke up in the middle of the night, wondering, "Why couldn't I get those 60,000 votes?"[31] Anyone who suggested that she and Rick Scott were essentially cut from the same cloth was proved wrong in the years to come, if not within days of Rick Scott assuming the governor's office.

CHAPTER FIVE

Missouri

AT THE RONALD REAGAN LIBRARY IN SIMI VALLEY, CALIfornia, during the second Republican presidential debate ahead of the 2016 election, candidate Carly Fiorina looked straight ahead. She punctured the air with her hand, and described, in staccato language and with tremendous intensity, a "fully formed fetus on the table, its heart beating, its legs kicking, while someone says 'we have to keep it alive to harvest its brain.'" That summer, every major news organization in the country, plus local radio stations and newspapers, had played or discussed videos billed as "investigative footage" that depicted Planned Parenthood staffers chatting about harvesting and selling fetal remains in cavalier tones, between sips of wine. The seven videos distributed by the Center for Medical Progress made Planned Parenthood's staff look callous, if not monstrous.

News outlets were slower to report that the Center for Medical Progress was a fringe group closely allied with the same antiabortion organizations that, among other positions, condoned the murder of George Tiller, a physician who had provided abortions in Kansas until he was shot to death while attending church in 2009. The antiabortion activists who had made the video cited as an inspiration and friend James O'Keefe, who had felled ACORN with his own stunts. Today, when relatively little time has passed, the public has already become accustomed to warnings about grand emotional appeals, deceptive framing, fake news, and outright lies. But back in 2015, Planned Parenthood's self-defense, its insistence that its employees were being framed, maligned, and directly lied about, required of the American public a paranoia and cynicism we were not ready to extend, especially not on behalf of abortion providers. Most Americans, apparently, did not believe—or want to believe—that Fiorina would look into the television and lie in such detail, with such conviction. Disentangling those lies would have required unthreading a whole knot of many Americans' most deeply held beliefs.

It didn't take a political mastermind to understand why Fiorina had invented wholesale a description of a baby's murder. The Supreme Court was on the ballot in 2016. For the Republican activist base, and many rank-and-file voters, control of courts was the ultimate strategic goal, the achievement of which, it was widely believed, would precipitate other long-held goals, including ending legal abortion and entrenching gun rights. By evoking abortion and guns, among the most emotional issues in American politics, Republican candidates played Reagan's old hand and reminded cultural conservatives that there could be no breach between them and the Republican Party.

For many national viewers, Fiorina's performance probably seemed like just one more charged moment in an endless spectacle. It was, however, perfectly timed: Congress had just opened investigations into Planned Parenthood over the propaganda videos. When Americans' eyes trailed over a related headline, many would undoubtedly remember that fictitious baby kicking its legs. Although researchers and government officials determined over the course of the next few months that the tapes had been edited to the point that they were fakes, by then it was too late. The evidence that exonerated Planned Parenthood did not dominate the news cycle as the original propaganda had. National attention had skipped on to the next outrages. Trump supplied plenty. On the state level, across the country, the Center for Medical Progress's fabrications had more profound repercussions than national viewers understood. A dozen states began their own investigations into Planned Parenthood, and legislators across the country readied antiabortion bills.[1] Those investigations were clues that might have tipped off national pundits and journalists that it was not inevitable that a pro-choice woman would be elected president the next year.

That summer the Missouri Senate set up the Sanctity of Life Committee with the stated purpose of investigating Planned Parenthood, which antiabortion activists and allied lawmakers had called "the enemy" for years. At the time, the state had only one remaining clinic that provided abortion, and it was well known that antiabortion activists wanted to shut down that one, too. After the Center for Medical Progress videos dropped in 2015, Republican candidates for office did their best to explode tiny bureaucratic questions into a scandal by continually threatening to hold government officials and doctors in contempt of court, holding press conferences with antiabortion protesters, and forcing the Department of Health director out of her job. A federal judge later found that the Sanctity of Life Committee's crusade against both Planned Parenthood and the Department of Health and Senior Services (deemed guilty by association for providing doctors' licenses) was motivated by political "animus."[2]

The crusade was also politically expedient. Republicans were still campaigning on "guns, God, and gays," as the saying goes. Missouri's transformation from a blue to red state was almost complete. In 2010, in lockstep with voters across the nation, rural Missourians had rejected local Democrats. "Jesus Christ would have lost if he ran as a Democrat" that year, explained one Democratic farmer who lost his race for District 18, the seat formerly held by John Cauthorn. Ahead of the 2016 election, Missouri Republicans held a supermajority in the assembly, with 25 of the 34 state Senate seats and 118 of the 163 state House seats. Then-governor Jay Nixon was a Democrat, but the assembly could override his veto power. And he would be term-limited out of office that year. The

Republican supermajority meant that there was a wide spectrum of conservatives, from centrists to Tea Partiers, in the assembly. They sometimes disagreed on important policy questions about issues like school funding, pensions, infrastructure spending, or the opioid crisis. But they all knew that veering from the party's long-winning pro-gun, antiabortion stance would have dire consequences for their political careers.

After 2010's redistricting, almost all Missouri districts became easy wins for either Democrats or, more often, Republicans. Most elections for Missouri state lawmakers, then, were decided on primary day, when only very partisan voters tend to show up. Many Missourians involved in politics assumed the Sanctity of Life Committee was a political stunt; the committee's chair was running for state attorney general. His competitor in the Republican primary, Josh Hawley, was advertising that he had been on the legal team that represented the craft store Hobby Lobby in the landmark Supreme Court case over whether employers can refuse to cover employees' contraception on religious grounds. (Hawley, who would win the AG contest, would go on to defeat Senator Claire McCaskill in her 2018 reelection bid.) In outstate Missouri, and in many regions of the country, the culture wars were a losing proposition for Democrats, and even centrist Republicans.

One Republican candidate for governor toured the state saying, "We don't want another St. Louis," a reference to the unrest after Ferguson. Her primary opponent, Eric Greitens, in one of his most discussed campaign ads, sat behind a mounted machine gun and sprayed bullets rapid-fire while a male voice said, "Eric Greitens is under attack from Obama's Democrat machine. They're trying to steal another Missouri election. But Eric Greitens is a conservative warrior." His campaign website read, "No person should have their tax money taken from them, and spent on organizations like Planned Parenthood, that engage in activities that are, quite simply, barbaric." The received wisdom was clear: to win a Republican primary, candidates needed to establish their anti-contraception and antiabortion laurels and commitment to gun rights and white identity politics.

★ ★ ★

Ahead of the 2016 election, Missouri lawmakers became obsessed with the idea that Planned Parenthood might be trafficking "dead baby body parts." I drove to the Missouri capital, a grid of steep hills overlooking a river, in early January, the first week of the legislative session, to watch hearings on abortion-related bills. What happened in Jefferson City that month would set the tone for that all-important election year. A dozen bills restricting contraception and abortion had already been filed. Missouri was still a testing ground, and national antiabortion groups were sure to try out their most extreme measures to see if Missouri's Republican supermajority would help pass them to secure their coveted Missouri Right to Life endorsement. On Tuesday, January 13, just after seven-thirty in the morning, Hearing Room Two was already almost full. Soon it was overflowing. The bill up for discussion, Senate Bill 646, would have required abortion providers to send the whole embryo or fetus to a pathologist so the state could ensure that no part of an aborted fetus had been sold. Missouri law already prohibited physicians from harvesting tissue, but the requirement would have created a complicated new process for abortion providers and the state.

At that point, I had traveled to multiple red states where I had interviewed dozens of people about abortion. A couple of years before, I had stood outside an Arkansas clinic where thirty or so white men in cargo shorts mistook me for a patient, surrounded me, and screamed about genocide until the police were called. And yet the simpatico relations between the antiabortion activists and elected officials in those Missouri hearing rooms stunned me. It wasn't just that pro-choice lobbyists were outnumbered and so couldn't persuade moderates. There would be no persuasion. No lawmaker was going to waver, at least not publicly. Missouri lawmakers openly expressed their personal beliefs as their motivation to restrict abortion. Usually, on the public stage, antiabortion lawmakers and activists say their proposed restrictions will protect women's health. In 1992, in the major *Casey* ruling, the

Supreme Court permitted states more leeway to restrict abortion but said their restrictions couldn't infringe on women's health, which is why the false claim that abortion causes women psychological distress, infertility, and other problems is so important to the antiabortion movement. But in those Jefferson City hearing rooms, nobody bothered with the pretense that their legislation prioritized women's health. In response to Planned Parenthood physician Dr. David Eisenberg testifying that abortion is an extremely safe procedure, Senator Jeanie Riddle, who represents District 10, retorted, "I just think the babies wouldn't say that, probably."

When the hearing was over, I rode the elevator with four men—two antiabortion lobbyists and two legislators' aides. One lobbyist shook his head; Eisenberg's argument that fetal tissue donation could contribute to life-saving research, he said, was like the Nazis' experiments on the disabled. "Ends justify the means," one aide said. "Repugnant," said the other.

That afternoon, for two hours, I watched a House hearing about whether Planned Parenthood was trafficking "dead baby body parts." The conversation was circular, always coming back to, "How can we be sure they aren't?" The only person who pushed back was Stacey Newman, the gun reform activist and former Democratic Party staffer, who had been representing District 87 in St. Louis since 2009. Her work advocating against gun bills had inspired her to run for office. Newman was then the chair of the assembly's Progressive Caucus, the largest group of Democratic legislators. The temerity that made Newman appealing to primary voters in St. Louis put her completely at odds with nearly everyone else on the committee. She kept interjecting that none of the Republicans' claims were based on evidence. It was easy to see how having to listen to dozens of hours of antiabortion propaganda from fellow lawmakers over the years would make it very difficult for a pro-choice feminist to speak in the nuances that define abortion for most voters.

The frenzy over "dead baby body parts" also demonstrated how much harder it is to dispel a lie than to spread one. Hearing that there was no evidence of wrongdoing only inspired lawmakers to say they needed to dig deeper. During later hearings, committee chair Diane Franklin, who displayed a Missouri Right to Life award on her desk, read in a sharp, authoritative tone from reports published by the Heritage Foundation (a major think tank at the center of the Reaganite conservative movement) and Alliance Defending Freedom (another conservative Christian legal group that has won multiple Supreme Court "religious freedom" cases that limited gay and reproductive rights). When the Planned Parenthood advocate said a report wasn't true, Franklin accused her of "hiding something." After watching many hours of similar hearings over several months, I had the impression that multiple—if not the majority of—Missouri state lawmakers genuinely believed there was a distinct possibility that physicians were encouraging women to get pregnant for the sole purpose of having abortions so that said physicians could sell and profit from the fetal tissue. It was almost like Pizzagate—when in 2016 a man fired shots into a DC pizza shop because he believed a viral conspiracy theory that Democratic staffers were running a child sex ring in its basement—except that those taken in by the bizarre fiction were lawmakers with the power to pass laws affecting thousands of women's access to health care.

The most fervently antiabortion legislators had command of the agenda. Disputing their false claims meant becoming their target. "The Republicans fall in line" would be a phrase I would hear again and again from Democrats describing the culture in the capitol. As then Representative Stacey Newman told me, lawmakers' opinions on guns and abortion are "fixed," unlikely to move during a hearing or assembly debate. Instead, Newman said, "The dial moves on Election Day."

Leaving the capitol that day, deflated, I wondered whether maybe the reproductive rights strategists working out of DC and Manhattan were right—maybe Missouri and other so-called fly-over states were lost causes, and so should be left to fend for themselves. But ceding those states risked ceding large swaths of the nation to people who rejected medical science and whose campaign to end legal abortion was closing clinics that provided low-income patients with cancer screenings and prenatal care.

Over forty years after *Roe*, antiabortion donors and activists had built a social movement that could serve as an exemplar, and Missouri remained one of its strategic battlegrounds. After decades of investment in local efforts, antiabortion advocates in Missouri had a solid presence. There were at least fourteen antiabortion organizations in the state, four of which were headquartered within walking distance of the capitol dome. With so many antiabortion organizations, they could each focus on a single strategy if they chose. Missouri Family Network, for example, primarily lobbied, while 40 Days for Life protested outside clinics; Concerned Women for America, through "legislative liaisons," proposed bills, and Vitae helped antiabortion centers market to pregnant women. Missouri Right to Life's presence latticed the whole state, with two regional offices plus ten local chapters. Its political arm consistently out-fund-raised Planned Parenthood and NARAL's local political arms.[3]

Sam Lee, a lobbyist who cowrote the Missouri laws upheld in the landmark *Webster* case, told me that the dominant view in Jefferson City is that "our legislation should be put out there as sort of a litmus test or a voting record." Missouri Right to Life ranked and endorsed legislators based on whether they "would be the best and most effective voice for the unborn." The ranking system was (and remains) punitive enough that any perceived sympathy for Planned Parenthood—even voting for a bill that expanded contraception access—endangered an endorsement. Antiabortion and gun rights organizations were excellent at shepherding those very partisan voters to the polls, so Republican lawmakers were eager to sponsor their bills. The NRA and the "no compromise" Missouri Firearms Coalition also issued endorsements, rallied voters, and kept in regular touch with lawmakers.

In contrast, local pro-choice advocates were stretched thin and still working under the framework established by the federally focused abortion rights groups back in the 1970s. As antiabortion organizations have pushed onerous incremental state laws, the largest abortion rights groups have had more reason to battle in the courts, perpetuating the cycle of investing in litigation rather than cultural programs that might change hearts and minds, or local organizing that could buttress the supporters and upstart community leaders already scattered across the country. National umbrella organizations like Planned Parenthood and NARAL tend to invest in state affiliates only if those states are important to national elections. Ahead of the 2016 elections, NARAL Pro-Choice America, for example, worked to build a political infrastructure in swing states like Colorado and Iowa, but not Missouri.

State affiliates for groups that endorsed reproductive rights—Planned Parenthood, NARAL, and the ACLU—were largely responsible for raising their own funds. In states where there was already vocal support for abortion rights, local organizations had less trouble coming up with donations to promote candidates or initiatives. For example, in New York State, where abortion restrictions are rarely advanced, there are five regional Planned Parenthood political organizations, which in 2013 had a combined revenue totaling nearly $700,000. Compare that with Planned Parenthood's political arm for all of Missouri, which took in $113,314 that year. Planned Parenthood and the ACLU raised tens of millions of dollars of donations within weeks of Trump's inauguration. The ACLU is hiring a few more staffers in regional offices, including organizers, but federal work commands the most resources. As we will see in coming chapters, the distribution problem extends beyond abortion rights; progressives advocating on the state level for education, immigration, and climate change reforms also say that donors tend to give to big-name groups they recognize, and—unlike their right-wing counterparts—those national groups don't necessary equip local leaders with what they need.

Some thought Planned Parenthood and other pro-choice groups were putting the cart before the horse when they spent on elections. Pamela Merritt, a reproductive rights advocate in Missouri, said, "For the last decade, the reproductive rights movement, which is mostly led by Planned Parenthood, from a political lens, has focused almost exclusively on an electoral strategy." They focused on mobilizing supportive voters. "Not a bad theory," Merritt said, "but the problem is that nobody has been doing movement work. Now we have the absence of movement infrastructure in states that did not have an electoral significance." That work is more than canvassing or making robo-calls the week before an election. "Movement work is constant and consistent messaging about how much you believe in the power of your ideas and why other people should believe in the power of your ideas too," Merritt told me. Changing the culture requires listening to and speaking with people in person, over time. Merritt explained that the Democratic Party often "messages to voters as if we've done movement work," sending out a slogan as if people are going to understand and agree with the underlying problem or principle.

In the last couple of decades, a network of independent organizations—like Merritt's Repro Action—has emerged to try to fill the vacuum in local organizing, new messaging, proactive model legislation, and more. Many of those organizations were founded by women of color in response to their marginalization by the mainstream women's movement, and they advocate for what they define as reproductive justice—the right to have autonomy over your body and to parent or not parent in a safe community. Advocates working within the reproductive justice framework embrace multiple causes, from trans rights to racial justice, that they see as part of one overarching movement.

When I arrived in Jefferson City that January of 2016, NARAL Missouri had a new executive director, Alison Dreith, who saw her new job through a reproductive justice lens. Dreith, then in her mid-thirties, had worked for Missouri Progressive Vote Coalition, which had sought to mobilize voters and coordinate interest groups in the tradition of the Colorado model but had folded after running out of money. Before that, in her twenties, Dreith had worked odd jobs, protested capitalist policies and behemoths like NAFTA and the IMF, and caravanned with punks and anarchists. When protests had broken out in 2014 in Ferguson, fifteen miles from her house, it never occurred to Dreith not to go. In late

2015, after she was offered the executive director job at NARAL, she weighed whether to accept, trying to convince herself that she could command and develop a political organization, cycling through platitudes about rising to challenges. She was an irreverent empath. She saw herself as an activist. And she was clear-eyed about how lonely the fight for abortion rights would be in Jefferson City. Still, she decided that accepting the NARAL position was another opportunity to fight for what was right.

When Dreith was offered the job, the state organization had about $20,000 in the bank. When she started, she was the only full-time employee. Her new life required incredible fortitude. That first Tuesday in January, and on many other mornings that followed, Dreith woke up around 5 a.m. to make the two-hour drive to Jefferson City, where in hearing rooms she made public arguments in support of a practice most people in the room believed was murder. Missouri lawmakers were required to give only twenty-four hours' notice before a hearing. That meant advocates who wanted to oppose or support a bill often had to scramble to get to Jefferson City. The long stretches of farmland and highway separating the state capital from Kansas City and St. Louis may seem incidental, but they created a major logistical disadvantage for local Democrats and progressives. In comparison, the two-mile slide from New Era's house to the capitol building in Denver seemed luxurious.

That legislative session, antiabortion bills were proposed and discussed at a frantic pace. As spring arrived, Dreith stayed in rapid-response mode. In April, the legislature advanced antiabortion legislation almost every day it was in session. On May 5, the House debated a constitutional amendment that would grant fertilized eggs legal personhood—thereby prohibiting not only abortion but also some forms of contraception and potentially fertility treatments as well. On the floor of the assembly, Republicans repeatedly asked, "When does life begin?" A failing of the reproductive rights movement is not having an effective answer to that question, which has humiliated countless advocates and pro-choice legislators over the years. At the microphone, on the assembly floor, they sputter, redden, or repeat a line that cannot help but sound like a dodge. It is a hard question to answer, especially because people who support abortion rights tend to see the question in shades of gray, and nuance does not translate to political posters, or to witty or authoritative comebacks during public jousts. And so it went that day. The next day, the amendment passed 110 to 37. With just a few days of the session left, the Senate wouldn't have time to vote on it. It wouldn't become law. But by hurrying the resolution to the floor, House leadership had taken the temperature of the assembly: an overwhelming majority was willing to support a resolution that would make abortion illegal, without an exception for the life of the woman.

Just over a month after the Missouri legislative session ended, though, the scales seemed like they might change for women, health care providers, and reproductive rights advocates in red states. In late June 2016, in *Whole Women's Health v. Hellerstedt*, the Supreme Court had declared unconstitutional multiple Texas laws mandating that abortion providers meet many more requirements than surgical centers that provided other kinds of procedures (like glaucoma treatments, for example). The court ruled that those laws made it so costly and complicated to offer abortion procedures that they effectively shuttered clinics and in turn created an "undue burden" for women living great distances from the nearest provider. That ruling was a major coup for reproductive rights advocates. It limited how much leeway state lawmakers had in establishing restrictions on abortion providers. Justice Anthony Kennedy, the longtime swing vote on abortion rights, had sided with the clinics, and in turn with disenfranchised women. It was widely believed that reproductive rights advocates were looking toward a time when states' punitive abortion laws would be challenged and invalidated one by one, thanks to the precedent set that sunny morning. Clinics had been forced to close in Missouri when its similar laws first passed, but after that 2016 ruling, Planned Parenthood began the process of dramatically expanding its abortion services in Missouri. For a few brief months, it was possible to believe that women's rights weren't as precarious as they appeared from the gallery overlooking the assembly floor in Jefferson City.

★ ★ ★

Guns remained another flash point in Missouri politics—and in states nationwide. In 2008, in *District of Columbia v. Heller*, the Supreme Court had amended the meaning of the Second Amendment for the first time in seventy years and decided that a thirty-year-old DC gun restriction was unconstitutional. That ruling affirmed that people, not only militias, have the right to own guns. But the landmark *Heller* decision did not establish a broad right to carry arms in public, nor did the justices clearly articulate how much leeway states have in regulating gun ownership. Since 2008, the NRA and other gun advocates have sought to pass state and local laws codifying the right to carry in public to achieve their long-term goal of winning a Supreme Court precedent enshrining public carry as a constitutional right.[4]

In an election year like 2016, the odds were high that Missouri would loosen its gun laws. Like Missouri Right to Life, the NRA was considered indispensable to Missouri Republicans, and invincible. And like antiabortion attorneys, NRA strategists were experimenting in Missouri to see what might be possible nationwide, as they had been doing for decades. Republican candidates and NRA lobbyists still counted on each other to advance their respective interrelated goals. By that January of 2016, Missouri lawmakers had rolled out multiple bills that would loosen restrictions on gun ownership, guaranteeing that lawmakers would have a chance to earn NRA endorsements.

Missouri was poised to enact the nation's most permissive gun laws. Before the legislative session began, Republican senator Brian Munzlinger, who had won the District 18 seat in outstate Missouri, filed a bill that eliminated requirements for training or a background check before being able to carry a concealed weapon in public. Even by Missouri standards, Senate Bill 656 was extreme. It wasn't the only radical bill. That same year, another Republican with a sterling approval rating from the NRA proposed a bill that would have allowed all felons, including those convicted of murder, rape, and kidnapping, to own guns after serving time. Meanwhile, Stacey Newman introduced five bills restricting gun sales and ownership. No one expected those gun safety bills to get a hearing, let alone make it to the governor's desk. Sure enough, as soon as lawmakers reconvened in Jefferson City, they pushed Senate Bill 656 through the committee process, increasing the odds it would be voted on by the whole assembly.

The years of disinvestment in local organizing for gun control—now called "gun violence prevention"—was still evident in Missouri as 2016 began. But as with reproductive rights, a small but vigilant and growing cohort of women was pushing against what had long been considered inevitable. They and their respective allies used different strategies, but they were all working to reverse patterns that had been established back in the 1970s, and they were all, slowly, brick by brick, building an opposition.

In a leafy suburban neighborhood in St. Louis County, just outside the city limits, Becky Morgan was working from home for Moms Demand Action for Gun Sense in America. Morgan's father had been shot twice in the head and killed in 1991, when she was nineteen. After the shooting at Sandy Hook Elementary School in 2012, Morgan was distraught, thinking of her father and her own kids. She realized she had never processed losing her dad. She came across Facebook calls-to-action written by Shannon Watts. In Colorado Springs, Watts ran her own public relations consultancy; she had previously worked for the state of Missouri and companies like Monsanto. In the weeks and months after the Sandy Hook shooting, Watts put her PR experience and the wide reach of social media to use. She coordinated with a group of women in New York, drummed up money and volunteers, and sketched out a plan for what would become Moms Demand Action, a nonprofit advocacy group that would organize local chapters and mobilize mothers (and, later, people who are not mothers) nationwide.[5]

By the time Morgan joined Moms Demand, gun violence was more visible to the broader public than back when Stacey Newman showed up in Jefferson City with only a homemade binder of statistics. In 2006 Mayors Against Illegal Guns formed. The Joyce Foundation lent support, as did New York City's mayor Michael Bloomberg. At that time, throughout the country, there were already dozens of local anti-gun-violence efforts. It was still rare, though, for foundations and megadonors to throw their weight behind political solutions to gun violence. Then a rash of highly publicized shootings happened, including one in an Arizona parking lot where a gunman shot Representative Gabby Giffords and eighteen others, killing six. When Watts tapped away at her keyboard that night in December 2012, after the murders at Sandy Hook, people across the country were looking for somewhere to channel their exasperation. Watts and her team devised a top-down approach, developing materials and protocols so that volunteers on the ground could just "plug in and go." Thousands of Americans immediately involved themselves. After a high-profile campaign resulted in Starbucks asking guns owners not to carry in their stores, Bloomberg's group approached Watts about a merger. Mayors Against Illegal Guns and Moms Demand Action folded into one organization, Everytown for Gun Safety. Suddenly Moms Demand had access to a much deeper coffer, plus professional staffers who could help with legal work, lobbying, and marketing. And national gun violence prevention strategists finally had a burgeoning network of activists in cities and small towns from coast to coast.

By 2016, Moms Demand had chapters in every state. The same enormous logistical and funding questions that have long thwarted local organizing didn't dissolve overnight, of course. Local organizers were still absorbing significant costs. Moms Demand's nationwide grassroots network was sustained by unpaid volunteer labor, including for state chapter leaders, like Morgan, who said she devoted at least twenty hours per week to the cause, often more during the legislative session. The regional chapter in Southeastern Missouri was given just $400 that year to cover costs like gas, flyers, food for events, and much more. Chapter leaders routinely subsidized event costs. Because so much of the work is unpaid, many of the women with leadership positions within

Moms Demand are white, middle class or affluent, and supported by their spouses. Much like Newman before them, then, Moms Demand activists are easy fodder for talk radio hosts in the business of stoking class resentment. Gun rights enthusiasts and their shills often riff on "gun-grabbing soccer moms" and "Bloomberg's bitches." None of this is lost on the Moms Demand volunteers, who are routinely harassed on social media and in person. Armed men have shown up at public Moms Demand meetings, and attendees—dismissed as fainthearted because they are mostly middle-aged women—have had to talk them down.

Moms Demand's branding was both a strength and a weakness. Many on the left champion inclusiveness as a core value; movements made up mostly of financially comfortable white women are never going to adequately agitate for the reforms that will benefit the majority of Americans. Moms Demand Action works closely with law enforcement, and its members span the political spectrum. There is also a strong argument that conservative white lawmakers are more likely to identify with and take seriously testimony from someone like Morgan, with her blond ponytail and quick smile. Her consistent presence in Jefferson City hearing rooms, and the gravity of her loss, made it impossible for Republicans in those rooms to dismiss gun violence as a problem for "those people," in barely veiled racist language.

"[There] was one time I felt like my testimony stopped legislation in its tracks," Morgan told me.

Moms Demand volunteers had organized a crowd of people to attend the public hearing for a bill that would have allowed convicted violent felons to carry guns. The room was packed. Morgan remembered the committee chair telling her there was time for her to speak for only a couple of minutes, less time than others had been allowed. She put aside the testimony she had prepared and improvised, telling the committee that the person who had murdered her father would be up for parole in two years.

"As tough as it is for me and my family to go to Chillicothe, Missouri, to say to the parole board, 'Please don't release this person,'" Morgan remembered saying, "I have to come here and ask you to not make it legal for this person who shot my dad two times in the head to own a gun again." She remembers looking them all in the eye and sensing a shift in the room.

"Even the Republicans," she recalled. "Their demeanor changed, they leaned in, they were empathizing with me."

"It's hard," Morgan said of testifying in public, but "my dad's not here. He can't speak for himself, so it made me glad that I could do that. I could be his voice."

The bill disappeared. "It's one of those victories that doesn't get a lot of attention, but it's what 'Moms' like me are doing in statehouses across the country," she said. Quiet wins like those may be hard to quantify in a grant application. And they may be barely perceptible to a public accustomed to high political drama. But during moments like these, when the tenor of a hearing—or even of individual lawmakers' attitudes—shifts, activists like Morgan realize that a greater change is possible, and they are more likely to be motivated to keep going, against long odds. Those tiny, incremental wins are what the gun reform movement has been missing for decades, as national strategists focused on federal lawsuits.

The strategic choices of Moms Demand Action also made it more difficult for their opposition to discredit their activists as anti-gun zealots. Moms Demand doesn't trade in leftist rhetoric, an intentional decision by Shannon Watts and Michael Bloomberg. Watts, who had established a strong corporate career, has been called out for underplaying if not misrepresenting her professional and political experience, repeatedly describing herself as a "stay-at-home mom who was folding laundry" when news of Sandy Hook broke.[6] Watts intuited that Americans would better respect her authority if it was rooted in her motherhood and her "outsider status." Even more significant is another messaging choice, one that distinguishes Moms Demand Action from their failed predecessors: the group explicitly emphasizes support for the Second Amendment and invites gun owners to join their calls for reform.

"Every once in a while, when we say what our platform is, that we support the Second Amendment, I can see some people shut down," Morgan said, describing leading meetings in her Democratic neighborhood in St. Louis. But she believes that "this is the smart, strategic, pragmatic place to be." In Jefferson City, Moms Demand's middle road, dismissed by their critics on the left as compromised, looked a lot like pie-in-the-sky idealism. But their low likelihood of immediate success did not deter Morgan and her fellow volunteers, just as it hadn't deterred Dreith. All that winter and spring of 2016, Morgan, like Dreith, tracked bills, searched for volunteers, drafted testimony, consulted with experts, and coordinated meetings in St. Louis and trips to Jefferson City. Senate Bill 656 moved through committee after committee. In its final form, the bill would codify "stand your ground," meaning Missourians would have the legal right to shoot if they felt they or their property was threatened, and permitless carry, meaning in Missouri it would be legal to carry a gun without training or a permit. Researchers at Texas A&M had found that homicide rates increased around 8 percent after stand-your-ground laws were enacted. Sheriffs from small towns, and the mayors and chief law enforcement officers from Kansas City and St. Louis, voiced opposition to the bill. Though the Missouri Republican Party had adopted the slogan "Blue Lives Matter" in response to multiple shootings of unarmed black men by police officers, when it came to gun legislation, lawmakers disregarded the advice and requests of law enforcement. Late on May 13, the very last day of the 2016 legislative session, Missouri passed Senate Bill 656 and became the first state to pass a stand-your-ground bill since Trayvon Martin had been killed in 2012.[7]

The battle over Senate Bill 656 had been intense, and it would not end on that May evening. Governor Jay Nixon, a Democrat, still had to sign the bill into law, and Morgan was determined to continue efforts to oppose it. She arranged for a meeting with the governor's staff and brought along other survivors of gun violence. Governor Nixon did veto the bill. But Senate leadership called for a special session that would convene in September to vote on whether to override the governor's veto.

Morgan and her fellow Moms Demand Action activists didn't expect that they would stop Senate Bill 656 from becoming law, but they redoubled their efforts anyway. Everytown's DC staff told Morgan to organize in outstate districts—the "heavy lift" that gun reform advocates had been avoiding since the 1970s. As part of their "losing forward" strategy, they would lay the groundwork for future campaigns in the very places where traveling gun shows set up their tents and tables of Glocks and AR-15s for sale. The national office recommended that Morgan organize two kinds of gatherings: private meetings with elected officials in their home districts and public meetings with community members in those small towns.

That summer, Morgan and another volunteer began the logistical nightmare of setting up meetings in nine far-flung towns. They wanted to organize opposition to the newly passed bill, to dissuade the supermajority Republican legislature from overriding the governor's veto. "It was a lot of work," Morgan told me, laughing. They made cold calls using a voter register file that Everytown had purchased. Morgan asked around, searching for anyone who knew someone living in various small towns. She sent Facebook messages to strangers. They called Democratic clubs and women's groups. For each meeting with an elected official, they hoped to find a Republican, a Moms Demand volunteer, and a survivor of gun violence. Morgan asked local volunteers from those towns to contact their representatives to set up the meetings, but few representatives responded to their e-mails or calls. The public meetings, though, were well attended, all things considered. Finally, Morgan arrived at Hillbilly Bowl, a long, white-paneled building with a restaurant and defunct bowling alley, in Kimberling City, a town of two thousand residents. She passed out stationery and asked the twenty-five or so people who had shown up to write letters to their representatives explaining why they disagreed with Senate Bill 656. "If you're a gun owner, please include that in your letter," she told them.

In Jefferson City that summer, the veto override special session loomed. Since the bill had passed the assembly, local media had paid it more attention. In just one of several op-eds written against Senate Bill 656, St. Louis police chief Sam Dotson wrote, "This bill poses serious public safety risks."[8] To shore up support for an override, in case legislators were wavering, the NRA's national office dispatched seven lobbyists to Jefferson City. On September 14, the day the assembly would vote, Moms Demand convened over two hundred people in the capitol rotunda, where they invited gun owners to speak against the bill.

The assembly overrode the governor's veto of Senate Bill 656 by a wide margin, mostly voting on party lines. It was a loss for Moms Demand, without question. Missouri's gun laws became among the most permissive in the nation. But Morgan saw a silver lining: those seven lobbyists the NRA had sent. Someone else might find in that same fact justification for cynicism or defeatism. But Morgan realized that the NRA had fought. It had been at least a decade since the NRA had needed to fight in Missouri. She heard that some Republican senators privately disapproved of the bill and regretted being forced to vote on it. They feared they were damned no matter how they voted on such a radical bill—the same backlash that had awaited many Missouri Democrats no matter how they voted on gun bills. Moms Demand and their allies, by Morgan's calculation, had inched a step closer toward their goal of making guns a thorny issue, instead of an obvious way to round up voters and donations.

★ ★ ★

On a humid afternoon during soybean and cotton harvest, I drove to Cape Girardeau—Rush Limbaugh's hometown, in the southeastern reaches of the state—to attend the local Moms Demand Action meeting. The meeting was run by Lynda Stewart, who had started the group when Becky Morgan told her there wasn't one nearby that she could join.

"I decided by my silence I was enabling the gun lobby," Stewart told me later. She lived in a small town edged by cotton fields near Missouri's southern border, true "little Dixie," but decided to host the meeting in Cape Girardeau. That summer, Stewart started casting around for local Democratic leaders who might show her the ropes of political work, which was slow going. For its first two months, the Southeastern Missouri Moms Demand Action chapter had two members.

As I drove toward Cape Girardeau, voices on the radio talked nonstop about "gun grabbers." That morning, on his nationally syndicated radio show carried by Missouri stations, Glenn Beck read aloud tweets from Nelba Márquez-Greene, whose six-year-old Anna was murdered in Sandy Hook elementary school in 2012.

On Twitter, Greene had written, "As a mom who had to bury a child I care less about perp color, but how come we never talk about angry white men with guns?"

"You know what that sounds like?" Beck asked, laughing, "You absolutely care about the perp's color! You hear about angry white men *all the time*!" Beck said he felt terrible for Greene, and then said her tweets proved that "these are not people who are going to help us charter a way forward to come up with good solutions, good policies and laws for America. These are people who are lashing out because they cannot control their emotions."

Two days earlier, on Monday, October 2, 2017, the country had woken to news that a gunman had hauled more than twenty assault weapons into a Las Vegas hotel room perched above a country music festival and shot into the crowd, killing fifty-eight and injuring more than eight hundred people. Originally, the Moms Demand meeting was supposed to be the Southeastern Missouri chapter's anniversary party. Stewart had e-mailed me, "Did I mention that there will be cake?" After the massacre, she called off the celebratory flourishes. She worried about what to say; she felt a responsibility to offer attendees a worthy response to the tragedy. The meeting that evening ended up becoming a memory I called upon many times over the course of reporting this book and when reading the news and trying to make sense of our nation's course. It was also an experience that helped me understand what people meant when they talked about building a movement rather than winning an election.

When I arrived, Stewart told me that she had asked Felice Roberson to lead an invocation to start the meeting. She and Stewart made a point of showing up at all of each other's events. Roberson's teenage son, Quinton, had been shot and killed in 2015. Roberson had subsequently founded Stop Needless Acts of Violence Please, a local group that worked with the police department to create an anonymous crime tip-line, knocked on doors to turn out voters for school board elections, organized marches, and prayed in the streets. Roberson wanted to make her organization an official (c)3, but she didn't know how to navigate the process—and even with a discount, the IRS filing fee was $400. When we met, she had made T-shirts to sell to raise funds. Roberson was living proof that the nonprofit system was not designed to advance the ideas of people who are not already connected, at least tangentially, to wealth and power.

About twenty of us sat at tables that formed a U-shape in a recently refurbished library room. Most attendees were white women who appeared to be over fifty and brought with them tubs of baked goods.

In attendance that night was a Democratic candidate for Congress, Kathy Ellis, a social worker who had decided to run because she was so moved by the Women's March, as well as Kathryn Swan, a Republican state representative. After Roberson's prayer, Stewart gave a PowerPoint presentation about all they had done that year. She said that before starting the group she never could have imagined that she would meet with Senator McCaskill.

After Stewart opened up the conversation, Ellis said, "I live daily with the challenge of working with clients who are very depressed and who have access to guns."

Across the room from her, a black woman sitting beside Roberson spoke next. "I have a mental disability. My diagnosis is paranoid schizophrenic. It hurts me when our society demonizes these people. It makes it hard for me to get out there. People will stigmatize and stereotype me, like this man that shot everybody."

The air in the room shifted. Some people leaned forward, others held still.

She kept going, saying she wished that Americans would collectively ask, "Where did we go wrong as a society?"

"I'm hoping, because this was so horrendous," Stewart responded. "The casualty count is so high. I don't think we can go on. I hope that this is a watershed moment and change happens."

"I know we have the Second Amendment," the woman said.

"I'm here. I'm actually a gun owner. I actually own several assault rifles," said a white man with long brown hair and a beard, wearing a T-shirt and cargo shorts. "I was horrified by Sunday. And I come from—I supported—Gun Owners of America, which is the extreme right group. They're the group that's further than the NRA. I worked to get permitless constitutional carry in this state. And I'm horrified by that."

His voice wasn't self-righteous or plaintive. Nobody in the room spoke as if they were obviously right, or someone else was obviously wrong.

He talked about the importance of gun locks and safes, especially for parents, ending with, "I don't want a child being shot."

Stewart responded by talking about how Moms Demand Action includes gun owners.

When the meeting was over, the woman who had said she was schizophrenic and the man who said he had helped pass Senate Bill 656 approached each other. They stood and talked, nodding and smiling, by the dessert table. Whatever passed between them was not going to change the nation's political landscape; it was not going to silence the radio hosts or Twitter trolls or rewrite our laws or change political campaigns. But something real was passing between them, between everyone in the room that night. That moment was possible only because Stewart and Roberson had put out an open invitation for Missourians to meet in person, in a public space, together.

When everyone else had gone, Stewart remained, seated beside Representative Swan. They were leaning toward each other, and Swan was silent as Stewart spoke.

★ ★ ★

If everything said on talk radio, if everything that happened in Jefferson City, wasn't enough proof that the culture wars kept

Republicans in power, November 8, 2016, had made it inescapably clear. Missourians elected antiunion, antiabortion, and pro-gun Republicans up and down the ticket, from the state assembly to the presidency. Trump and Greitens winning their elections on the same night made fatalism very tempting. It would take another eighteen months before the major cable networks and newspapers would detail how abortion rights and the potential for gun reform were in peril, hanging in the balance of the changing Supreme Court, but on that night local activists like Dreith and Morgan foresaw what would happen.

During that election cycle, the Republican Party and its megadonors had used rhetoric about guns and abortion to ensure fealty to their economic interests. Missouri billionaire David Humphrey and his family, heirs to a construction materials company, worked with Americans for Prosperity and spent at least $2.75 million targeting pro-union Missouri Republican lawmakers.[9] Incumbent representative Shelia Solon, a Republican from a middle-class suburban district near Kansas City, had voted against right-to-work, the antiunion bill promoted by Americans for Prosperity, and other business lobbies. Americans for Prosperity had threatened to oppose her in her reelection campaign if she did not support their bill, but Solon said that she had surveyed her constituents and received clear indication that a majority supported union rights. The antiunion donors spent at least $500,000 on negative ads against Solon, and roughly $1 million against another pro-union Republican woman candidate. The Missouri Republican Party gave Solon no support, which she attributed to her pro-union vote. "I was outspent five-to-one," she said.

The negative ads did not highlight Solon's pro-union stand, however. Instead, the ads attacked her for not having "family values." While in office, Solon had sponsored a bill that proposed allowing pharmacists to prescribe birth control. "I'm pro-life," she explained. "If you're pro-life I would think the biggest thing would be to reduce unplanned pregnancies to begin with." Solon lost the primary to the billionaire-backed challenger, Dan Stacy, who also won the general election. "I think it's going to strike fear in hearts, unfortunately, of legislators," Solon said. "It's no longer representing your constituents and the folks back home, or even your party and what your party wants, it's going to be about a couple of billionaires."[10]

The Republican legislature and Greitens kept their promises, and in 2017 Missouri passed a right-to-work law. Unions then organized to put on a 2018 ballot an initiative that would allow voters to override right-to-work. Because many of their members had voted for antiunion lawmakers, the unions had to wage an expensive battle to undo those lawmakers' decisions. The AFL-CIO, a progressive union, rounded up over one thousand volunteers, knocked on eight hundred thousand doors, and made nearly one million phone calls. A wide array of progressive organizations and church groups helped get out the word, too. Missouri voters showed up, even though the vote was held in August, and they were unequivocal: 67 percent voted against right-to-work, and 33 percent in favor. Roughly half of Republicans who voted opposed right-to-work. In national outlets, the results were heralded as a labor victory, which it was, and as a bellwether of Democrats' possible reassertion in Trump country, which it wasn't.

★ ★ ★

The majority of rural Missourians were not going to have a mass conversion and suddenly disavow the soundtrack of their lives, the voices from talk radio and Fox News. Abortion and guns were not going to be minor issues anytime soon. Democrats and progressives were still finding ways to gradually make inroads. That year, 2018, Democrats ran a candidate in every district, including in places like John Cauthorn's District 18, where they hadn't won in over twenty years. In the tradition of Howard Dean's fifty-state strategy and in step with the DNC's new mandate, the Missouri Democratic Party was trying to reestablish itself in every corner of the state. Talking with Crystal Stephens, who ran as a Democrat in District 18, brought home what those candidates were up against. Stephens had disagreed with members of her local county Democratic club over whether, for example, they needed to add the state party's nondiscrimination clause to their bylaws. Many members of the club were cultural conservatives in their seventies or older who, she said, acted more like Republicans—defending the Confederate flag, openly disparaging LGBTQ people, marching in antiabortion parades, posting pro-Trump messages on Facebook. Some of them also opposed the idea of Missouri expanding Medicaid. One final straw for Stephens was a club leader beginning their meetings by praying for Trump. When she objected, they questioned her morality and said she wasn't a Christian—which they meant as an insult. Another problem was that its members did not want to use Act Blue, the online fund-raising platform that connected candidates with donors all over the country, which sabotaged their chances. "They are so stuck in the past, they are afraid to change anything," she told me. She and a cohort of progressives defected and started their own Democratic club.

That summer, Stephens had about $2,000 in campaign funds and no campaign staff. "More than money, we need people out there walking," she told me. Her opponent was Cindy McLaughlin, a board member of the Missouri Club for Growth, a pro-business group with a national arm that had raised at least $10 million for Josh Hawley in his campaign against Senator Claire McCaskill before 2018 even began. The Missouri affiliate was funded by Rex Sinquefield, Missouri's other resident right-wing billionaire, who told fellow University of Chicago alums, "If you get involved on the local level, you will be amazed at how much influence you can have." In 2014 alone, Sinquefield donated $10 million to sixty-eight state campaigns in Missouri. Connected to Sinquefield, McLaughlin was set. By that summer, she had $200,000 in her campaign fund. Stephens said that put her at a disadvantage from an optics standpoint, too: "People aren't listening to somebody who doesn't have money, because, let's face it, they think that money is intelligence, and that's not true. We can't buy intelligence."[11]

The issues, like abortion rights, that put Stephens at odds with not only the Republican candidate but also her fellow Democrats were everywhere, so woven into the backdrop that they were somehow almost invisible. Racism and sexism and reflexive deference to Christian groups' politics were too much for any one person to combat. "It's like everybody puts up this brick wall around their heads, and it's so hard to knock down those bricks because they've been taught these things for so long . . . and they think it's normal and it's not," she said. Plus, few if any of her neighbors had heard of ALEC or understood campaign finance laws. The young people with perspectives broadened by travel tended to move out permanently. Multiple people told me that "Missouri's biggest export is young talent." Those who remained were "in a constant state of struggle and survival, so they can't pay attention to anything else," Stephens said. She believed that keeping people living paycheck to paycheck was in itself a way of diverting opposition.

If Republican billionaires and antiabortion and pro-gun strategists had a lock on places like District 18, Democrats and progressives needed to try something different altogether. A group of Missourians had an idea, the seed of which had been planted years earlier, in 2013. That year, a coalition had tried to get on the ballot an initiative that would have capped the rate for payday loans at 36 percent. At the time, the average annual percentage rate in Missouri was so high that if someone borrowed $100 from a payday lender, within a year she could owe $455. Democratic lawmakers had repeatedly tried to pass regulations through the statehouse, but their efforts failed. Payday loan companies were major political donors. To get around their direct political influence, the coalition of reformers, including church groups, began gathering signatures to get the initiative on the ballot. Payday loan companies and Republican politicians and political action committees threw hundreds of thousands of dollars into stopping the initiative, including threatening the church leaders and starting front groups that confused their opponents' message.[12] The reformers' initiative didn't make it on the ballot. As they regrouped, the reformers realized that they were going to continuously face the same problem. They needed to diminish the influence of massive corporate donations, or they were always going to lose.

Around the same time, State Voices was forming the latest incarnation of a Missouri organizing table, this one called Missouri

Organizing and Voter Engagement Collaborative (MOVE). Its director was Molly Fleming, a former community organizer, who had helped coordinate signature gathering for the payday loan initiative. MOVE sought to unify movements for people of color and for labor—groups that for generations business organizations and politicians had strategically driven apart in order to "divide and conquer." Meanwhile, St. Louis politics was changing as the post-Ferguson generation of ascendant leaders were organizing and running for office.

By 2018, reform-minded Missourians had an ambitious ballot initiative that they wanted voters to pass. CLEAN Missouri didn't aim to change one policy arena; it aimed to disrupt the system. Its multiple provisions included transferring the responsibility and power of drawing district maps from legislators to a neutral bipartisan commission, which would prevent incumbents from rigging the map to protect their seats or party; restricting campaign contributions to state legislators; banning lobbyist gifts over five dollars; requiring state legislators to be subject to open-records laws; and limiting political fund-raising by candidates. If passed by voters, those new provisions would have a dramatic effect on reducing the influence of incumbents, lobbyists, and dark-money political action committees.

CLEAN Missouri was presented as a bipartisan coalition and initiative, and it won the vocal support of multiple high-profile Republican community leaders, but local reporters acknowledged that its redistricting reforms would benefit Democrats. Under the current system, Republican incumbents made sure the game was played on their board. With 2020 redistricting fast approaching, CLEAN Missouri's redistricting provision could deliver appreciable results as soon as 2021. George Soros's Open Society donated $300,000 to MOVE, which in turn donated $250,000 to CLEAN Missouri.[13] Other progressive groups based throughout the state, including the union SEIU and NARAL Missouri, helped turn out volunteers to gather signatures to get the initiative on the ballot. For progressive leaders, changing the underlying power dynamics was the only way forward. Dreith told me, "I am putting every egg

I have in that basket." CLEAN Missouri would later pass, potentially creating an opening for Democrats and progressives who were willing to play the long game.

★ ★ ★

Dreith decided that NARAL Missouri would also focus on proactive work—in St. Louis, close to home. During the 2017 legislative session, Missouri lawmakers proposed at least forty separate bills that pertained to abortion. Lobbying against onerous bill after onerous bill in Jefferson City was draining morale. And for once there was energy to seize—starting the day after the 2016 election, people flooded NARAL with donations and requests to volunteer. "People needed something to be excited about and to know that the resistance was in their neighborhoods and cities and towns," Dreith said. NARAL Missouri began handing out endorsements for St. Louis races, which were held during odd-numbered years.

NARAL also began organizing to pass a city ordinance that would protect St. Louisans against discrimination from employers and landlords based on their reproductive health choices. The St. Louis ordinance was based on a model passed around by reproductive rights advocates. After the 2016 elections, reproductive justice and rights organizations had accelerated their push for pro-active bills that would expand and codify abortion and contraception access in Democratic cities and states. In February 2017, the St. Louis Board of Alderman passed the nondiscrimination ordinance 17 to 10.[14] The practical implications of the victory mattered less than its ripple effects. The ordinance proved that Missouri lawmakers could unify around a reproductive justice measure and that NARAL Missouri could help make that happen. National funders sent grant money, and local activists saw that a win was possible. Dreith's doubts about her fitness for leadership back in 2015 had proved unfounded: under her direction, NARAL Missouri had grown exponentially in terms of dollars, staffers, and volunteers. She hadn't needed to disavow her activist core; that was a source of her strength as an organizer and leader.

"I actually have less pessimism than I probably did three years ago," Dreith told me in the summer of 2018. NARAL Missouri and the local Planned Parenthood were invited to participate in meetings for the newly coalescing progressive infrastructure. This was a first; reproductive groups historically hadn't been embraced by local old-school Democrats, who were opposed to abortion (or afraid voters would be). "I think we're getting a lot of the long-due recognition," Dreith said, because progressive organizers finally saw the power in Planned Parenthood's long list of supporters and NARAL Missouri's ground game. She had worried that as time passed after the 2016 election the new NARAL supporters would disappear again, that the new frenetic energy in St. Louis would subside, but that hadn't happened yet. That campaign season, NARAL Missouri had funding to hire more organizers and canvassers, and for many more months, than in previous years.

In St. Louis, the new progressive leaders had much broader support than when Dreith first showed up at Black Lives Matter protests in 2014. White moderates had just experienced reality checks—first on election night 2016, and then in August 2017, when white supremacists marched through Charlottesville, Virginia, and one of them deliberately drove his car through a crowd of antiracism demonstrators, killing Heather Heyer and injuring twenty-nine others. "White people in St. Louis who had once, you know, questioned what we were doing in the streets for black lives had their second awakening and were just like, 'Holy shit, the kids in Ferguson were actually speaking the truth,'" Dreith said. The progressive electoral movement that had grown out of the Ferguson protests was continuing to gain traction. That summer, in the 2018 Democratic primary, Wesley Bell, a former defense attorney, challenged and defeated Robert McCulloch, the long-time St. Louis County prosecutor who had chosen not to charge the police officer who shot Michael Brown. That victory was resounding proof that progressive organizing worked.

At the same time, the stakes of coming elections were increasing, especially for women. And, nationwide, another awakening was about to occur. Early that summer, Justice Kennedy announced his retirement. That meant that Republican state lawmakers would likely have much more leeway in coming years. President Trump was made to understand that he had won over skeptical right-wing donors and Evangelical voters precisely for this moment. Trump was all but required to make his choice from the Heritage Foundation and Federalist Society's roster of judges vetted specifically for their antiabortion track records. At the time of Kennedy's retirement, there were already thirteen cases concerning abortion laws moving through the federal court system. Any one of those cases would provide judges an opportunity to chip away at abortion rights.

Beyond that, if in coming years Missouri passed a new law that shuttered its remaining clinic, reproductive rights groups might not even challenge the law. Missouri was in the Eighth Circuit, an infamously conservative circuit. An unfavorable ruling for the clinics could mean establishing a precedent for the whole region, a gamble that cautious lawyers would hesitate to make. If lawyers challenged a circuit ruling all the way up the chain to the Supreme Court, the justices could gut *Roe* again, as they did in *Casey*, only more completely this time. But most court watchers assumed that the Supreme Court would not unilaterally overrule *Roe*, which could spur intense political backlash, instead continuing to allow states more and more leeway, keeping abortion hypothetically legal while also making it all but impossible to end an unwanted or dangerous pregnancy. In immediate terms, that meant that in red states across the country, like Missouri, the next legislative session would bring a torrent of antiabortion legislation, plus bills designed to whittle away at conservatives' other longtime targets, like unions rights, environmental protections, voting rights laws, and more. A conservative court was also unlikely to reverse *Heller* and uphold stronger gun laws, a blow to Moms Demand Action advocates and others who had imagined a day when the gun violence prevention movement finally advanced its own incremental legal strategy.

Dreith was thirty-seven. She didn't feel so young anymore. The prospect of getting arrested felt very different than it had a decade earlier. In 2017, the St. Louis police teargassed her while she was protesting the Stockley verdict, an experience that left her shaken. Nonetheless, Dreith traveled to DC and to Judge Brett Kavanaugh's confirmation hearing. Before Christine Blasey Ford publicly testified that Kavanaugh had assaulted her, before the nonstop coverage dominated all forms of media, before hundreds of women protested, and before she was arrested and held for hours in police custody, Alison Dreith understood what was in jeopardy. She stood up. As officers pinned her arms behind her back and dragged her out of the room, she called out, "I had to leave the state of Missouri to seek my abortion . . . Poor women are going to be sent to back-alley abortions."[15]

CHAPTER SIX

Colorado

I TRAVELED TO DENVER TO SEE WHAT THE YEARS OF INvestment in Colorado state politics had manifested. As I met with local organizers, advocates, and lawmakers, what took shape in my mind as the crown jewel of the "progressive infrastructure" was not something I had thought to look for when I set out. During one of my early conversations for this book, a progressive political strategist told me, emphatically, that progressive state lawmakers across the country were by definition all special people. That statement struck me as somewhere between odd and unbelievable. In Denver, I finally saw what he meant. When I met Ian Silverii, a Brooklyn, New York, native and director of Progress Colorado, the progressive media outfit, I told him that the Coloradan politicos I had spoken with seemed to share a quality that I didn't know how to articulate. They didn't rant at me with self-righteous fury, even when Trump came up, and yet they weren't passive either. They seemed animated by pragmatism and idealism in equal measure. I didn't have to finish my thought before he agreed. Silverii gave a counterintuitive explanation: Coloradan progressives were good at their jobs because at one time or another they had all both won and lost.

"The 'elections have consequences' spiel that you hear everywhere is very real for all of us," Silverii said. "The way we talk about it here is that it evaporates like this—" He snapped his fingers. From a national perspective, Colorado was clearly trending blue—the state hadn't chosen a Republican presidential candidate since 2004. But on the ground, on the state level, the situation was more precarious. At the time, in 2017 and 2018, Colorado's governor was John Hickenlooper, a moderate Democrat with strong allegiances to oil and gas. The state House was controlled by Democrats. In the state Senate, Republicans held one and then two extra seats—enough to give them the power to kill envelope-pushing progressive bills. The legislature had been in gridlock for four years, since 2014. I underestimated that fact when I arrived.

By that time, almost fifteen years after the Gang of Four first laid their plans, the network of progressive organizations outside of the party—the fabled infrastructure—was still in place, still a model. Staffers from organizations focused on different issues, like Conservation Colorado, Mi Familia Vota, and One Colorado, still met regularly and coordinated their efforts. However, several people (unnamed in this book) told me that the ongoing situation was precarious. Local organizations didn't exactly have an open spigot of endless support, as some national strategists and donors seemed to believe. Tim Gill still operated his foundation but had mostly removed himself from partisan politics after gay marriage was legalized nationwide. Rutt Bridges was focused on his new passion for electric cars. Jared Polis was pursuing his own ambitions, namely his run for governor. If at any time Pat Stryker, the remaining primary benefactor, decided to move on, the local nonprofits who mobilized progressives would feel the hit. The infrastructure was vulnerable. Just like nonprofits across the country, many of the organizations on the ground in Colorado were in perpetual fund-raising mode, relying on short-term, relatively small grants.

Maybe the progressive infrastructure hadn't delivered consistent electoral wins, maybe it was too hard to tell whether the network of political nonprofits was achieving more than the sum of their parts, but a bench had been built. The Coloradans working in the statehouse and in those political organizations were talented and committed, and they were sticking around. A nexus of the ascendant political class was New Era Colorado, the youth voting group that Steve Fenberg and his friends had started. I kept meeting people and learning that they had interned, volunteered, or worked for New Era. The Speaker of the Colorado House was Crisanta Duran, the state's first Latina Speaker, elected to the House in 2010 at age twenty-nine, and one of New Era's early board members. On November 8, 2016, Leslie Herod was elected to represent Denver's District 8 in the Colorado House, and Steve Fenberg was elected to represent Boulder's District 18 in the state Senate. Herod was the first openly gay black representative to serve in Colorado; she ran on criminal justice reform, a statewide universal health care system, and abortion rights. Fenberg listed among his top priorities creating a statewide carbon tax and cracking down on oil and gas companies, some of the state's biggest political donors. Neither Herod's nor Fenberg's win was an upset; their districts were among the most liberal in the state, if not the country. They were joining a new generation of progressive lawmakers who represented Coloradans in the state capitol. Several other early New Era staff, volunteers, and interns had graduated to become local elected officials, lobbyists, and organizers. Barely in their mid-thirties at the oldest, already political veterans, they knew how to be effective leaders. New Era was both the product and a catalyst of a thriving progressive politics.

To appreciate what the New Era cohort's achievements signify, first we have to step back and appreciate the wins and losses that Silverii mentioned—the ones that set the stage for the politics of today. It is too easy, especially after the 2018 midterms, to cast Colorado as following some arc of progress, slowly but surely. In fact, party control has bounced back and forth ever since the Gang of Four started their spending spree. "I was the deputy caucus director in 2010. I lost the House by one seat that was determined by 197 votes," Silverii told me. Before that, in 2007, for the first time since 1962, Colorado Democrats had won a complete trifecta—governorship, House, and Senate—the culmination of the Gang of Four's investment. In 2010, the year of the nationwide Obama backlash and "shellacking," Colorado Democrats lost five seats in the state House. "It was a bloodbath," Silverii remembered. Colorado Democrats scrambled for another three years to regain control. On November 5, 2012, buoyed by voters who showed up to reelect Obama, Democrats won control of the House with a nine-seat majority. John Hickenlooper was governor. They had their trifecta again. A few months later, as soon as the legislative session began, Democrats began steamrolling ambitious bills, many of which Republicans had blocked during bitter fights in previous years. Their agenda that year exemplifies just how much can be achieved on the state level. In the spring of 2013, over the course of just a few months, Colorado granted DACA recipients eligibility for in-state tuition rates, codified civil unions for gay couples, strengthened Colorado's clean energy standard, and expanded Medicaid, which cut in half the number of uninsured people in the state.[1] And, that April, Colorado Democrats pushed forward a package of gun safety bills that was considered a possible model for the nation.

The previous July, during a midnight showing of *The Dark Knight Rises*, a gunman had sprayed bullets into a movie theater in Aurora, Colorado, killing twelve people and wounding fifty-eight others. The Colorado state House representative for Aurora's District 42 was then Rhonda Fields, whose son had been shot and killed in 2005. Sandy Hook had just happened. Gabrielle Giffords had just been shot. Fields decided that she would sponsor legislation that created background checks for gun sales and limited high-capacity magazines. Beth McCann, Herod's predecessor, cosponsored a bill that required universal background checks. Those bills met intense resistance from the beginning.

As lawmakers debated the bills on the assembly floor for hours, gun rights activists drove a parade of trucks and Humvees around and around the perimeter of the capitol grounds, leaning on their horns. The constant blaring was audible from within the stone walls of the building. Meanwhile, inside, Republicans tried procedural maneuver after procedural maneuver. In January, gun rights protesters had gathered at the capitol, where a speaker told the crowd, "Folks, don't make a mistake, they are out to take our weapons from us in totality," echoing the fears that John Cauthorn and his neighbors in outstate Missouri shared.[2] The national press and activists across the divide followed the Denver hearings with anticipation. "Universal background checks are more popular than Jesus, and you couldn't get a single Republican to vote for them," Silverii said. But the Republicans couldn't stop the Democrats, who had the majority and control. That spring, the assembly passed and Hickenlooper signed new laws requiring background checks and limiting high-capacity magazines.[3] The package of legislation was heralded as a national model.

Then, just weeks later, gun rights enthusiasts, led by the Rocky Mountain Gun Owners—a Colorado-based group whose members think the NRA is "a bunch of literal snowflakes," as Fenberg put it—fought back. They decided to recall two Democratic senators, including the Senate majority leader. Recalls had never been considered a serious possibility. They were unprecedented. Those senators would have to defend their seats. Millions of dollars from outside interests—national unions and Michael Bloomberg on one side, the NRA on the other—poured into those state elections. In September, the two targeted Democrats were voted out, replaced by Republican gun-rights supporters.[4] The senators' falls were chilling, both for Colorado Democrats and for gun reformers nationwide. Every person I talked with about Colorado politics brought up the recalls. Local organizers had celebrated that they were on the cusp of a new Colorado progressivism. Keara Fenzel, a former New Era organizer and current political director for the Colorado AFL-CIO, remembered thinking, "Oh my gosh, everything's going to get done! This is a new age for Colorado!" Instead, the recall elections vacuumed up resources, leaving less for other races. Democrats would lose the state Senate in the 2013 elections. "Our big dreams for legislative progress were quashed," Fenzel said. They weren't going to have another crack at ambitious proactive bills unless they held on to the House and won back the

Senate. During the 2018 legislative session, before the midterm elections, that goal was still elusive.

After the 2016 elections, state Senate Republicans had the slimmest possible majority over Democrats: one seat. In 2018, after one Democrat changed her affiliation, Republicans had an advantage of two seats. The respective majority parties in the House and Senate still dictated which committees would consider which bills. Those assignments, which at a glance seemed like crushingly boring minutiae, were in fact part of the chess game that the majority party played to maintain control. That one extra senator meant that Republican leadership decided whether to send bills to their appropriate committees—like a Medicaid bill to a heath committee—or to Military Affairs, known as the "kill committee," where the Republican majority axed Democratic bills. Fenberg said, "Generally, if it's a Democrat bill in this committee, it dies. Almost always." Both parties were guilty of that calculated partisanship; House Democratic committees also scuttled Republican bills.

At a glance, the Colorado state Senate seemed purple, but because Republicans could set the agenda, in effect the chamber was solidly red. "That's the thing people don't realize," Fenberg told me. "Everyone always says, like, 'Well, it's seventeen to eighteen. You can get a Republican to be reasonable on different issues and things.' That's true, but only for bills that make it onto the floor. If it goes to committee, and it goes to [the State, Veterans and Military Affairs] committee, you never have the chance to convince a Republican, because the three Republicans in that committee will almost always kill the bill. It's not about having eighteen votes. It's just simply about having a majority. That's all that matters."

Close elections and divided chambers kept Coloradans on their feet, Silverii said. "You're in the trenches with people all the time, and you're fighting these fights, so you get close. It's that bunker mentality," he explained. That notion didn't stand out to me as especially important at the time. But later it would. Over the course of reporting this book, I learned the difference between optimism and hope. Optimism could be dangerous. But hope was necessary. You fight like your life depends on it only when you have reason to think you can succeed. In some places, a realistic assessment of progressives' odds led to fatalism. It seems illogical to go all in when you absolutely know you're going to lose for the tenth time. Coloradan progressives could believe in their work without being deluded. They weren't softened by certainty.

Colorado's pioneer heritage, its libertarian culture, and its relative youth as an American state also shaped the culture, as did the razor-thin wins and losses, the constant urgency, the constellation of allies, all of which made the work satisfying. The work was also made less grim by demographic changes occurring in Colorado, and especially Denver. The influx of new voters can't be minimized as a factor that contributed to Democratic and progressive gains. Statewide, a generation of Hispanic young people were coming of age and able to vote. In Denver, developers were throwing up the same kinds of glass-plated luxury rentals they were building in gentrifying neighborhoods nationwide. The city had become a hot destination for recent college graduates, and a hub of the tech industry. In Denver, as in many American cities, the air was thick with tensions over rising costs, displacement, and interlopers changing the city's culture. That Denver, a state capital, was attracting young educated people from across the country set Colorado apart from most other states, where capitol buildings are moored in small, grim cities far away from dense Democratic neighborhoods. Colorado was an attractive place to live and an exciting place to work in politics. And that, too, explained why so many of the people I met in Denver impressed me. "This stuff is hard, and there aren't a ton of jobs, so the wheat and the chaff kind of get separated pretty quickly. The best people stick around," Silverii said. "No one's getting rich doing this. So you have to have a fire."

★ ★ ★

I first saw Leslie Herod at work in the summer of 2017, when she appeared on a panel at a conference sponsored by the Public Leadership Institute—a group that supports progressive state legislators, started by Gloria Totten and the focus of her energy since

Progressive Majority had folded into Wellstone Action, a larger Minnesota-based outfit, in 2015. In those DC conference rooms packed with state legislators, many of them awkward, Herod was poised and confident, and people kept approaching her. The theme of that conference, which Totten repeated from the stage, was to be bold. Conservatives, Totten told the crowd, had been in the minority when they whipped up their plans, which were then way outside popular opinion. They had shifted the narrative toward them and their ideas by being bold, by not relenting, for thirty-plus years. She urged the progressive lawmakers to borrow elements of that tack—to figure out their constituents' problems, pose bold, progressive solutions to those problems, and to keep coming back with envelope-pushing proposals even if they never made it out of a committee hearing room. Democrats and progressives had been defensive, reactive, and they needed to be proactive, to establish a narrative, reframe the conversation, remind people that they had ideas and resolve. When Totten and I spoke later, she cited Herod as a state legislator who exemplified living in that boldness and pushing a proactive agenda.

When Herod and I next met, it was November 2017, and she had invited me along on a ride out to the Larimer County Community Corrections Facility in Fort Collins, about sixty miles north of Denver, not far from the Wyoming border. That visit to the corrections facility was one step in exactly the kind of long, proactive process that Totten had emphasized was so important. First, Herod had identified a problem that she and her neighbors wanted to alleviate. That year, felony- and drug-related deaths were spiking in Colorado. In Denver, the prisons were overcrowded. Downtown, outside McDonald's and Fig & Olive alike, addicts paced the streets, passed out on sidewalks. Retail workers were finding dead or dying people sprawled on the floors of their store bathrooms. Some argued that by legalizing marijuana in 2012 Colorado had invited addicts from around the country and enabled drug abuse among its residents. The devastation, though, stretched well beyond the state's borders. In 2017, some seventy-two thousand Americans died from opioid-related deaths.[5] The nationwide opioid epidemic was killing so many young people that the average life expectancy for Americans dropped for the second year in a row.

Herod had met with the Colorado Criminal Justice Reform Coalition to get more information about how corrections programs worked. Through them she learned about the alternative sentencing program at Larimer County Community Corrections. The program took an approach very different from that used in standard corrections facilities. Inmates could complete their sentences piecemeal, a day or two at a time, on the condition that they maintained jobs, to keep them tethered to the world outside. Staff weren't armed. Offenders wore their own clothes. In another wing of the building, the county ran ninety-day rehabilitation programs for those arrested on drug-related charges. The jail was the only place in the county that offered free rehab. There was a monthlong wait list. That fall, Herod wanted to show the program to Denver's district attorney, Beth McCann. When they went out there, I rode along.

As part of our tour, we were taken to a room in the rehab wing where several women were chatting. While the rest of us visitors assembled near the wall, arms crossed, Herod moved to the center of the room.

"How many of you have been in corrections before?" Herod asked.

Several of the women raised their hands. Some of them seemed healthy, while others wore profound markers of their struggles. One woman couldn't focus her eyes; another kept pulling on her white sweatshirt. Several simultaneously looked young but had faces hardened and wrinkled like stiff masks. A few of the women talked about appreciating the program, especially the intensive counseling, which they had never previously received.

"I'm Representative Leslie Herod, and I represent District 8 in Denver. My sister has been in and out of corrections for years," Herod told the room. She reminded the women that once they served their time and were off parole, they had the right to vote in Colorado. Then she explained that she sat on the state's Judiciary

Committee, which often needed people to come testify about what was happening in correctional facilities.

"I want to hear from you," Herod said. She called out her office phone number.

Herod finished by telling them, with a glint of excitement in her voice, that she and her colleague Representative Faith Winter had passed legislation to make sure that women in correctional facilities had access to tampons. Before that, women had needed to appeal to corrections officials to prove that they had a medical need. Was tampon access going to change the macro problems with the criminal justice system? No. But it restored a measure of dignity to women in Colorado corrections. As Herod talked about the tampon bill, the women erupted into cheers, some with tears in their eyes.

We moved on to more rooms, where Herod greeted inmates with the same big smile, repeated her message about voting and testifying, and gave out her office number. In each room, with the wide-openness of the newly sober, inmates described how at the Larimer County facility they had been offered counseling for the first time, and it had changed their outlook on life.

During the car ride home, Herod and the district attorney talked about the program's impressively low recidivism rates, the moving testimony from its inmates in recovery. Herod's long-term goal was to make an analogous program work in Denver. With the state chambers gridlocked, Herod knew she probably couldn't pass an ambitious bill in the statehouse. There might be an opportunity on the city level. Herod was well positioned to make something happen. After years of immersing herself in Colorado politics, Herod had connections to people in elite positions: the busy Denver district attorney, for one, had accepted her invitation to drive out to Larimer County. And, as we will see, Herod was able to mobilize people in Denver to take action.

Herod was going to try to create a progressive solution regardless of whether the program was guaranteed to be enacted. Creating a new mental health program in Denver was inevitably going to be complicated, even amid a dire addiction epidemic that cut across race, class, and partisan lines. The most influential policy in Colorado in recent memory, a remnant of the pre–Gang of Four era, still put a chokehold on what lawmakers could do to solve their constituents' problems. That measure, the Taxpayers Bill of Rights, known as TABOR, still affected the entire state. It is impossible to understand what Herod and her allies were up against every time they wrote a bill or proposed a program without understanding TABOR, which has severely restricted government spending in Colorado. Bruce Douglas, a committed antitax libertarian activist, worked for years before TABOR finally got on the November 1992 ballot. TABOR would require the state to annually return to citizens all unspent dollars via rebates and to ask voters to approve all new tax increases via ballot initiatives.[6] There was an elegant simplicity to the principle behind the proposal, the beautiful idea that the people could directly check the state's overreach. In 1992, Ross Perot was running for president; libertarians got themselves to the polls. On the ballot was also Initiative 2, which prohibited Colorado and local governments from giving residents protected status from discrimination on the basis of sexual orientation. That proposal brought out the "religious freedom" set, which also tended to favor small government. On November 3, 1992, TABOR and Initiative 2 both passed.

Since then, Colorado lawmakers have invented some workarounds, but for the most part TABOR has them in a knot. Despite how fair the proposal sounded in theory, in practice TABOR has forced so many complicated maneuvers to fund road construction and the like that even some Republican lawmakers publicly disapproved of it. TABOR also kneecapped public school funding. Americans for Prosperity, the Koch brothers' organization, has asked Colorado lawmakers to sign pledges to keep TABOR intact before they receive endorsements and donations. Conservative lawmakers in at least thirty states have tried to enact similar policies, with the help of Americans for Prosperity and other groups. So far legislatures and voters in each of those states, including in solidly Republican ones, rejected the proposal, until 2018, when Florida voters approved a similar measure.[7]

TABOR's survival in Colorado shows the limits of a progressive movement funded by billionaires. Dismantling TABOR would seem like an obvious priority; its death would create a structural change that would pay ongoing dividends for Democrats' agenda. But TABOR is hard to unravel because of a cleverly built-in catch-22. The law prevented the legislature from passing any multi-issued tax law, and because TABOR touches almost everything, any attempt to change it would require passing a multi-issued tax law. As an alternate plan, outside political groups could work to gather thousands of signatures to put an initiative on the ballot that would ask voters if they wanted to eliminate TABOR. But that would require a massive statewide campaign to persuade people to pay more taxes. Carol Hedges of the Colorado Fiscal Institute estimated that such an attempt would cost roughly $12 million. Who could be asked to put up the money? The very same wealthy donors whose taxes would almost definitely increase meteorically should TABOR die and the legislature be free to tax away. Whereas the Koch family could fund Americans for Prosperity as a straight investment, if left-leaning donors funded an anti-TABOR crusade, they would be funding the direct diminishment of their wealth and power. There it was, a concrete example of the very different incentives that guided right-wing and left-leaning donors.

The fate of the antigay ballot initiative that passed the same night as TABOR back in 1992 throws the situation into relief. Back in 2007, soon after Democrats won control of the statewide trifecta for the first time in fifty years, they enacted the Colorado Anti-Discrimination Act, which prohibited discrimination on the basis of sexual orientation or religion, and voided the 1992 antigay measure. (As of 2018, only twenty-one states have laws that prohibit private employers and landlords from discriminating based on sexual orientation and gender identity.)[8] Gay rights were a priority for the Gang of Four. Gill and Polis, after all, were gay. Tim Gill would cite that 1992 initiative as his motivation for involving himself in local politics and galvanizing hundreds of other gay political donors to flood state elections. The spectacular shift in our culture and laws toward giving gay people—and to a lesser extent queer, nonconforming, and trans people—more dignity and freedom is often cited as proof that a social movement can deliver concrete legal, political, and cultural gains within a generation. It is worth noting, however, that LGBTQ people include extremely wealthy and well-connected white men—and their children, friends, business associates, and so on. Many LGBTQ political outfits steered by those men's priorities made gay marriage the centerpiece of their cause, instead of pushing for labor or housing discrimination protections that arguably could have benefited the most vulnerable. Tim Gill's decision to elevate members of the gay community, especially in philanthropy and politics, had been instrumental in helping Leslie Herod and others build a career in Denver. But now that Herod was in a position of power, she had to work around a system that stymied social change for disenfranchised people. If Herod wanted Denver to raise taxes to start new mental health or drug treatment programs, she was going to have to persuade the taxpayers themselves to help. It didn't matter whether it was guaranteed to work; she was going to try.

★ ★ ★

That fall, New Era was still running from a grayish-green two-story house on North Humboldt Street, in the residential neighborhood of City Park West, a mile and a half away from the gold-capped capitol dome, a fifteen-minute glide on a bicycle. It was then operating the largest youth civic engagement outfit in the country. Lizzy Stephan, a transplant from New York State, had taken over the executive directorship in 2016, when she was twenty-six years old. New Era's primary objective remained registering young people to vote. Its goals had expanded, though, to include an advocacy arm and an internship program that taught young people how local and state government worked. That undertaking was more radical than it first seemed. In Colorado, as across the nation, young people still voted less often than older people, especially retirees. Because older people voted so reliably, they were able to install politicians who did not address climate change, stagnating wages, debt, and other accelerating problems that disproportionately hurt young people. It was still New Era's mission to change that. A long-standing myth said that young people didn't vote because they didn't care. Stephan told me that research showed that a sizable portion of young people didn't vote for the opposite reason: they considered voting a weighty responsibility and didn't feel knowledgeable enough to make a choice. She considered it New Era's job to relieve young people of that feeling, through education and empowerment. Just like its founders, its current leaders wanted to help other young people grasp the levers of power—while they were still young, and for life.

New Era's bread and butter remained registering voters ages eighteen to twenty-nine. By 2018, Stephan said, voters ages eighteen to thirty-five made up one-third of Colorado's electorate. "We have to focus on voter registration in order to close that participation gap," Stephan said. "There's certainly a whole set of issues we need to focus on there, but registration is number one." Once young voters were registered, the likelihood that they would vote almost matched that of older generations. The 2016 elections had been New Era's biggest cycle to date; they ran a $1.6 million operation that registered 55,367 voters. New Era, like many nonprofits with an electoral arm, multiplied their staff in the summer and fall during election years. The offices buzzed with energy, and dozens of staffers fanned out across campuses and neighborhoods. In 2018, at peak campaign season, they were dispatching seventy-eight staffers, who registered 43,695 voters.[9]

One of their cornerstone issues was election integrity, a topic that Stephan acknowledged didn't strike most twenty-somethings as particularly "sexy." However, the long American tradition of officials blocking citizens—and, in particular, black citizens—from casting a ballot necessitated vigilance. Along with Common Cause and the League of Women Voters, New Era made itself a watchdog, following up with the Board of Elections and polling sites if they heard of any problems. Being a custodian of the voting process was not glamorous work. Much like office workers who don't see the crew that cleans up at night, voters could be forgiven for not appreciating the presence of groups like New Era, whose efforts were measurable only in the absence of messes. Several incidents during the 2018 elections brought national attention to election integrity. Among the higher-profile instances was Fair Fight Action, a group backed by Georgia gubernatorial candidate Stacey Abrams, filing a lawsuit alleging that state election officials had "grossly mismanaged" the election, thereby reminding national audiences that their local election officials' actions had real consequences.[10]

New Era, meanwhile, had bigger ambitions than a single election cycle. That core staff remained to organize and advocate on local legislation and work on off-year local elections set New Era apart from other massive get-out-the-vote outfits like Next Gen. Its guiding principles set it apart, too. New Era staff worked from the assumption that the political system was designed to give ordinary people the impression that it was complicated and serious and beyond their comprehension. That front of grandeur and incomprehensibility discouraged all kinds of political action, from voting to running for office. In big and small ways, all year long, New Era sought to break down that façade.

To that end, from their Denver and Boulder headquarters New Era ran programs designed to demystify the political process. Their youth-led advocacy shop focused on economic justice, abortion rights, climate change, and election access. "Most young people are multi-issue people," Charley Olena, the advocacy director, explained. "They see how climate change is also an economic justice issue. They see how reproductive rights is also an economic issue. They see how all these issues are racial justice issues." Access to contraception and abortion, for example, is a financial issue for multiple reasons; if women can't control their fertility, they can't control whether they can show up for school and work, and whether they can afford housing and other basic needs, not to mention day care and the many costs associated with raising a child. Reproductive justice is also a racial issue for a myriad of reasons, including that black American women are dying in pregnancy, childbirth, and the postpartum period at higher—and rising—rates compared to white women. Activists of their generation understood how seemingly separate issues were interrelated.

New Era's advocacy arm often solicited volunteers to testify on state legislation. When New Era brought interns to the capitol, with its heavy chandeliers and portraits of suited men in gilded frames and heeled aides wearing blazers, they explicitly pointed out that "power and privilege [were] playing out in ways that [were] presented as normal," Stephan said. During the legislative session, staff asked if interns wanted to testify in hearings. Legislators regularly treated people who came to testify with varying levels of disrespect—from straight-up bullying to passive aggression (like continuously tapping away on a laptop without looking up while someone talked about a dead family member). Similar forms of belittlement were routine in hearing rooms across the country, where almost nobody paid attention to, let alone challenged, how state officials talked to members of the public. In 2013, when the controversial package of gun safety bills was being considered, New Era interns testified on behalf of a bill that banned concealed weapons on college campuses. "We had a lot of old, white, male Republican legislators saying, 'You kids need a gun on campus so that you don't get sexually assaulted,'" Stephan recalled. "We had interns in our program who were sexual assault survivors who were wanting to tell their story but scared as hell about how they were going to be treated." When preparing them for their capitol visit, Stephan explained, "we're not only saying, 'Here's what you need to wear tomorrow.' We're also saying, 'How messed up is it that you need to wear that to talk to your legislators who work for you?'" When prepping interns for questions they could receive from a hostile committee member, New Era staff also asked questions like, "How terrible is it that a legislator is about to intimidate you up there?"

That constant modeling of questioning power dynamics was built into everything they did, including the executive director's leadership within the organization. Stephan didn't just write a budget; she showed younger staff how she wrote the budget. She told interns that they could fund-raise without being especially shiny charismatic fancy people. Whereas after the 2016 election there was a burst of pop-up leadership training sessions, Stephan said she thought of leadership development as lasting "five to ten years." It got complicated for her, the executive director, leading a staff barely her junior, when she had to ask herself, "'How do I train them to contest for power?' Including with me. How do I give them enough tools that they can say, 'Lizzy, I think that this is a spending priority and you don't, and here's what's next.'"

New Era's messaging about empowerment and possibility wasn't just a collection of throwaway lines. They had accomplished tangible, real-world achievements, the kinds of wins that seasoned operatives struggled to pull off. New Era made one of its biggest waves in 2011, when it helped secure a David and Goliath–style victory. The city of Boulder was considering two ballot measures that would create a new city-run energy distributor. If the measures were approved, Boulder residents would stop buying electricity from the investor-owned energy company Xcel, which ran coal plants and had no plans to build additional renewable energy sources in the near future. Whereas names like Philip Morris or Exxon or Geo Group each in their turn became shorthand for the nefarious arms of American business, utility companies don't have the same widespread reputation as underhanded profiteers. As we will see when we return to Florida, their benign image is undeserved; on the state and local level nationwide, utility companies form a major corporate lobby that often advocates against the public interest. If Boulder broke away from Xcel, its officials and residents could choose to run their city on renewable sources of energy.

New Era drove much of the effort against Xcel. They ran ads that said DUMP XCEL. There is no replacement for hitting the pavement. Their staff and volunteers knocked on thousands of doors and made countless phone calls. Xcel Energy spent $960,689 discouraging people from voting for the measures, whereas proponents spent $106,760. On Election Day, by the slim margin of 142 votes, Boulder became the first city in the country to vote to break away from its investor-owned utility. "I think that was New

Era's doing," a Boulder City Council member told the press. Then, in 2013, they defeated Xcel again. Steve Cole-Schwartz, director of the Partnership Funds, which distributes civic engagement philanthropic dollars, told me, "It's incredible on its own. And the fact that that win is attributed, rightly, to them by industry, by political players in the state, by national philanthropists like myself, that is a secondary, undercover, incredibly important win that stabilizes that organization's political influence for the long term." It is even more remarkable, Cole-Schwartz said, that "a *youth* organization is understood to have done that. That credit didn't get taken away from them by some old white dude's organization in DC or New York or San Francisco."[11]

New Era's advocacy arm wasn't educating young people in hopes that they would be effective in the future. They were trying to change young people's internal narratives about power while simultaneously working toward ambitious policy goals in real time. One of the most salient examples of their work was their attempt to pass state laws that would help people with student loans. "We see [student debt] as one of the major things that is holding back our generation from seeing economic stability and economic success," Olena, New Era's policy director, told me. As of 2018, some forty-four million Americans were carrying roughly $1.5 trillion in outstanding student loans or education-related debt, a sum that had roughly tripled since 2006. New Era's advocacy work on student debt was proactive, motivated by the same principles that guided Herod when she organized the visit to Larimer County Corrections. Just as Gloria Totten and others had preached, their advocates were proposing solutions to people's real and urgent problems, regardless of whether those solutions had a chance in hell of being enacted that year. By choosing to focus on student debt, they weren't just playing into ideological or cultural wars. And they forged relationships with both people in elite positions of power and the ordinary people who supported their cause.

New Era's first attempt to pass statewide protections for student borrowers was in 2015, when its staff helped generate support for a bill that would have capped the interest rates lenders were allowed to charge for student loans. An especially galling moment for New Era staff came during those hearings. Staff remembered that after a current college student testified about her debt burden and loan rate, a legislator said, "I just Googled it and I found a better rate than the one you have." The student was humiliated. Still, testifying before hostile legislators invigorated young people, Stephan told me. "That experience of testifying in the legislature in those adversarial conditions is completely transformative for young people," Stephan said. "They can see the forces that are maintaining the status quo, protecting bad actors, right in front of them."

Republican-controlled committees squashed the bill capping interest rates. It didn't seem likely to pass without power shifting in the legislature. Then another route presented itself. In 2015, Connecticut unanimously passed the nation's first "Student Loan Bill of Rights," which required student loan companies to have licenses, thereby giving the state authority to crack down on companies that mishandled students' loans and contributed to their delinquency or default. The bill zeroed in on student loan servicers—the companies that acted as intermediaries between the federal government and student borrowers (and were often not lenders themselves). Those student loan servicers were subject to fewer regulations than mortgage lenders or credit card companies. In 2017, New Era and Representative Faith Winter decided to try to pass a "Borrower's Bill of Rights" in Colorado. That bill couldn't get past the Republican Senate, either. But in January 2018, as the Colorado legislative session began, the need for heightened protections were made clear: the federal Consumer Financial Protection Bureau and the states of Washington and Illinois sued Navient (formerly part of Fannie Mae)—the largest student loan company in the nation, which handled some $300 billion worth of loans for more than twelve million borrowers—for "systematically and illegally failing borrowers at every stage of repayment."[12] The suit charged that Navient had created obstacles to repayment, deceived borrowers and steered them toward more expensive options, and failed to accommodate disabled borrowers, including injured veterans, leaving them with more interest to pay.

Despite those charges, there was scant hope that Congress would act to protect student borrowers. State legislatures had an opportunity to achieve what Congress couldn't—or wouldn't—but their members would prioritize such legislation only if they felt enough pressure. New Era organizers and students met with staff from the office of the Republican attorney general, who as a result of their conversations issued her support for the bill and eventually asked the federal government for more protections for student borrowers. New Era's Olena also approached the United Veterans Committee of Colorado, and they rallied their members, who tended to be very different from the motley crew attracted to New Era.

The idea that failure was just part of the process was a central tenet of organizing. Representative Winter, the Student Borrower's Bill of Rights sponsor, told me that organizers "think about building a movement. Whereas others are thinking about winning this one bill." Having a bill die in committee didn't deter her from trying again, because she was working slowly, persistently to wear down the opposition and build a coalition that would win in the long term. Winter said that her generation of Coloradan Democratic lawmakers were especially effective because several of them, like her and Steve Fenberg, had been organizers. They had spent their formative years learning how to empower people to advocate for themselves. They also understood the technicalities of the political process.

Many of the people I met who were affiliated with New Era had a similar openness, the kind of confidence that allows a person to be candid. They didn't hesitate to tell me that they had stumbled, erred, or embarrassed themselves, and that stood out, especially since politicos often trade on insider knowledge and prestige, or, worse, slickness and puffery. When working with young people, one former New Era staffer told me, "There needs to be space for failure. You're not trying to expect that people who are doing this for the first time [are not going] to fail . . . You just want to do whatever you can to make them fail quickly and learn quickly so that you can make progress together." That was an idea that several people brought up. Matt Singer, who had cofounded Forward Montana during the same years New Era was founded, told me that he had originally been panicked because he didn't know how to read a financial statement. Then he realized that no one was born with that innate ability, and he just needed to ask for help. Multiple people who had worked or partnered with New Era told me that the experience rid them of their impostor syndrome. That was a profound transformation. If young people could stop looking around and wondering if they were doing it right, they could do what they thought was right. And that outlook was more likely to appeal to people like them. New Era's ethos was: Come as you are.

The progressive infrastructure had supported local organizing outfits, which gave lawmakers like Fenberg and Winter that experience early in their careers. And because many of those organizations were still thriving, they were still giving young leaders like Olena a chance to become experts on the legislative process before they turned thirty. If Olena decided to run for office one day, she would have a huge head start in understanding how to rally support for her bills. "We have been an important part of the talent pipeline," Stephan told me. Over a decade after its founding, New Era alums were everywhere. Cofounder Joe Neguse was running for Congress. New Era alums were also running for city- and county-level positions. Matt Singer, the youth organizer from Montana, had recently moved to Denver and was working for Movement Voter Project, which dispatched funds to races around the country. Among other efforts, in 2017 he had helped orchestrate donations to NAACP chapters in Alabama that called every voter in their rolls to make sure they got out to vote for Senate candidate Doug Jones, who went on beat Roy Moore for a longtime Republican seat. By the time I met them, in different ways, they had become the decision makers.

★ ★ ★

Herod and Fenberg had managed to pass proactive legislation during their freshman terms, the 2017 legislative session. In February 2018, I flew to Denver to see what day-to-day life during the legislative session was like for state lawmakers like them. Fenberg and Herod wore their ambitions differently. Herod was all magnetism, the center of gravity in any conversation, certain to find her way to center stage, with a giant smile. Fenberg shrugged a lot, made self-deprecating jokes, and didn't fill pauses. During committee hearings I watched him repeatedly zero in on the issue at hand, in a tempered tone. While no politician (or person) is perfect, they struck me as genuine—and effective. They weren't the only Coloradan officials who disarmed and impressed me. Representative Mike Weissman apologized for being short on time—he had spent the weekend helping a constituent move. Then he refused to let me buy him a cup of coffee, citing ethics rules. Senator Rhonda Fields, as described earlier, ran for office, where she succeeded in passing gun reform laws, after her teenage son was shot and murdered. With our federal government in freefall, with daily news items about payoffs and lies, I found the mere existence of these people reassuring. In a political culture, furthermore, where "outsiders" were increasingly glamorized, I was also struck by how much of Herod's and Fenberg's competence came from their previous experience as—in Fenberg's words—"political hacks."

"I think we [the New Era cohort] were able to have a lot of the lessons that people are having now, back then," Herod explained, "which makes me more effective now." During her freshman year, while she pushed her bold bills, Herod had actively sought out Republican partners. She cosponsored a bill banning civil forfeiture (law enforcement's ability to seize citizens' assets without charging them with a crime) by partnering up with Republicans, including Senator Tim Neville, the leading gun rights enthusiast. Likewise, that year, when she first joined the Judiciary Committee, she specifically chose a seat next to Representative Cole Wist, a Republican who represented District 37, just outside Denver. "I wanted to sit next to a Democrat on one side, a Republican on the other. I did that in all my committees. Just so I could figure out what they were thinking and how they think," Herod explained. During her years working at CU Boulder and with New Era she had learned that she couldn't accomplish anything if she understood only her own side's point of view. "I know what happens when you think you have the only good idea and that their opinions don't matter and they're just wrong," Herod said.

Her fellow New Era cofounder, Joe Neguse, knew and spoke highly of Wist, so Herod sought him out. They formed an alliance that grew into a friendship. She asked Wist to cosponsor the Child Mental Health Treatment Act. The state's law required many parents of mentally ill children to give up custody if the child was going to be eligible for Medicaid's mental health programs. Herod wanted to change that. "It's an expensive bill, so I needed a Republican cosponsor," she told me. She knew that she could frame the bill as a matter of family values and fiscal responsibility. Wist agreed and signed on as a cosponsor, which hugely increased the bill's chance of passing the Republican Senate. She also asked Wist to work with her on a bill that would limit the number of beds in private prisons. Opposition to private prisons is a calling card of the left. But she had already learned how to talk about criminal justice reform in the language of conservative values, framing the issue as one about checking government spending and overreach.

It was a credit to Colorado's political culture that lawmakers there often worked with members of the opposing party. Years of having a split chamber, with control bouncing between the parties, meant that lawmakers had no choice but to solicit support across party lines. But in statehouses where Democrats were in the minority, as in Missouri, they also had to work with Republicans if they were going to accomplish anything. Missouri Democrats told me that after they collaborated with Republicans, their primary opponents sent out mailers maligning them as turncoats. In liberal pockets of cities like St. Louis or Kansas City, primary voters were looking for the most progressive possible champion. But, realistically, given the power dynamics, for that champion to have any voice, to deliver tangible results and pass legislation, she needed to have the personal skill and the political latitude to work with Republicans as often as possible—in ways that didn't compromise progressive values. Herod told me that she had honed her political skills throughout her twenties because "I was invested in, quite early, with New Era, with the Gill Foundation, with the LGBT movement, with black folks, with progressives."

Herod and her friends had come up in a political environment where donors and political leaders invested in their rising generation of talent. I am not implying that their friends were successful only because the Gang of Four and the Roundtable had laid the groundwork for them. When I asked Alice Madden, former House Speaker and an early member of the Roundtable, how she thought the wave of investment and strategy facilitated the careers of the New Era cofounders and their friends, she demurred, saying that she wouldn't take any credit for their success away from them. It is true that there is no work history at a nonprofit that would enable most people to pull off, with a smile, what I watched Leslie Herod accomplish on one ordinary Tuesday that February.

What I happened to catch that Tuesday was also evidence of how many issues state lawmakers juggle at once. Ahead of that day, Herod had been in closed-door meetings with other Democratic leaders and local activists. The week before, Republican state lawmakers had voted to withhold funding for the Colorado Civil Rights Commission, which evaluated claims of discrimination. That coming June, the US Supreme Court was slated to rule on *Masterpiece Cake Shop v. Colorado Civil Rights Commission*, over whether a baker had the right to refuse to make a gay couple a wedding cake. The Civil Rights Commission had ruled against the baker. That week in Denver, Republican lawmakers implied that if the Supreme Court overturned that decision, the commission's credibility would be shot, so even with the case pending they couldn't guarantee its funding. Herod was among those who wanted to push hard against any changes. The moment offered a chance to stake out a moral high ground. "People think that Democrats aren't fighting for them. We need to create the conversation," Herod said, explaining her rationale. "We've seen what happens when you don't frame the narrative," she told me later.

Plus, the notion of civil rights protections struck a chord with so many—religious minorities, disabled Coloradans, immigrants, black people, gay people: "When you can thread a needle that will attach so many people, thread that needle." Democratic lawmakers and advocates from groups like ACLU Colorado, Colorado Cross-Disability Coalition, and One Colorado, a gay rights organization, drummed up interest in a rally.

That Tuesday in the early afternoon, as a couple hundred people stood on the plaza outside the state capitol, with their backs to the distant Rockies, Herod addressed the crowd. She was just as much in her element as when she had moved to the center of the room in the corrections facility and talked about voting rights. The crowd cheered. After the rally broke up, Herod spoke with reporters and went inside and took her place on the Judiciary Committee. Then, roughly an hour later, she and her Republican colleague ducked across the hall, where they presented their Child Mental Health Treatment Act. That was the pace of the legislative session, which demanded incredible stamina from lawmakers. Within the span of a couple of hours, Herod had gone from giving a rousing speech in front of a crowd to talking to reporters to listening to testimony to politely answering technical questions about Medicaid from the panel. That was just one afternoon, the day I happened to be at the capitol, not some special day. Herod's schedule was breathless all year long.

★ ★ ★

The next day, I met Fenberg in his office across the street from the capitol. His dog, Ellie, a German shorthaired pointer mix, was there, too. "Today's committee is going to be grueling," he said.

Fenberg sat on the Senate's State, Veterans and Military Affairs Committee, known around the capitol building as "the kill committee." When Colorado Democrats first told me that the "kill committee" existed so that Republican leadership had a place where they could ax Democratic bills, I was skeptical, just as I was skeptical when Missourians told me that Republican leadership scheduled the hearings that were important to progressives in different rooms at the same hour so that their staff was spread thin. Claims of a bureaucracy rigged against them sounded paranoid, a little desperate. Now, having spent more time in state capitols, I understand that an unfathomable amount of pettiness and jockeying is in fact par for the course. Alice Madden told me that during her first week as the House minority leader she had helped herself to some Post-it notes. The clerk told her, "You don't get those. Those are for the majority party." Day-to-day work was full of those tiny indignities for members of the minority party. When the Democrats regained control of the Senate after the 2004 election, Madden and other leaders tried to implement "the Golden Rule" by changing the most absurd of the procedures. Hearing schedules would be announced ahead of time, for example, creating a chance that people could actually show up.

Of course, despite some nods toward creating a fairer system, Democrats did not change the underlying structure when they were in power. Colorado law required all filed bills to have a hearing. Deciding which committee hears a bill, Fenberg said, "is like 80 percent of [the bill's] fate"—and those decisions were still made with partisan calculations in mind. That winter of 2018, because Republicans held a majority in the Senate, they controlled the Senate's State, Veterans and Military Affairs Committee. Few of the bills sent there would have anything to do with veterans or the military. Instead, that committee would consider the bills that Republican Party leadership wanted crushed. Make no mistake: in the state House, where Democrats were in charge, they made similar calculations to prevent Republican bills from advancing. As Fenberg said, "Both sides are guilty."

Members of both parties also undoubtedly considered it a moral and strategic imperative to kill their opponents' bills. There were multiple reasons Republican leadership might want to send a bill to be "suspended indefinitely" in State, Veterans and Military Affairs. The simplest reason: Republican officials and voters openly didn't support the policy. Second, the bill could potentially create a fault line between Republicans. In an election year especially, it could be dangerous to have officials vote on the floor about a hot-button issue that could potentially alienate part of their base. Almost nobody paid attention to how state officials voted in committees, but if a bill concerning a salient issue was green-lighted through committees and made it to the floor for debate and a vote, local news crews would be on alert. Advocacy groups could pack the gallery. Voters would be paying attention to what happened with schools or guns or gas drilling. On the flip side: During an election year it could be dangerous to allow a Democratic-sponsored bill to make it to the floor, especially if its sponsor lived in a swing district. Even if the whole assembly didn't pass the bill, that Democratic sponsor could use footage of herself arguing for, say, student debt relief, in campaign ads, in speeches.

Senate Democratic leaders had assigned Fenberg to the State, Veterans and Military Affairs Committee. He wasn't going to have much direct impact on the outcomes of the votes; those were all but decided. His role was to be the Democrats' voice of dissent. Because he represented a solidly Democratic district, Boulder's District 18, he was the right person for the job. He could vote against bills promoted by power brokers like the Rocky Mountain Gun Owners or gas companies without worrying that he would be maligned and lose his seat. He explained, "My job is to ask questions of witnesses to make the arguments that, like, 'It's ridiculous that they're killing this bill,' or to say, 'This is a crazy nut-job bill and here's why,' so then we get our argument out there."

The reality of partisan machinations made Fenberg want more Democratic members of the assembly, regardless of their position on any given issue. Only with control of the assembly could Democrats quickly crush, say, a gun or abortion bill that the majority of the party opposed. In that scenario, if they won control of the assembly with a few extra pro-gun rural Democrats, bills loosening gun laws still were unlikely to make it to the floor, whereas the Democratic coalitions' favorites had an excellent chance: "That's why it's really frustrating when people try to make everything a litmus test, because it's like, I don't really care if one of our people is good 60 percent of the time in a really difficult swing district where you need to be pretty moderate, but if they win, that means

80 percent of our bills pass, whether they vote for them or not. It's just about numbers."

Fenberg ran through another set of problems: First, industries like oil and gas dumped huge sums into the political process. They funded candidates and lobbyists. Fenberg said that before taking office he hadn't grasped the magnitude of lobbyists' influence. Whereas lawmakers and aides were constantly rotating in and out, lobbyists were often long-term fixtures with institutional knowledge. They almost always knew infinitely more minutiae about particular issues and the lawmaking process than lawmakers did. State lawmakers didn't have the staff to research much of anything, let alone everything related to the seven hundred or so bills that would be discussed each year. Each lawmaker was allotted funding for one part-time aide, paid fourteen dollars an hour. Fenberg subsidized his aide's salary out-of-pocket, even though his own was $30,000, which he supplemented by bartending on the weekends.

"Every two years there's a new crop of people [in the legislature] that just don't know anything about what they're doing. They don't know how to write a bill." Insecurity is par for the course. Everyone is pressed for time. "The lobbyists know that, and they're smart," Fenberg said, so they'll approach legislators and say, "'I have bills that are already crafted, and I'll do all the work for you. I'll count the votes. I'll work the talking points. I'll work the media angles. You just have to put your name on it.'"

That reality of the day-to-day life of a state lawmaker is a major reason that it matters that groups like Americans for Prosperity and the NRA and corporate lobbying firms from giants like Amazon and Chevron keep stables of well-connected surrogates in state capitols. Fenberg held up a fact sheet sent to him from an advocacy group. That was his only arsenal to play defense against one of the bills to be discussed that day.

We went to the hearing. The room was already filling up when I took my seat in the audience, around one-thirty in the afternoon. One of the items on the agenda that day was SB18-114, which would have created a grant for public schools to teach students about depression and the warning signs of suicide. Colorado's youth suicide rate was one of the highest in the nation, and national suicide rates for middle schoolers had doubled between 2007 and 2014.[13] Teachers, administrators, parents, and students from around the state took turns addressing the panel. Parents held up pictures of dead children. A middle-school student talked about being institutionalized. "Government is not the answer," one member of the committee said, summing up the reigning point of view. The committee voted, and the bill was "postponed indefinitely."

There was no fanfare for the parents who had spoken, no applause. The ordinary people who show up to speak in statehouse hearings have often encountered a painful problem that they need addressed; why else would they have traveled there, to open themselves up and ask for help from a panel of strangers? The setting—the formal titles and protocols and thick drapery—cut against how raw the stories are. When someone is done speaking, the committee chair says thank you, the person gets up, and the next person sits down. During the many hours I spent watching hearings in statehouses across the country, I was struck by the futility of most political theater, yes, but also the ordinariness of personal courage.

Around three-thirty that afternoon, a flood of people came into the hearing room. Most of the crowd looked well under forty years old, although many older people filled the chairs, too. Herod, Senator Brittney Pettersen (another New Era alum), mental health workers, and city officials had encouraged people to show up. It was time to discuss SB18-040, which proposed creating a pilot program in Denver for safe injection sites for drug users, plus needle exchange and other harm-reduction programs. The idea was that if addicts had a place to use drugs without the threat of arrest, someone would be there to supervise and give them Naloxone if they overdosed, reducing the chance of death. Herod and Pettersen were not sponsoring the bill, but they nonetheless were among those trying to drum up support for it, as a broader effort to address the addiction and mental health crisis in the city and state.

A few weeks earlier, Herod and Pettersen and a delegation of Denver city officials had traveled to a safe injection site in Vancouver that had been visited by 3.6 million people, without a single one dying, since its opening in 2003. The program was shown to have reduced overdose deaths and ambulance calls. Boston, Philadelphia, and San Francisco had similar sites. Seattle and New York City were in the process of setting up theirs. That year, 2018, throughout the country, including in Florida and Missouri, city councils and state legislatures were considering new ideas to help reduce opioid addiction and deaths. If Colorado passed the safe injection site bill, it would be on the cutting edge of addressing the opioid epidemic.[14]

In the hearing room, there was standing room only. Along the walls, the crowd was two or three people deep. In their calls to action, both Herod and Pettersen had publicly spoken about family members who had struggled with debilitating addiction. Breaking down stigma, connecting with constituents first as people, then as officials, was part of their project.

"This is a national-level crisis," said one of the bill's cosponsors, Senator Kent Lambert, a Republican who represented District 9. "There are problems at various levels of government and various levels within the health care and pharmaceutical industries where we need to change the practices we've had in the past because frankly they're just not working very well."

Herod and Pettersen entered the room together and stood by the door, giving little waves to people they knew in the crowd.

Only one person, an administrator for the University of Colorado, testified against the bill. "It is saving the life for that one injection. That very same person will go out and inject many other times," she said.

"I think you can make the same argument for seat belts," Fenberg said. He reiterated that tax dollars would not be used to fund the sites.

Then other people in the room issued their support. Mothers testified about the day that they learned that their child had overdosed and died. A pharmacy owner described doing CPR on someone who died in front of him. A retail worker said that people regularly shot up and sometimes overdosed in the store bathroom, telling the committee that "people who work minimum wage should not be cleaning up biohazardous waste." Medical professionals, social workers, and former addicts argued for the creation of a safe injection site. The attorney general's communications director testified: "The office of the Attorney General supports this bill." Representatives from the Colorado Department of Health and the Colorado Medical Society and the Colorado Chapter of the American College of Emergency Physicians testified in support, too.

After two hours and ten minutes of testimony from at least thirty people, the committee took its vote. At 5:55 p.m. the bill was "postponed indefinitely." As the room emptied, Pettersen stood by the door. She thanked people for coming and repeated, "This is not over."

I checked my phone and saw news of a mass shooting at a high school in Parkland, Florida.

A new crowd shuffled in, but it was dramatically smaller than the injection site crowd. Senator Tim Neville, one of the founding members of Rocky Mountain Gun Owners and a Florida native, presented SB18-097, which proposed allowing Coloradans to carry concealed handguns without a permit. One of Neville's sons, Joe, was a lobbyist for Rocky Mountain Gun Owners; another son, Patrick, was serving in the Colorado House. With their growing political clout, the family was considered a cross between the Kennedys and the leads in *Duck Dynasty*.[15] Neville presented the concealed carry bill every year, and every year it advanced through committees, throwing red meat to the same voters and donors who had won the Senate for Republicans back in 2013, which in turn gave Republicans the power to operate this committee and quash whatever proposals they chose. Every year, the Democratic House blocked the bill's passage. Sure enough, that night, at the very same time that Florida emergency workers were tending to wounded students, and parents were receiving word that their children were dead, the committee voted on party lines to advance Neville's bill.

The hearing dragged on, with several more bills to go. Fenberg periodically slipped out of the room to take his dog Ellie outside. He had stashed her in the Speaker's office after his aide went home.

Fewer and fewer people remained in the audience. It was seven, then eight in the evening, on Valentine's Day. Newspaper editors from small-town papers appeared to testify against a bill that would have cut down on notices that provided one of their few remaining forms of revenue. The bill was passed along, meaning the small-town editors were dealt another loss. When Senator Irene Aguilar, a physician, asked the committee to support her bill that would have prevented pharmaceutical manufacturers and wholesalers from price gouging, the hearing had been running for over seven hours, and there were fifteen people in the room, most of them on their laptops. That bill was, of course, "suspended indefinitely."

I texted Fenberg that I was going to leave.

"A miracle is about to happen though," he wrote.

"I can't tell if you are joking," I replied.

The day before, Fenberg had been surprised when the committee voted to "suspend indefinitely" SB 18-150, a bill that would have allowed felons to preregister to vote before their parole was completed. Fenberg had based the bill on one New Era had helped pass in 2013 that allowed sixteen- and seventeen-year-olds to preregister so they wouldn't lose a chance to vote because of when their birthday fell. Fenberg had talked through the felon preregistration idea with each of the members of the kill committee and had gotten enough promises of support. After the bill was unexpectedly killed, Fenberg asked each of them what had happened. One of the Republicans apologized; he had lost track of the bills and accidentally voted to suspend indefinitely. Before that day, I probably would have thought something snarky about that lawmaker. But blanking out for a moment was totally understandable, given how heartbreak and tedium blurred together for hours on end. The very last action of the hearing that night was a reconsideration of 18-150, Fenberg's once-dead bill. They voted again. The room was almost empty. The Republican lawmaker changed his vote, and the bill was off to the next round of consideration. A couple of months later, Governor Hickenlooper would sign it into law.

That one vote was enough for Fenberg to have achieved something that day. He freed Ellie from the Speaker's office, and they walked down the grand marble staircase of the rotunda, surrounded by ornate gilded railings and rose onyx walls and murals of pastoral scenes. Ellie scrambled down a few paces ahead, with her leash sliding down the stairwell behind her. Fenberg would drive an hour back to his place in Boulder, then get up and be back on the floor of the Senate at nine the next morning.

★ ★ ★

When Republican leadership sent the Borrower's Bill of Rights to the kill committee, Olena saw the writing on the wall. "I was disappointed," she said. But she added that they "failed forward." More people showed up than the previous year. News outlets covered the bill. They had new partners working with them. "Ultimately the arguments of the industry lobbyists were more compelling," Olena said. Rallying states' attorneys general and legislatures to protect student borrowers became all the more important just six days after the Student Borrowers' Bill of Rights was suspended indefinitely in the Colorado Senate's kill committee. On May 9, 2018, the Trump administration's Consumer Financial Protection Bureau announced that it was collapsing the office tasked with monitoring student loan servicers, a move that critics said would weaken the department's investigation of the giant loan servicer Navient.[16] New Era would be back at it the next year, Olena told me. "A lot of times efforts like these are three, four, five years' efforts, which is frustrating. Organizing is really powerful, but it doesn't change things overnight. I think there are a lot of different places we can look and say, 'Yeah, we are making progress. Yes, we pushed, we've moved the needle on this.'" And the next year, as it would turn out, they would face entirely different odds.

★ ★ ★

In the late summer and fall of 2018, Colorado Democrats made flipping the state Senate—and thereby banishing the Republican kill committee—one of their ultimate goals. They targeted five seats, needing to flip at least two to win the trifecta, if they could hold the House and elect Jared Polis governor. The race for Colorado's state Senate became one of the most-watched in the nation. Fenberg was in charge of raising soft money for the state Senate races—a pressure-filled job. His many hours spent in the kill committee meant he had a personal stake in making sure that his side flipped the balance of power. "I'm motivated to do it," he said. Representatives Faith Winter and Brittney Pettersen were both running for highly contested state Senate seats. The previous infusions of cash into Colorado state legislative races had "created a soft money monster," as Alice Madden put it, and elections now commanded staggering sums of cash. Outside political groups spent an incredible $5.3 million in the race between Faith Winter and her Republican opponent—roughly $2.4 million of which was spent in support of Winter.[17]

In different ways, that election season the New Era founders and their friends were all hustling. New Era cofounder Joe Neguse was the so-called establishment Democratic candidate for the Second Congressional District. And another old friend and cofounder, Lisa Kauffman, was directing Jared Polis's campaign for governor; by late summer she was managing sixty-eight staffers. Herod, meanwhile, was working close to home, leading the charge to pass a citywide ballot initiative, dubbed Caring 4 Denver, that would create a new 0.25 percent sales tax within the city of Denver to generate funds for community-based mental health and addiction care programs. There was an outpouring of support for the measure, and the team had hit the pavement; they had gathered twice as many signatures as they needed to get the measure on the November ballot. When they held an event at the city's Museum of Contemporary Art they were forced to turn people away because its rooftop terrace had reached capacity. But when I talked to Herod just before the election, she was still a little nervous, unsure the initiative would pass.

On November 6, 2018, the New Era cohort had an excellent night. Caring 4 Denver passed. Joe Neguse was elected to Congress, a soon-to-be member of the freshman class. Friends of New Era Faith Winter and Brittney Pettersen were elected to the Colorado Senate, meaning the Democrats gained the majority. Fenberg wouldn't have to endure being the voice of Democratic dissent on the kill committee anymore. Instead, he was voted Senate majority leader. Lawmakers like Winter and advocates like Olena could push for solutions to problems like student debt, knowing that they had a real shot. And because Jared Polis was elected governor, there was a good chance he would sign their bills into law. Of course, it wasn't all rainbows for progressive Coloradans. The formidable influence of libertarian activists and political spending by the oil and gas industries was clear that night, when Colorado voters rejected a ballot initiative that would have raised taxes to repair major roads and another that would have banned oil and gas drilling in close proximity to homes. Still, in the new year a new generation of lawmakers and advocates would have a chance to try again, with some but not all of their obstacles cleared away.

CHAPTER SEVEN

Florida

IN EARLY SEPTEMBER 2017, ZENIA PEREZ WAS AT HER parents' house in Miami, resting on sandbags they had put in the doorways, anticipating flooding. Hurricane Irma was approaching. The news predicted a seven-foot storm surge. At the time, Perez was working from home for Justice Democrats, a political action committee headquartered in Tennessee that is devoted to electing candidates who don't accept private prison money. (Their biggest profile win by far would be New York congressional candidate Alexandria Ocasio-Cortez, although the public seemed to believe her success had come out of thin air.) Her coworkers urged Perez to drive up, escape the storm. Perez didn't think of leaving. Her mother and brother worked at Costco, her father at a hardware store, where crowds were showing up last minute to buy supplies. Her family couldn't get off work and go, and Perez wanted to stay with them. "We were stuck," she said.

Resting on the sandbags, Perez was watching a video about climate change that had popped up in her news feed. Her dad was nearby.

"Climate change," she remembers her dad saying. "I worked so hard. I've almost paid off my house. And I'm going to lose it."

That caught Perez's attention. She rarely if ever talked politics with her parents.

"My dad voted for Trump," Perez told me, "and he said something like that."

"I think climate change will make the difference," she said, when I asked what it would take to get more people involved in progressive politics in Florida and turn the state around. "I live in Key Largo now, and I talk to my neighbors, and everyone here is kind of Republican, but when it comes to climate change, everybody sees eye to eye."

By the time Hurricane Irma whipped through Florida, Republicans had ruled the state for twenty years. After multiple rounds of careful gerrymandering, Republicans still had a strong majority in the state legislature. From 2011 through 2018, during his eight years as governor, Rick Scott handed the reins of the state to corporate interests with the legislature's sanction. In doing so, he exacerbated many of the old problems, like poverty and racial disparities, that had been intractable for hundreds of years. One of his first acts as governor was reducing the budget for public schools by $700 million. His administration and the Republican legislature refused, on principle, to accept billions of federal dollars to expand Medicaid to cover the working poor, denying roughly eight hundred thousand low-income Floridians health care coverage; by 2017, about 13 percent of Floridians were uninsured, the fifth-highest rate in the nation. The state, meanwhile, rolled out subsidies to corporations, and when some of his fellow Republicans blasted what they called "corporate welfare," Scott said they were anti-jobs. Scott also consistently touted that jobs had been created during his tenure. Almost half of those jobs paid less than $10 an hour. In 2018, almost three million Floridians lived in poverty, bringing in less than $24,300 for a family of four. During his eight years in office, the gap between the rich and the poor in Florida had expanded. The United Way of Florida's most recent report, conducted in 2015, found that 44 percent of Floridians could not afford basic necessities like food, housing, and child care. And at the same time that Floridians were struggling with those "old problems," the obstinate ones that have persisted across generations, a new problem of epic proportions was presenting itself.[1]

It goes without saying that Florida, a low-lying limestone peninsula, is especially vulnerable to losses related to climate change. Even leaving sea level rise aside for a moment, there is no way to adequately express how central the whole subtropical natural world is to daily life in Florida. The unmatched beauty of the place—the turquoise bays skimmed by pelicans, reeds waving in the Panhandle's marshes, Spanish moss dripping from giant oaks—is why so many people love living there. Floridians across the political spectrum, like Perez and her father, understand that their safety, the stability of the local economy, and the value of their homes is directly connected to the integrity of sand dunes and aquifers and the Everglades, as well as the foresight of public officials planning for energy production and road pumps. Despite (or perhaps because of) that shared ethos, there is hardly a better example of the dire consequences of Democrats losing on the state level than how the Rick Scott administration thwarted action on climate change.

In Florida under Scott, age-old and oncoming problems were compounded. "We have almost three million people in Miami-Dade County, and 58 percent of those are either poor or working poor, living paycheck to paycheck," said Caroline Lewis, who in 2010 founded the CLEO Institute, a Miami-based nonprofit dedicated to educating the public about climate change. And those already disenfranchised people were on the front lines, living in regions that will be among the first to be destabilized by rising seas. "When the science-oriented folks understand the degree of vulnerability, their efforts are heightened. They're so angry." Lewis emphasized that climate change was about much more than the seas rising. "Quite frankly, I think we can drive away from the sea," she said, so she considered conversations about the coasts a "gateway drug" to get audiences to care about the impending "salt water intrusion and freshwater vulnerability, food vulnerability, heat and health changes, migration changes, and shifting populations."

In the face of those fast-accelerating concerns, at the helm of the state most vulnerable to climate change, with the nation's third-largest population and economy, Rick Scott led a wholesale rejection of environmental science. His actions had far-reaching implications. The governor of Florida chooses who will head the agencies and commissions that oversee the state's real estate developers and agribusinesses and utilities companies—all of which, if left unchecked, can wreak havoc on water supplies, air quality, and the climate in general. Under his direction, Florida enacted environment-threatening measures at a breathtaking clip. "When Governor Scott was elected, literally the entire culture in Tallahassee as it relates to the environment changed 180 [degrees] overnight," said Jonathan Webber, deputy director of Florida Conservation Voters. Among other actions, Scott reduced the budget for environmental regulators by $700 million.[2] His appointees to run the state's environmental agencies were clear political hires chosen from the very industries they were supposed to be regulating. The state, for instance, gave multiple real estate developers authority to issue land-use permits.

Scott was breaking the bipartisan Florida tradition of environmentalism—or, at minimum, a tradition of voicing support for environmentalism. His motivation was not difficult to trace. For all its supposed absurdity as "the weirdest state," Florida embodies a very typical American irony: its economy relies entirely on growth, and yet that growth imperils the very thing that drives the growth. Roughly one hundred million people visit Florida every year. Somewhere between five hundred and one thousand people move to the state every day. The way to capitalize on those people is to pave another parking lot, construct another row of beachside condos. Dwelling for too long on the fact that the bulldozers will ultimately destroy the natural beauty that draws in the newcomers doesn't keep the economy booming. Pointing out that seas are rising and the state's drinking water supply is diminishing doesn't help sales. The only way to keep real estate prices high, to clear the permits for another hotel, to celebrate the numbers that show that more jobs are coming to the state (even if half of them pay less than $10 an hour), is to pretend that growth can be sustained indefinitely. The mirage must go on. The same is true under capitalism in general—markets must expand or they collapse—but in Florida that abstract reality was and is visible in real time, in Rick Scott's decision to fire scientists and empower energy company executives, in the acres of strip malls, and most recently in plans for the $4 billion megamall and casino named American Dream slated to be built in Miami.[3]

The experience of Jim Gross, a geologist who had been working in his field for over thirty years, was emblematic of what he called the "dramatic, abrupt, quantum change" after Scott became governor. After 2010, career scientists were purged from state agencies. Gross had worked at the St. Johns River Water Management District, the agency tasked with monitoring water-related projects and real estate development permits in central Florida. The district is required by law to create plans for the region's water supply. Under the previous governor, Charlie Crist, a centrist who is now a Democrat but was then a Republican, the administration had signed off on a years-long, multi-million-dollar project assessing the region's water supply and laying out a preservation plan. Gross told me that his team completed the massive undertaking in December 2010, a month before Scott was inaugurated. But their findings were "tossed in the garbage can." Gross had never seen that happen before. Under Jeb Bush, their findings were used to develop action plans. Under Scott, Gross remembered, "A chill went through the office." That summer of 2011, 120 of his colleagues were fired. Over the next few months came another round of firings that government scientists told local newspapers were "targeted" because of their opposition to the administration's actions. Scott was living up to his promises in his 2011 inaugural address, when he said that "taxation, regulation, and litigation" were "the axis of unemployment."[4]

The next year, Gross and his team were once again tasked with conducting a study on the region's water supply. After they had done over a year of work, their findings were set to be heard before a public board. But in June 2014, Gross says, the executive director of the St. Johns River Water Management District, Hans Tanzler, and the second in command, Jeff Cole, called him to the director's office. Gross said that the directors explained that word had come down from the governor's office that their findings were unacceptable. Their report had deemed a tract near Jacksonville "water resource cautionary," an official designation for areas that already or will soon have water resource problems. Scott was seeking a second term. He was also actively recruiting companies to relocate to Florida, to deliver all those jobs he had promised in his first campaign. Gross read between the lines: the governor couldn't risk having an honest appraisal of Florida's environmental vulnerabilities put on the public record right ahead of the election. Gross told me he left the meeting "half laughing, half crying," because "we're talking about essentially the whole water supply of the entire district."

"We would have had to actually falsify data to meet the task the governor was asking for," completing a report that said there were no absolutely water problems, Gross told me. "I'm a licensed geologist," Gross remembered saying. "You're asking me to break the law." Some district staff were asked to change the report. Then Gross was fired. And so were Cole and Tanzler and several others from the district. They were among the scores of scientists forced out of their positions during the Scott administration's eight years.

His was both a staggering and typical story. Volumes upon volumes could be written about the myriad ways that Florida's political establishment privileged big businesses over people, but for the sake of simplicity in coming pages I will focus on how Florida officials stymied—and continue to stymie—efforts to combat climate change, and the Herculean, urgent, yet-to-be-won battle to change that obstructionism. This example, this story, indicts the energy company executives who have a chokehold on the Florida legislature. It shows the real-life ramifications of harms that sometimes seem academic—money in politics and gerrymandering. It shows why the governorship matters. It illustrates the magnitude of what happens under the cover of darkness (and right out in the open) in statehouses, and it demonstrates that ensuring state officials represent the will of the people is a matter of life and death. Though Florida Republicans and their allies drove much of the action by, for example, firing scientists and handing regulatory bodies to industry insiders, this story also indicts past and current iterations of the Democratic Party, the legacy environmental groups, and the left's donor class writ large, all of whom failed to turn voters against the officials who defied their values and acted against their best interest.

* * *

There is nothing subtle about the moneyed, transactional culture of Tallahassee. Political science research has found that, as the *Harvard Business Review* summarized, "state governments, in fact, are considerably more corrupt than their counterparts on the national level," and "state-level corruption is likely to directly or indirectly affect most Americans on a daily basis." Florida consistently ranks as one of the most corrupt states. But beyond the straight-up corruption, pay-for-play politics is the norm. In one of the more absurd examples of what a lobbyist can secure for a client, in 2015 the rapper Pitbull received $1 million from a secretive state contract in exchange for his mentioning Florida's "sexy beaches" during concerts, at a time when the average salary for Florida teachers was $47,780. Utility companies are among those with the most to gain from political spending, as they are well aware. In another instance of pay-for-play that seems like a joke but was real, lobbyists for Florida Power & Light, the state's largest utility and a major political donor, flew the chairman of the state Senate's energy committee on a private plane to the Daytona Raceway, where the chairman wore a leather jacket stamped with the parent company's logo, waved the race's start flag, hosted a fund-raiser wherein he brought in roughly $10,000 for his political action committee, then toured Disney's Epcot Center with more lobbyists. A month later he fast-tracked multiple pieces of legislation favorable to Florida Power & Light, including one that, had it not died in committee, would have allowed the company to charge Florida electricity customers for the company's exploratory fracking in other states, a practice that the Florida Supreme Court had disallowed the previous year when it decided that shareholders should shoulder those costs. The meaning of all that wasn't difficult to parse. "[Utility companies] get their way because of the money they contribute," said Susan Glickman, Florida director of Southern Alliance for Clean Energy.[5]

The peril created by that kind of political spending is difficult to adequately convey. Any overture that pits energy companies' political machinations against the welfare of humanity may sound like an exaggeration. Even people who do not consciously reject climate science passively reject the reality that it reveals. It is very difficult to move through an ordinary day while also holding in mind what is happening on a global scale. "The disinformation campaign to create doubt was successful," as Caroline Lewis put it, "therefore, people just thought that we were a bunch of crazies, just like alarmists." As of the writing of this book, evoking mass destruction is not hyperbole. Any potential technologies that might be able to rid the atmosphere of the overload of carbon that is warming the planet are untested. Experts give mixed opinions on whether any posited solution might be effective.[6] The only known preventive measure is to dramatically cut carbon emissions immediately. A 2018 United Nations report said we have about twelve years to dramatically reduce carbon emissions to minimize the catastrophic effects of rising global temperatures. Prospects for making those changes became even more dire after the election of Donald Trump, whose administration scrapped a number of key Obama administration policies, including the Clean Power Plan, which aimed to decrease emissions by cutting energy from the utility sector.

The Trump administration also allowed states to roll back their own emissions standards.[7] State governments were already important to utility companies—and in turn climate science. Currying favor with lawmakers is a cornerstone of utility companies' business strategy, in Florida and elsewhere. When the electricity grid was first built, the priority was getting reliable service to as many people as possible. Relying on a patchwork of countless local electricity distributors just didn't make sense. The federal government decided to allow utility companies to operate as monopolies within their regions, under the condition that they would adhere to guidelines put in place by government commissions. In different states the commissions operate under different rules, and in some cases their members are elected, but the general outline of their duties is roughly the same. These commissions are "a very dark corner of state government, which most Americans don't know about," said David Pomerantz, executive director of the Energy and Policy Institute, a watchdog group for the energy industry. The utility companies "thrive on that because it means they're able to manipulate the commission without very many people watching."

"These public utility commissions that nobody's ever heard of probably collectively have much more say over [the energy industry] than almost anything that president Trump can do," Pomerantz said. The commission sets emissions standards and the rates that customers pay for electricity. In Florida, it also guarantees Florida Power & Light a rate of 11.7 percent return on equity. At the risk of stating the obvious: because electricity is the backbone of modern life and the economy, those rates affect every other cost Americans have.

Florida's utility companies (and most others nationwide) are Wall Street investor–owned private businesses. Pomerantz pointed out that their executives' fiduciary duty is to ask themselves how they can make the most money for the company and its investors. The Public Service Commission's role—at least on paper—is: "We represent the public interest. We represent the customers to make sure that they don't get taken advantage of by this company who's got a profit motive." This balance has become especially fraught since the emergence of alternative forms of energy. Energy companies have had even more incentive to dictate who is appointed to commissions so they can squash threats to their monopoly from third-party solar companies and other forms of clean energy that could potentially cause what the *Wall Street Journal* dubbed a utility "death spiral." Because these commissions have so much influence on respective states' energy policies, local activists from across the country have zeroed in on them as a crucial battleground.

In Florida, as in thirty-seven other states, the governor appoints members of the Public Service Commission. It is hard to overstate how much political influence utility companies have bought in Tallahassee. Integrity Florida, a nonpartisan watchdog group, found that Florida's four largest utility companies gave $43 million to state-level candidates, political parties, and political action committees in the 2014 and 2016 cycles alone. They gave mostly via political action committees, which allowed them to give above the cap of $1,000 per candidate per cycle. The Republican Party of Florida received a chunk of the funds—$5,289,574 total from 2014 through 2016. The Democratic Party of Florida was a distant second, taking in $926,283 in those years. Those are only the direct political contributions. Between 2014 and 2016 Florida's four main utility companies gave roughly $9.4 million to Associated Industries of Florida and the Florida Chamber of Commerce, the biggest and most influential business groups in the state. Leaders of the utility companies also sit on the boards of these business groups. And the utilities were in the capitol's meeting rooms, too. According to a 2018 Integrity Florida report, utility companies employed more than one lobbyist for every two state legislators in Tallahassee. Those lobbyists were from Tallahassee's premier firms, including Ballard and Holland & Knight. And utility company lawyers had direct input on energy-related bills.[8]

Rick Scott was a top recipient of utility company political donations. According to a report by the Florida Center for Investigative Reporting, during Scott's 2014 reelection campaign utilities gave $600,000 to his Let's Get to Work PAC. They also gave $670,000 to the Republican Governors Association Florida PAC, which gave $500,000 to Scott.[9] To underline the point: in a single campaign cycle, utilities gave over $1 million to help elect the person responsible for appointing the committee that would oversee them and determine their profits.

The utility companies' investment in the Scott administration paid off. In 2010, the five-person commission had declined to allow the electricity rate hike the utilities wanted. "The retribution was swift and unapologetic," the *Tampa Bay Times* editorial board wrote later, in a pointed letter. The Florida Senate refused to confirm two Public Service Commission members and pushed out two more, leaving four out of five positions for Scott to fill. That may seem like bureaucratic minutiae, but it is a huge deal. "The PSC has typically followed the wishes of Tallahassee's ruling class" since Scott took office, the *Tampa Bay Times* wrote. Scott appointed utility industry insiders and his political allies, including a restaurateur who was an early supporter and had no industry experience (and kept receiving new appointments until in 2018 he was elected Florida's chief financial officer). Those commissioners gave the utilities much more latitude, allowing them, for example, to charge Florida ratepayers for that exploratory fracking in other states. And most importantly, Scott's commission undid what few gains had been achieved on the climate front. Before Scott took office, the commission had required utility companies to meet new—but still very modest—energy efficiency goals. The companies asked Scott's commission if they could scrap those goals. In 2014, the commission agreed, gutting the predetermined efficiency goals by over 90 percent, even though those standards had been more permissive than those in many other states. Florida Power & Light's parent company, Next Era, after all, boasted on its own website that it is one of the country's leading producers of wind and solar power. The company could lobby to produce more clean energy in Florida, but it doesn't, because Florida lawmakers don't put enough pressure on the company's decision to instead rely on coal, gas, and nuclear power.[10]

Massive political spending by utility companies also kept Republicans and conservative incumbent Democrats in charge—and that meant not only regressive environmental policies but also no Medicaid expansion, no increased minimum wage, no gun reform, no new policies to help address the statewide teacher shortage.

★ ★ ★

Corporate influence in Tallahassee wasn't the only reason Florida's environmental protections were precarious. In a state where concern for the natural world was woven into the culture and transcended party affiliation, it would seem that polluting industries and their sympathetic lawmakers would meet strong resistance. There are myriad interlocking reasons that the environmental movement thus far doesn't have enough muscle to create concrete change on the state level in Florida, many of them familiar because they are the same reasons campaigns for abortion rights and gun reform failed to reach their potential. The first issue was that Rick Scott's climate denialism caught Florida's progressive and environmental groups flat-footed.

For a long time, nationwide, environmentalism was the province of the ultra-wealthy, painted as a luxury concern. In 1892, the Sierra Club was founded as a way for men to explore mountains, and from there it morphed into a fancy picnic club, wherein rich white people traipsed into the wilderness with tents and feasts, believing that in the wonder of mountaintop vistas they would see the face of God. That legacy left its mark on environmental organizations, often run by wealthy or middle-class white people whose emotional appeals usually centered on the preciousness of the natural world, saving a tree frog, or the Amazon. Even the word "environmentalism," with its emphasis on everything *around* people but not people themselves, speaks of that history and fails to adequately express everything that the movement seeks to protect, which includes every one of us. That legacy lived on. "Frankly, a lot of environmental funders aren't very progressive," one philanthropy observer told me, adding that they don't necessarily conceive of themselves as political. Nationwide, much of the cash supporting environmentalism came from a handful of institutional funders, like the Rockefeller Family Fund, instead of from small donors or explicitly political outfits. Those foundations gave the bulk of their funding to a relatively small number of big brand-name organizations, like the Sierra Club, the Nature Conservancy, and the National Wildlife Federation. That concentration of wealth and decision-making power exacerbated multiple long-existing patterns. Only recently have foundations begun to aggressively fund climate-related projects, and too rarely have they supported sustained community organizing in the United States.

The Sierra Club, as one example, kept its focus on gridlocked Congress, even as state commissions slashed and burned local protections. In Florida, the Sierra Club had a few paid staffers, including an organizer based in Tampa, and a network of scattered volunteer-run clubs whose involvement ranged from fifteen people meeting for cookies, as one person put it, to larger-scale events. But they were not going to wage war. During the Scott administration, and for years before, whom did the Florida Sierra Club send to stand in opposition to the fleet of white-shoe lobbyists who roved the capitol halls on behalf of Florida Power & Light (and US Sugar and BP and all the rest)? Every year the Sierra Club hired a lobbyist who worked in Tallahassee during the three-month legislative session and then decamped to Maryland, where for much of the year he wrote and performed in pirate-themed musicals at the Jolly Roger Amusement Park. He was in a position similar to that of reproductive rights or gun reform advocates: outrageously outmatched, constantly playing defense, and trying to rouse public outrage over arcane regulations whose devastating implications made sense only after a fair amount of explaining. They needed to be there, if for no other reason than to bear witness, but how could those individuals possibly turn dozens of legislators against the interests that guaranteed them reelection?

It wasn't as though nobody cared. All across Florida, there were dozens of local environmental groups, many of which focused on their particular region or cause. Local efforts were often successful and brought together neighbors from across the partisan divide. Julie Hauserman, a longtime progressive advocate, reporter, and editor of Florida Phoenix, a news site focused on state government, explained that the environmental movement is "local because it *is* local. In other words, what matters to you is what's near you." Someone might not realize they care about water quality until their canal is threatened. Glickman of the Southern Alliance for

Clean Energy—one of the relatively few lobbyists who traveled to Tallahassee to advocate for clean energy—told me about helping to block coal plants in rural Florida. As climate issues have moved to the fore of environmental concerns, volunteer groups like 350.org—which organizes online campaigns and mass demonstrations to oppose new oil, coal, and gas projects and advocates for renewable energy—have formed chapters in South Florida and Orlando.

Compared to those local efforts, organizing people across issues and regions and influencing state policy proved to be much more difficult. Sometimes an outside billionaire would contact a local progressive to ask what could be done to whip up an environmental movement, but the feeling on the ground was that movements could not be manufactured. Donors had to invest and hand over control when a genuine outpouring gathered force. There was also that familiar pattern of funders "doing something for a little while and then just moving on to something else," as Hauserman summarized, when real change "takes a long time."

Yes, combating the utilities was yet another David versus Goliath struggle. Yes, of course, nonprofits and activist groups were going to be outmatched by giant corporations. Sure, maybe hiring expensive lobbyists to talk to a majority Republican legislature would be a waste of money. But why couldn't they raise money for elections, to get better allies in office? At least theoretically, lots of Floridians supported the green groups' ideals. Why couldn't those people be galvanized? As with other causes, the scale of the resources available to green groups was only part of the problem. Laura Reynolds spelled out two primary problems that thwarted a unified statewide movement to pressure lawmakers to prioritize environmental protections: first, Florida's environmental groups weren't explicitly political organizations, and second, the groups that did wade into politics received funding from none other than the industries that they were supposed to be fighting.

That was true—environmental groups in Florida didn't have sizable (c)(4) political organizations that could raise political dollars and in turn influence elections. Without a way to influence elections, they couldn't compete with the utility companies and others that dumped millions into political action committees. Meanwhile, for years, rationalizing that their backs were up against a wall, the Florida Democratic Party and its candidates had accepted funds from polluting industries. Many of their candidates took passive positions. When I spoke with members of the Florida Democratic Party about the party's struggles, several times I heard the refrain, "You can't say you're the party of the people and accept sugar money." Reynolds said, "A lot of our Democrats have gone to the dark side because they are being funded by sugar [industry] money or something else. The environmental community can't afford or isn't willing to fight to fund them to stay clean." Others told me that the bipartisan appeal of environmentalism actually dissuaded Democrats from staking out strong positions; if a position wasn't going to differentiate them from their Republican rivals, they figured it wasn't worth a stump speech.

Then there was the second category of environmental organization: the co-opted organization. This category was more complicated. The Everglades Foundation was Florida's biggest in-state environmental funder. In 2016, the fund parceled out roughly $1.2 million worth of grants to parks and conservancy groups around the state, none of which were political organizations that would hold lawmakers accountable.[11] The Everglades Foundation, meanwhile, was allied with the same groups and people who were actively working to dismantle environmental protections. The foundation was funded by the same Republican donors—like its board chair, Paul Tudor Jones—who gave hundreds of thousands of dollars to help Rick Scott get elected not just in 2010 but also in 2014, well after anyone involved in Florida politics could plead ignorance about his agenda. The Everglades Foundation's CEO, Eric Eikenberg, is a former senior lobbyist for Holland & Knight, the firm that represented Florida Power & Light and sugar companies, and a trustee of the Florida Chamber of Commerce, which lobbied alongside the utility companies and donated to Scott. The Everglades Foundation's legislative director from 2010 to 2012, Noah Valenstein, was also simultaneously founding two political companies that took in at least a million dollars working with Republican candidates and PACs. In 2017, Valenstein was the only person Scott interviewed before naming him director of the Department of Environmental Protection. Michael Sole, Florida Power & Light's former vice president of state and government affairs, was on the board of the Everglades Foundation when Scott named him head of the Florida Fish and Wildlife Conservation Commission. Everglades Foundation staff and board members appeared with Rick Scott during events and publicly celebrated Florida's land buys. The foundation consistently released statements that started with "We applaud Governor Rick Scott."[12]

One of the Everglades Foundation's closest partners, Audubon Florida, was the environmental group with the largest statewide presence, with roughly fifteen thousand members who belonged to scattered local groups. Those members had the potential to be a massive force of boots on the ground in local and statewide political efforts, but Audubon chose to organize bird-watching walks and plant sales, not political events. Their membership tended toward older white people, many of whom might have voted for Scott because they supported his low-tax policies or agreed with his rants about Obamacare. In 2016, the national organization gave its Audubon Medal to Paul Tudor Jones, the billionaire Scott donor. Around the same time, Reynolds spearheaded a lawsuit against Florida Power & Light after a government report showed the company's facilities had polluted a bay near Miami that fed into a local aquifer. Reynolds had been director of the Tropical Audubon Society, a South Florida–based chapter of the organization, which operates under the umbrella of the state and national arms. Reynolds told me that after she filed the lawsuit against the utility company, Audubon denied her funding she had received for years and pressured her out of her role.

How was someone reading the newspaper supposed to know that a spokesperson for a group called the Everglades Foundation or Tropical Audubon might be abetting climate change deniers? As Reynolds put it, "Audubon and the [Everglades] Foundation give these candidates cover when they need environmental greenwashing." When those organizations lend their supposed green credibility to politicians, Reynolds explained, those politicians "have enough from them, so they don't need Sierra Club or League of Women Voters." If other green groups pushed back, they risked seeming like true fanatics, and groups like the Sierra Club already seemed fringe to many. The co-opted groups neutralized the dissent of legitimate environmentalists, who were already struggling to make their voices heard. Calls for conservation became a kind of cover—allowing politicians and donors to appear "pro-environment" as they blocked efforts to address climate change, which would have required systemic changes, not just land buys. These disingenuous maneuvers gave officials like Scott a counterclaim to any charge that they were "anti-environment."

* * *

Despite being outnumbered and outmatched, Florida climate activists proved, at least once, that it is possible to defeat the utilities and create the kind of real, concrete change that perpetuates itself. One story offers a glimpse of how the battle might be won again, both in Florida and elsewhere. It began with a moment of realism: after Rick Scott took office, a cadre of clean-energy advocates took a hard look at the utilities' grip on Florida's lawmakers and decided that they needed to change their strategy. "Just standing up at the Public Service Commission or at the legislature or wherever else wasn't going to get you the good outcome, because the game is essentially rigged," said Susan Glickman. Glickman had worked for Tobacco Free Kids in the early 2000s, when they helped pass a statewide ballot initiative to ban smoking in Florida's workplaces. "If it was up to the Florida legislature, we'd still be smoking in restaurants. People had to take it to the ballot," Glickman explained. It was the same strategy ACORN used to raise the minimum wage back in 2004, and that the Voting Rights Restoration Campaign would use in 2018 to restore voting rights to felons. Glickman and her colleagues at Southern Alliance for Clean Energy came up with a ballot initiative that would allow third parties to sell rooftop solar. If the initiative passed, it would essentially break up the utility's monopoly and open the gates to more changes.

The groups that rallied together for the Solar Choice Amendment were strange bedfellows. "It was an amazing coalition," Glickman said, including business groups like the Florida Retail Association and environmental outfits like Greenpeace. Glickman worked closely with Debbie Dooley, a Tea Party cofounder and the current head of Conservatives for Energy Freedom. The Southern Alliance for Clean Energy and their partners hired paid canvassers to try to gather enough signatures—almost seven hundred thousand—to get the initiative on the November 2016 ballot.

That spring, state lawmakers heard rumblings about the initiative and decided to write their own bill in support of solar energy. Glickman was surprised as she watched the bill advance through committees, and she counted its success as a side effect of their work on the Solar Choice Amendment. The legislature voted to put on the ballot Amendment 4, which if approved by Florida voters would give tax breaks to homeowners and businesses that used rooftop solar. (Florida's legislature wasn't allowed to abate taxes without voters' permission.) The amendment would run on the August 2016 ballot, which seemed like a concession to the utilities, because fewer voters turned up for summertime elections.

That summer, a curveball came at the green coalition. Consumers for Smart Solar, a new group, announced its "consumer friendly" solar-related Amendment 1, which was planned to run on the November ballot. That amendment consisted of a tangle of complicated phrases that seemed to imply that it would promote rooftop solar but in actuality would put in place new rules making it more difficult for homeowners and businesses to control their own solar power. It turned out that Consumers for Smart Solar was really a front group supported by the state's utility companies.[13] Running a successful ground campaign is "like building an empire for this short period of time," Glickman explained, and that year the utility companies were late to the game. "But who cares? They have all the money in the world." Something similar had happened in 2010, when a progressive effort called Hometown Democracy tried to pass a ballot initiative that would have reined in real estate developers but was thwarted when the Chamber of Commerce whipped up its own ultimately more successful counter-effort.

The state's four largest energy companies spent over $20 million promoting Amendment 1. Other groups funded by the fossil fuel industry bankrolled the effort, too. A Koch network–sponsored seniors group, 60 Plus, donated more than $1 million.[14] Consumers for Solar Choice also sought out alliances and hired politicos whose image would lend them credibility. Among the Tallahassee insiders chosen to lead the front group's effort was Screven Watson, a former executive director of the Florida Democratic Party who had also been a lobbyist for the sugar industry. Consumers for Solar Choice took $100,000 from the Koch-affiliated National Black Chamber of Commerce and even received an endorsement from the Florida NAACP. Caroline Lewis of CLEO said, "I think the messaging by FP&L was scaring [the black community] into thinking that prices would rise, that they would not be able to afford continuous energy."

"They did everything they could to confuse people," Glickman said. She had to keep a Post-it note with the two names stuck to her computer so she herself wouldn't mix them up. Glickman also remembered confronting Consumers for Smart Solar canvassers wearing Solar Choice Amendment T-shirts. The rival campaign tripped up every aspect of the green coalition's ground game. When the coalition's canvassers approached passersby, those passersby often said, "Oh, I already signed that," and the canvassers would try to slow them down long enough to figure out whether they had signed the green coalition or utility-backed petition. The front group also kept increasing the price-per-signature they were willing to pay signature gatherers, spiking the costs for the green coalition, which had far fewer resources. The green coalition was soon sinking the untenable sum of $350,000 a week on signature gathering.[15] Then, because the green coalition had less to show than donors expected, for more money sunk, it became even harder to convince donors that they were within striking range and worth another donation.

The green groups hadn't gathered enough signatures in time. Their initiative wouldn't make it onto the November ballot. The front group, however, had gotten enough. Floridians would vote on the deceptive measure. In August, meanwhile, voters went to the polls to vote on the measure the legislature had sponsored. An astounding 74 percent of voters approved of the legislature's Amendment 4. Floridians unequivocally supported green energy.

As November approached, the green coalition took to social media, dispatched canvassers, and did everything they could to urge Floridians to vote "no" on Amendment 1. Any question about whether Amendment 1 was a corporate plot to undermine voters' previous support of solar power was settled in October. The *Miami Herald* published a transcript from an audio recording of Sal Nuzzo, a vice president of the James Madison Institute, a free-market think tank that operates from a redbrick house a few blocks from the capitol and receives support from Florida's electric utilities. At a state energy policy conference, Nuzzo told the crowd that the front group's Amendment 1 was "an incredibly savvy maneuver" that "would completely negate anything [the pro-solar interests] would try to do either legislatively or constitutionally down the road." He went on to recommend to fellow attendees: "As you guys look at policy in your state, or constitutional ballot initiatives in your state, remember this: solar polls very well." And so, he said on the open mike, it might be necessary to "use a little bit of political jiujitsu" and "use the language of promoting solar" even when pushing policies that did the opposite.[16] In November, Florida voters overwhelmingly rejected Amendment 1. The defeat wasn't the game-changing win that the green group had initially hoped for, but their relatively small, underfunded team of "feisty activists," as Pomerantz called them, still managed to defeat the utilities and prove that Floridians wanted action. That win gave lawmakers clear evidence that clean energy was overwhelmingly popular among Florida voters. It also began moving the market incentive toward clean energy, a shift that is slowly beginning to happen nationally and globally.

★ ★ ★

When I heard that several green groups were organizing a lobby day in Tallahassee, I made plans to join them. By that time, early 2018, I had spent enough time in "kill committees" that I understood, as Stacey Newman had told me in Missouri, that the dial would move on Election Day. Florida's best hope for new legislation, especially on the climate front, would be flipping its legislative chambers and installing a new generation of proactive Democrats. Still, I wanted to see who would show up, and how their lawmakers would respond to Floridians' requests for proactive legislation to protect the integrity of their homes. We didn't yet know that Justice Anthony Kennedy would retire, likely foreclosing hope that the Supreme Court would uphold environmental regulations in the decades to come and multiplying the importance of state protections.

On the evening of January 31, 2018, a couple hundred Floridians from across the state ate pizza and drank lemonade in an airy meeting room in the LeRoy Collins Leon County Public Library in Tallahassee. ReThink Energy Florida, a small local nonprofit that aimed to educate the public about clean energy, had organized the event. Several buses full of people who wanted to talk with their lawmakers had driven up from South Florida, an eight-plus-hour ride. In the library, the crowd listened to staff from the Sierra Club and the League of Conservation Voters give a quick rundown of the key issues and bills on the table that legislative session: a fracking ban; conservation funding; bills expanding renewable energy.

The people who had assembled in that public library to eat pizza and role play conversations about fracking didn't match that old archetype of the genteel environmentalist. Some of them—like the older men in Birkenstocks, with unclipped toenails—fit other stereotypes. A disproportionate number were white. But most of the crowd looked neither fancy nor down and out, in jeans and T-shirts or khakis and blouses. I sat between a twenty-year-old black woman from Miami who had lupus and a white mother of children with asthma, who called herself a "mom activist." They talked about pollutants' effects on health and climate change. Like Zenia Perez and her father as they waited out Hurricane Irma, they shared concrete concerns.

Once staff from the green groups distributed information sheets on the proposed legislation and advice for approaching lawmakers—professionalism was important, meetings were "not a time to vent"—the crowd began to disperse. Most of the people who had traveled from South Florida were staying at either the Econo Lodge off the Apalachee Parkway or the People's Advocacy Center, a new nonprofit a mile away from the capitol. After the presentation, I piled into an Uber with four people in their twenties who were staying at the center.

A mile from the capitol building, on a quiet block in Frenchtown, the city's historic African American neighborhood, the People's Advocacy Center occupied a two-story redbrick building. Inside, the foyer was decorated with mismatched armchairs and couches, the walls covered with signs and posters, many with the affirmations "Don't Stop Believing" in pink lettering, "RESIST" in black. As we entered, the sounds of conversation and laughter carried over from a side room, where members of Catalyst Miami, an organization dedicated to advocating for low-wealth communities, was hosting a reception for members who had also taken buses up from South Florida to lobby their legislators.

The center was the long-envisioned and newly realized dream of Karen Woodall, a longtime advocate who had previously used her own home to host people traveling up to Tallahassee. Woodall and her colleagues were working from the principle that the state government was designed to keep poor people out. The center would serve two main purposes: it would give people traveling to the capital an affordable place to stay, and it would serve as a hub for the progressive movement. One side of the building was dorms, the other offices for four nonprofit organizations. ReThink Energy would move in later that year. Proximity would give those groups opportunities to work together. "When you start seeing the immigrant rights groups working with Black Lives Matter, the Dream Defenders, the child advocacy group, that's very powerful," Woodall said. The Advocacy Center was about more than convenience. Most of the groups that Woodall worked with were poverty-based nonprofits that couldn't afford hotel rooms. Their groups often left home at four in the morning, went to a single meeting in Tallahassee, and then hauled back to Central or South Florida. It wasn't realistic to expect any meaningful change to come from those short visits with tired volunteers. "The goal is for folks that are underrepresented in the capitol and are most directly affected by a lot of these policies that they pass, laws they enact, to learn the process," Woodall said. "You can't do that when you don't have a consistent presence." Making their voices heard in the state capitol was particularly important because the state had overridden the hard work of city organizers. The Florida legislature had banned local minimum wage laws in 2003, preventing cities from raising theirs. After cities and counties passed wage theft ordinances, the legislature considered a bill that would have banned local wage theft protections. And after activists in Miami-Dade organized to pass a local paid sick-leave policy, Scott preempted their efforts by signing into law a prohibition preventing local governments from enforcing their own paid sick-leave laws. "They can't ignore you when you're inside and you're hanging around," Woodall said. This was especially true after the committee meetings, when legislators mingled with the lobbyists whose employers arranged their campaign donations.[17]

There were plans for murals, but that winter the Advocacy Center's cinderblock bedrooms were painted white. Some were dorm-style with bunk beds, others were smaller, with inflatable mattresses or sleeping bags unfurled on the floor. There was an improvisational spirit, a contagious energy about the place. Downstairs, the Catalyst Miami members chatted with the ReThink Energy volunteers. Upstairs, the bedrooms' furnishings were as bare as they could have been and the bathroom was shared, but I wished I had planned to stay there, not at a grim motel on the other side of town. If you were going to think about the sea reclaiming the city you loved, starting during your lifetime, if you were going to wonder whether it would be ethical to have children, knowing that they would probably end up climate migrants, it was better to do so in good company. That was part of the plan, too. Hurried one-day visits weren't just ineffectual from a policy point of view. Scrambling didn't give people time to find sustenance in meeting new people who cared enough to make the journey to Tallahassee. Spending the night, Woodall explained, "gives people time to have a safe place and to know each other better and hear about each other's issues and say, 'Yes, we want to support that.'"

★ ★ ★

The next morning, I was reunited with everyone in the Florida capitol building. The building often pictured in news reports—two-storied, white-gabled, old-fashioned—isn't really the Florida capitol anymore. Instead, since the late 1970s, Florida's business has taken place across a brick-pave courtyard, in the twenty-two-story vertical building where central hallways are made of miles of beige terrazzo with brown flecks, imported from Italy. The first thing we encountered after passing through the metal detectors at the entrance was a life-size cardboard cutout of Pope Francis, ready for photo ops, and a table where Catholic Church representatives passed out invitations to a special Mass for elected officials. (A couple of hours later, when I was standing outside watching ReThink Energy's rally, two gray-haired women wearing red sweatshirts that said in white block letters I AM PRO-LIFE asked me what was going on. When I explained and mentioned the pope's encyclical on climate change and asked if their church group ever lobbied for environmental causes, one replied, without a touch of irony, "No, we focus mostly on life issues.") In the lobby, standing at the elevator bank surrounded by suited men and women carrying dossiers, I could have imagined that I was in the lobby of an upscale law firm if not for the pope, the clusters of teenagers representing Future Farmers of America in matching blue corduroy jackets with gold stitching, and the prevalence of 1980s-style hairdos and shoulder pads.

The ReThink Energy crowd dispersed in small teams and went to find their legislators. Later on, I caught up with one cohort that included a college student, a sociology professor, and two former Bernie Sanders organizers, all of whom had traveled great distances to get to Tallahassee. They were in good spirits, telling me that all the elected officials they had spoken with so far had been receptive. We filed into the office of Representative George Moraitis, a Trump supporter who had recently become the head of the Broward County Republican Party and represented Fort Lauderdale.

The ReThink Energy group talked about the proposed fracking ban first. I confess that I was surprised by how the group comported themselves as they countered Moraitis. That morning I had caught myself wondering whether the ragtag appearance of some of the volunteers might discredit more than bolster their cause. One participant, for example, had been wearing his plaid bathrobe as a jacket in the rotunda; it was unusually chilly in Tallahassee that week. I was reminded of how one legislator in another state told me that he asked the Sierra Club's volunteers not to show up to testify on behalf of a conservation bill because he didn't want it to be tainted by perceived association with "extremists." In Moraitis's office, the bathrobe was nowhere to be seen, and each member of the group cited data. They were persistent but professional as they explained how fracking could cause groundwater contamination. The college student offered to e-mail the representative peer-reviewed articles.

When the cohort asked for his support on a bill that would have expanded renewable energy, Moraitis replied, "I would prefer that it be a market-driven thing."

They went back and forth, Moraitis insisting on the free market, and the ReThink Energy group responding. A couple of minutes later, Moraitis's next appointment arrived, and we headed out. Once we were back in the hallway, the college student allowed his agitation to show.

"Florida Power & Light has a guaranteed rate of return!" he said. He knew exactly why the lines about the free market were absurd.

Several months later, in the summer of 2018, I talked with Erika Grohoski Peralta, who spent the 2018 legislative session as an aide to Democratic representative Annette Taddeo, who had won a surprise upset in a Miami special election. By that summer Grohoski Peralta was back in Miami working as an electoral organizer for the Center for Community Change, which seeks to build power within low-income communities. Grohoski Peralta told me she worked in the statehouse for only that one session because she was so put off by the culture of Tallahassee, where lobbyists and lawmakers carried themselves with a sense of superiority. We talked about how removed Tallahassee was from Central and South Florida. It seemed like a wholly different country from Miami. I told Grohoski Peralta how difficult it had been to watch young people from South Florida ask their officials—who are supposed to be public servants—to act on their behalf and see those officials flat out reject their very real concerns. My future was on the line, too. Those scenes, she told me, were nothing compared to what happened when the Parkland students visited Tallahassee a couple of weeks later. They were crying in the gallery as lawmakers voted against restricting the semiautomatic weapons that had just killed their friends.

"[Lawmakers] know that they have to appease their donors first. That is a complete failure of democracy," Grohoski Peralta said. "The fact that because so many people don't vote, and because elected officials know this, and because they constantly need more and more money to run campaigns, and elected officials and donors know this, the lobbying efforts [by most citizens' groups] are not very powerful." She used to think of lobbying as a means to persuade lawmakers. Then her outlook changed. Making phone calls to officials was basically useless. Elected officials rarely switched positions because of calls. Showing up in person mattered because it changed the person who showed up. *That* was the first step toward structural change. "Taking people up [to Tallahassee] and having them bring other people up, so they can see firsthand how much these people don't give a shit about them, is actually really important," she said. The organizers' job was to help transform "sadness and fear into hope and anger."

"The Parkland students, for instance, going up to Tallahassee and recording the students yelling at the governor, 'Vote him out,' was one of the most powerful, political things I have ever seen in my entire life. I was so amazed that sixteen-year-olds were telling them, 'We're going to vote you out.'" They understood that only new officials would meet their demands.

★ ★ ★

That year, 2018, Florida Democrats needed to resurrect themselves. On that, at least, everyone agreed. The summer before the midterm elections, in the deluxe Diplomat Beach Resort in Hollywood, just north of Miami Beach and some 460 miles and a world away from Tallahassee, party leaders organized for the make-or-break midterm elections. In 2016, within the party's committees and clubs, the Sanders-Clinton divide created an ideological fault line. Infighting worsened. "Unity" was a persistent theme in the 2018 conference speakers' addresses. The stakes for coming together to win were monumental. If Democrats could win the governorship, if they could squeeze out a majority in the state Senate, they could potentially enact proactive environmental measures and gun reform. They could expand Medicaid, and over eight hundred thousand uninsured Floridians would have access to health coverage.

That weekend, candidates for state offices pitched themselves to the party's legion of volunteers. Rick Scott was term-limited and was running for the United States Senate, challenging Democrat Bill Nelson, who had held his seat since 2001. In the mouth of a hallway in the hotel's conference center, the five Democratic gubernatorial candidates' teams set up folding tables and piled them high with branded swag. With two months before the primary, there were three presumed top contenders: former congresswoman Gwen Graham, the party's standard bearer, daughter of former governor Bob Graham; Philip Levine, founder and CEO of

Royal Media Partners, the parent of Royal Caribbean Cruises, and former mayor of Miami Beach; and Andrew Gillum, the mayor of Tallahassee, the favorite of the progressive caucus and a long shot by most estimations. Campaign and party staffers paced the halls. On the opposite side of the hall, dozens of preteen girls at "cheer camp," in tight ponytails, heavy stage makeup, and wearing booty shorts, twirled and flipped and chanted, creating an appropriately surreal backdrop.

By Saturday afternoon, on the Democratic Party side of the hallway, young people were also rushing back and forth, whooping, clapping, and chanting "Gillum" and "Levine." The competitive enthusiasm kept accelerating, until packs of young volunteers were running into conference rooms cheering. In those rooms, candidate after candidate—for attorney general, agriculture commissioner, state assembly—many of them first-timers, some of them primary challengers, stood up and made their case. Democrats were running candidates in almost every district. Several longtime party officials remarked from the stage that they had never felt so much energy at the annual conference.

In the preceding years and months, newcomers and new ideas had inspired a surge of energy outside the party structure, too. Campaign finance laws prevented most of those new players from coordinating with the party or candidates, but in practical terms their work would invariably lend muscle to Democratic candidates. After several false starts, America Votes had finally put together a Florida-based organizing table for the political arms of groups like the League of Conservation Voters and Planned Parenthood. They were targeting five state Senate seats, plus the governorship, just like their counterparts in Colorado. There was at least one other table, too, comprising the black and Latinx organization the New Florida Majority, which had full-time organizers and an expanding get-out-the-vote operation, and Organize Florida, an Orlando-based group, along with some others. Those groups were focused on day-in, day-out organizing on labor issues, affordable housing, racial justice, and climate change. In 2017 Organize Florida's c(3) educational wing had received an unusually long-term ten-year grant of over $2 million from the Ford Foundation to "mobilize and train leaders in Florida to create a more just and equitable society,"[18] giving its employees newfound stability and its membership the potential to become a local powerhouse because they could take on more ambitious work. During the long, tense primary season, those groups hosted gubernatorial debate-watch parties, where lots of Gillum supporters showed up. In the purely electoral realm, outside donors had also set up For Our Future, a progressive group that used analytics to target and market candidates to voters. Groups associated with the Indivisible movement mushroomed statewide. And in 2018, the New Venture Fund, a DC-based nonprofit, backed the Florida Phoenix, an online news outlet based in Tallahassee with the specific mandate of reporting on state government and politics. Its editor-in-chief was Julie Hauserman, the former local reporter and longtime progressive advocate. "There's so much bad behavior that goes on around the capital," Hauserman told me, that busy local reporters often "don't have time to pull back and ask some larger questions." The Phoenix would aim to fill that gap, and, she said, "we're going to lift up good ideas."

With that backdrop, the possibility that the Democrats could win back the governor's mansion and reverse Florida's calamitous course seemed very real. In those busy conference rooms, there were just so many people, people who had never before been there, never run for office, never volunteered, never considered themselves Democrats. The question that weekend was, which Democrat could pull it off? The common wisdom was, that Gwen Graham, cut in the image of her moderate father but leaning hard into her status as the only woman in the race ("I don't need a microphone, I'm a mom, I can shout!") would appeal to the widest cross-section of Floridians. I met college students who had been Republicans but after being repelled by Trump and awed by the Parkland students were volunteering for Graham. Their mere presence made a strong argument for the apparent wisdom of endorsing another round of "Republican lite" candidates. And yet Graham, who in Congress had voted for the Keystone Pipeline and limiting the Affordable Care Act, was claiming "progressive" bona fides, as was every gubernatorial candidate. Each was refusing money from the sugar and private prison industries. That was a major break from the Florida Democrats' long-standing tradition of tacitly accepting that corporations would buy influence in Tallahassee.

That weekend I spoke with several people who said that the party needed to shake up its habitual deference to milquetoast politicians and corporate donors and match the vigor and ambition of the rank-and-file voters and volunteers who saw no time to waste. But the shorthand often used in the national press—"the Bernie Sanders wing of the party"—didn't accurately capture all the Floridians I met who wanted to move the Democratic Party away from its old ways. Lots of them were former Clinton supporters. Lots of them were backing someone other than Gillum.

Trying to determine whether the party was correcting its course, whether it had a real chance of changing the power dynamic in Tallahassee, was confusing. One moment would bring uplift; the next, the deadening frustration of a "kill committee" hearing. If the mood, personalities, and slogans had metamorphosed since the 2010 election cycle, the Florida Democratic Party's core dilemmas remained. At the Diplomat Resort, as the gubernatorial candidates railed against how their predecessors privileged corporations over people, they stood beside the logo for one of the event's sponsors, US Sugar. The environmental community's big show, meanwhile, was a scientist who spoke in monotone about algae blooms while a PowerPoint presentation involving lots of charts and tables played to his right, leaving people in the room exchanging glances. This in a state where 74 percent of voters had just voted in support of clean energy incentives. It wasn't until Philip Levine jumped onstage and started waving his arms and shouting about climate change that the crowd came to life.

The party still did need to supplement its relatively scant resources. It still needed to stake out a moral argument, a narrative for voters. Committee members disagreed over how. During the conference, members of the party's executive committee voted on whether to prohibit the party from taking donations from private prisons. That would require cutting themselves off from the Democratic Congressional Campaign Committee, a main artery of support, because it accepted prison money.[19] Party leadership paused, fully cognizant of what they were up against. Republican allies had arsenals. A single political action committee specifically set up to target Nelson, New America PAC, already had roughly $8 million, $5 million of which was from a single hedge fund. In the end, the party officials decided to cut themselves off from private prison companies and the DCCC anyway, a clear break from its old ways.

Whether the party was trading its infighting for urgency was also unclear. Brevard County Democratic chairperson Stacey Patel, who had dramatically increased voter registration and volunteer numbers, won applause for saying that people were showing up in droves to local Democratic meetings because national calamities were spurring them to action, not because they wanted to organize spaghetti dinners. But, in deflating contrast, party committee members broke into a protracted, heated disagreement over bylaw tedium I could not follow. There was the moment when a speaker explained that unpaid party volunteers could legally coordinate with the extra-party progressive groups like For Our Future to make sure they weren't reinventing the wheel. But, no, a Broward County party leader chimed in to say that she would not, on principle, team up with those groups. That position bewildered me, frankly, even after I heard the rationale: If local Democrats worked with the outside groups they would end up deferring to those groups even if they didn't understand local nuances. That would derail the local party's progress in establishing its own programs. Those outside groups would be gone after the election. The Florida Democratic Party would not. "We can't keep thinking one election at a time. That just has to stop," that party leader told me, explaining why she preferred to focus on strengthening the party itself.

Florida Democrats faced so many dilemmas that it is unsurprising they often disagreed. As another party member summarized,

"There are the usual contests for power" between the various factions within the party, all wrestling for control of its next direction. Members from the state's far-flung regions all had an opinion on which territory needed more dollars and attention. Ideology and strategy preferences split party leaders and volunteers, too. Some wanted a clean break from the consultant-driven model. Others wanted to embrace this or that outside group. On one hand, those disagreements were a normal part of organizing people, and possibly the hand-wringing over these tensions was a distraction, a commotion on the surface of the real work that was getting done. On the other, the fate of eight hundred thousand low-income people's ability to access health care and the future carbon emissions of a state with twenty-one million people were riding, at least in part, on the effectiveness of those volunteers assembled in those conference rooms. The young people in particular seemed to comprehend the magnitude of the task at hand. I asked one twenty-something Levine volunteer whether she would help the eventual Democratic nominee no matter who it was. "Yes! Of course!" she said, as she threw her arms wide, laughing with the requisite gallows humor. "If a Democrat doesn't become governor of Florida, we're all going to die!"

★ ★ ★

"We're not going to sweep this state by running the same playbook of the last twenty years," Gillum said. The crowd cheered. It was Saturday night, and all the candidates were speaking, simultaneously, in different rooms that hooked around the hallway. The Gillum room was packed. "We're going to get there by getting voters, many of them who have been feeling left out, who are feeling unheard, who are feeling unreflected, who feel that they don't have a champion."

Gillum's very presence on that stage was a beautiful story, the kind that Florida Democrats had not told in a long time, if ever. Gillum was thirty-nine years old, black, the son of a bus driver and a construction worker, the fifth of seven children, the first of them to graduate high school. He advocated for establishing "Medicare for all," increasing state education spending by $1 billion, raising the minimum wage, and tightening Florida's gun laws and environmental standards. He was also potentially under FBI investigation. The bureau had sent undercover officers to Tallahassee to pretend to be real estate developers, and that summer the scant details about the investigation meant that it was unclear whether in cozying up to the "developers" Gillum had broken any laws. In the grand scheme of Tallahassee favor trading, his alleged conduct didn't seem like the most egregious of sins, but the fact that I was making those calculations at all meant that I had arrived prepared to be cynical about his candidacy. In the room that night the caterer, a Latino man wearing a white apron and chef's cap, smiled and nodded along from behind a tray of Cuban sandwiches in the back, taking in the room as everyone erupted in cheers. I, too, was transfixed.

Two months later, Gillum won the Democratic primary with 34 percent of the vote. Florida's late primary date often creates a scramble, especially for underfunded Democrats. In roughly ten weeks, the Gillum campaign had to galvanize at least four million Floridians, only half a million of whom chose him in the primary. Headlines catapulted him into national prominence, transforming him into a vessel of hope for Democrats nationwide. The local opposition to his candidacy was strong, and not subtle. You probably already know this part of the story. The morning after the primary, on Fox News, the Republican gubernatorial nominee, Ron DeSantis, said "The last thing we need to do is to monkey this up by trying to embrace a socialist agenda with huge tax increases and bankrupting the state." That DeSantis used the phrase "monkey this up" in reference to a black man seized the attention of local and national media. The racism directed at Gillum, and by extension all black and brown Floridians, would get worse before the campaign season ended. About ten days before the election, a robo-call from an Idaho-based white nationalist group called Florida voters and played audio of a man speaking in a minstrel-like voice, impersonating Gillum while jungle and chimpanzee sounds played in the background. The ad ends, "All the Jews gon' vote me, Andrew Gillum, governor of this here state of Florida." In the final debate of the long season, Gillum told the crowd, "I'm not calling Mr. DeSantis a racist. I'm simply saying that racists think he's a racist."[20]

If Gillum's campaign attracted hate-mongering, it also generated unprecedented enthusiasm. As soon as he won the primary, he was everywhere, the focus of anticipation from all corners of the country. Tom Steyer, the San Francisco–based billionaire obsessed with impeachment, gave Gillum's campaign roughly $2.8 million and sent another $7 million to groups working indirectly to elect him, including Next Gen and For Our Future, which were registering young voters around the state.[21] Other billionaires chipped in, too. The Collective PAC sent him at least a million dollars, and Gillum hauled in millions in small dollar donations. All told, by the end of his campaign Gillum had raised over $52 million. The atmosphere in Florida was supercharged. "I've never seen a governor's race so big before," Emmanuel George, a New Florida Majority staffer, remembered. "This felt like an '08 Obama situation." Politicos wondered whether inspired Gillum voters would buoy Senator Bill Nelson, widely known to be at risk by his Republican challenger Rick Scott.

Gillum's candidacy did not remake Florida's playing field. Democrats and progressives were still trying to defy similar hurdles, as in 2010 and subsequent years. Across the state, though, they were hustling. All summer, the Democratic Party had sent surrogates on a tour of rural counties to talk to people about Medicaid expansion. The party actively recruited and ran candidates for almost every state legislature race. When I met several of those candidates at the Diplomat Resort over the summer, they all described, with fervor, their unrelenting campaign schedules and get-out-the-vote plans.

Both the party and the progressive groups were using new techniques to bring people into the political process more organically. Democratic Party leaders were training their volunteers on how to have real conversations with people while canvassing. Several new electoral outfits were flanking the state, too. WIN Justice PAC—a collaboration between Planned Parenthood Votes, Center for Community Change Action, Color of Change PAC, and the union SEIU—was distributing an estimated $30 million among organizers in a handful of key states, including Florida, to mobilize young people and people of color. The League of Conservation Voters was hurling unprecedented funds toward Democrats in the final campaign sprint, too, and they believed they had a shot at persuading swing voters. For a year a toxic algae bloom—a byproduct of pollutants—had been traveling northward through the canals and streams that emptied into Lake Okeechobee in central Florida. The state hadn't funded the commission that was supposed to monitor algae in it waterways since 2001. By that summer, fish and even sharks and dolphins poisoned by the algae were washing up on Florida's beaches, and people were showing up at hospitals with respiratory problems. That was exactly the sort of environmental problem that sparked bipartisan outrage—possibly providing an opening for Democrats. Meanwhile, Organize Florida and the New Florida Majority were running massive drives to get people in South Florida to the polls. None of those programs had existed on that scale during the 2010 election, which had been so close. Democrats' Achilles' heel had always been low turnout in their strongholds, especially the minority-majority stretches of South Florida; these new strategies had to mean something.

On Tuesday, November 6, 2018, on the patio of the Little Haiti Cultural Center, local progressive groups hosted an election watch party. Music played over a dense, diverse crowd, many of whom were still wearing their sweat-soaked campaign T-shirts after knocking on doors all day—or, in some cases, all year. Many in the crowd belonged to nonprofit and volunteer groups and had been instrumental in getting on that year's ballot Amendment 4, the initiative that asked Florida voters whether they wanted to extend voting rights to nonviolent felons, "returning citizens" who had completed their sentences. That campaign had lasted over six years and was a joint effort involving not only the Florida Rights Restoration Coalition but also many other local organizations, including the ACLU of Florida, the New Florida Majority, Organize

Florida, SEIU Florida, and the Dream Defenders. Before the other results came in, Valencia Gunder, a local activist and founder of the nonprofit Make the Homeless Smile, took center-stage at the front of the patio to announce that Amendment 4 had passed. The crowd erupted in cheers and applause.

"Picking up petitions, filing lawsuits, hitting doors, filling out e-mails, you did it, Florida," Gunder said, her voice filling with emotion, the crowd's cheers overpowering her. "First time in Florida's history. People are going to get their rights back. For everybody who came and hit these streets with us, we thank you so much."

That achievement was a victory for organizing, a repudiation of the vestiges of the Jim Crow South, and a clear example of people being given the voice in our democracy that they deserve. It was also, potentially, the kind of change that could magnify progressives' power on the local, state, and national level, if enough returning citizens could be motivated to vote for them. This was exactly the kind of structural change that the left rarely laid plans to prioritize.

Moments later, the screens on either side of the stage returned to CNN and the Florida elections website. As the returns came in, those of us huddled on the patio did the math—it was becoming steadily less possible for Gillum to win. Nelson, too, was destined to lose. Republicans held on to their control of the state Senate; a progressive activist told me that their control in the legislature had never really been in question. Few people were dancing anymore. Faces were stoic. I watched one New Florida Majority staffer sling his arm around the shoulder of another, consoling him. When the final votes were tallied, Gillum had lost by thirty-three thousand of over eight million total votes. The same question that tormented gubernatorial candidate Alex Sink in 2010, and Democrats nationwide in 2016—why couldn't they close those slim margins?—would continue to haunt the Florida Democratic Party and the progressive apparatus. Dueling theories would inform the 2020 races, and beyond. Maybe it was because wealthy and middle-class Floridians were afraid their taxes would be raised. Maybe it was the FBI probe. By November, reports had emerged that the undercover FBI agents had given Gillum tickets to the Broadway musical *Hamilton*. Or maybe it was deeply etched cultural beliefs about "guns, Gods, and gays" that motivated Floridians. Maybe too many voters agreed with DeSantis, who unapologetically made anti-immigrant remark after anti-immigrant remark, rallied with Trump, and ran a campaign ad wherein he taught his toddler to "build a wall" out of blocks. The truth is probably some unquantifiable combination of all those reasons and more. Gillum later said that he believed it was the strength of Republicans' get-out-the-vote machine that delivered DeSantis the governorship. "[Republicans] get that their voters don't need a rally," Gillum said. "They don't need a parade. It is muscle memory, practically."

On the patio that night, I thought of the line I had heard so many versions of during the course of my reporting: "We can't solve climate change unless we solve racism." Progressives from across the country had told me this over and over, insistent that all battles are interconnected. I had half listened because I thought I knew what they meant, but it didn't really hit me, not the full weight of it, not until I was on that patio, thinking about the Public Service Commission appointments, the emissions that would continue to imperil the children standing near me, the Haitian neighborhood all around us, more in danger than the tracts of landlocked America where so many white people live, and the robo-calls with the minstrel voice and chimpanzee sounds. I had heard another talking point repeated, when growing up, that racism hurts white people, too. But that always seemed like a line. White supremacy, in all its many forms, has of course protected and glorified white people. Now, as long as one major political party is simultaneously the party of overt racist rhetoric and voter disenfranchisement and also of the industries who have a direct stake in stalling action on climate change, racism does threaten us all. Florida may be first in line, but, as the activists reminded me, we can't simply drive away from all the consequences of rising global temperatures.

And then there was the reality of how white supremacy shaped Democratic and progressive political funding—and the circumstances of everyone on the patio, all the people who had worked so hard to make Florida a fairer place. Many of the electoral organizations that had crashed into the state, like Steyer's Next Gen, would fold up and leave, presumably not to return until just before the next big election. Local groups like Organize Florida and the New Florida Majority would remain. In coming days and weeks, national progressive pundits would talk excitedly about Florida restoring felons' voting rights, claiming it as a bright spot they too were celebrating. But that amendment would change power dynamics only if enough people were registered and mobilized to vote—and if they voted for Democrats and progressives. There was no magic wand. As I write this, during the 2019 legislative session, Florida Republicans are advancing a bill that would require felons to pay their court restitution fees before they can register to vote. The bill may appear neutral. But Florida doesn't track restitution fees, so many felons don't know what they owe, complicating whether they would be able to pay their fees. That means the bill, if enacted, could potentially prevent hundreds of thousands of Floridians from being able to vote. The people now showing up in Tallahassee to protect Floridians' voting rights and registering voters across the state are the members and leaders of local Florida organizations, many of whom are black, brown, and low-wealth.[22] In other words, after the media and political operatives' spotlight moved, following potential 2020 presidential candidates the moment the 2018 midterms ended, Floridians—and especially low-wealth, black, and brown Floridians—were left to attempt another Herculean lift, one that would likely decide the fate of the Democrats in 2020, with major repercussions into the next decade and beyond.

EPILOGUE

WE HAVE ALL EXPERIENCED A MOMENT WHEN OUR frame of reference changed. Something that had always been there, right in front of us, was illuminated, gradually or in a flash. How could we not have seen it before? Dozens of politicos told me about a moment when they first saw what they now cannot unsee. Whether in the 1960s or after the 2016 election, the recognition was similar. Over the past few years, many of us have come to better understand our political system and how it affects our lives. "It's like Plato's cave," Zenia Perez, the Justice Democrats operative, told me, describing her own political awakening. In the Allegory of the Cave, people lived chained in a cave, captivated by fluttering shadows that a puppeteer projected on its walls. After a freed prisoner was able to leave the cave, he saw the sun for the first time. The light was painful at first. When he returned to the cave, he saw the shadows for what they were: blurry, one-dimensional, nothing like reality itself. Today, when issues like gerrymandering and voter suppression, lobbying and "fake news," are part of the mainstream political conversation, many of us have taken the difficult journey out of the cave. Now that we are here, what do we do?

The scale of the problems at hand, from racism to climate change, are so daunting that trying to face them—even for long enough to read a news story—can seem impossible. The twenty-four-hour news cycle hurls tragedy after tragedy at us, all of them outside our immediate control. In a way, writing this book provided me a reprieve from the grim spectacle that is the national news, even though I was thinking all the time about gun violence, carbon emissions, women's diminishing access to reproductive health care, and other grave problems. I met so many people who were getting things done in their cities and states. Their goals may be incremental, they may seem humble, but they are nonetheless necessary, concrete steps toward progress. For those of us overwhelmed with the dire state of our nation and world, local politics provides a venue where we can do something. It may not be in our power to curb all carbon emissions, but we can join together with our neighbors and push our states to incentivize clean energy. We may not be able to rid this country of its racist heritage, but we can advocate for local laws that will expand access to the ballot. We can't control that Justice Brett Kavanaugh is serving on the Supreme Court, but we can make sure that reproductive justice activists are not alone when they speak publicly about the importance of abortion and contraception. We can all help register voters.

I don't want to peddle some misguided *Lean In*–style directive that promises that if we just work hard and volunteer with enough enthusiasm, all our problems will disappear. We know that the campaign finance system and lobbying rules are rigged so that corporations have more power than most Americans. Increased participation does not necessarily change power dynamics or translate into a democracy that reflects the will of the people. (We do, after all, live in a country where the current president received three million fewer votes than his opponent.) Much of the change we need must come from the top. Foundations and megadonors can and should change their priorities and sponsor long-term community engagement and organizing, as well as space for ambitious idea-generation, instead of handing out short-term grants or last-minute campaign checks. Legacy interest groups can divert more of their resources to their local chapters. Nonprofits and state parties can hire and promote more members of minority and low-wealth communities who better understand how to work locally. Some foundations, donors, nonprofits, and local parties are already taking steps in those directions, and they can be role models. But the real truth is that the "nonprofit industrial complex" is not going to save us. There is no switch a billionaire donor or team of professional activists can flip on their own. All of those people and organizations are ultimately just trying to engage the rest of us. Without our sustained participation, we have nothing.

Voting is not enough. As Howard Dean told me, "If you just think you're going to vote every four years, you're going to end up with a Republican version of the world, which I guarantee you is going to be incredibly unpleasant except for people who are in [Congress]." Political scientists often refer to the "collective action problem," a catch-all for the many ways that personal incentives are often at odds with joining collective political action. In a sense, it's against each of our own financial and sometimes emotional self-interests to volunteer and donate when we could just sit back, let our neighbors do the work, and appreciate the gains when they come. When individuals weigh their life choices, they know (unless they are incredibly grandiose) that their decision to become an attorney for a coal or private prison company is not going to make or break those industries' existence, whereas choosing instead to be an environmental or immigrants' rights organizer will make all the difference in decreasing their earning potential and, more than likely, increasing their personal stress. We each weigh those kinds of trade-offs, though on a smaller scale, every time we decide whether to protest, volunteer, or run for office. But nothing will change unless we understand that our lives, and especially the lives of our children, depend on collective action. As my friend the climate reporter Abby Rabinowitz said to me recently, "We need to be as accountable to political action as we are to our families."

We can't allow ourselves to fall victim, yet again, to the "divide and conquer" strategy. We can't allow our disagreements with each other to prevent us from participating. Especially now, when the multiple Democratic presidential campaigns are slicing the party's coalition into ever smaller factions, and when Trump is shouting ever louder about immigration and abortion and other topics he latches onto exactly because they are divisive, we have to stay disciplined enough to stick together and to keep showing up.

We can also be smart about how we channel our participation. With all-important redistricting approaching, taking and maintaining control of state legislatures in 2019 and 2020 is paramount. Winning in the states is the kind of "two-fer, three-fer" win that sets up Democrats and progressives for escalating wins—or, if they lose, mounting losses. In 2018, Democrats won control of six state legislatures, where lawmakers began advancing proactive progressive reforms. Between 2017 and 2018, Democrats won eight more governorships. Now is the time to ensure that those victories were more than outliers in the general trend of Republicans gathering strategic power via the states. Democrats and progressives can't claim a genuine sea change yet.

Throughout the country, people are readying to advance and protect Democratic strength in the states ahead of 2020. The National Redistricting Action Fund is trying to undo Republicans' disproportionate power by winning targeted state elections and rallying support for fair districts. Early in 2019, under the leadership of Eric Holder, the Action Fund announced a merger with Obama's political arm Organizing for America. Between now and the 2020 election, their plan is to mobilize supporters, especially in ten key states, to win state legislatures that control district maps. That is but one effort designed to overcome Democrats' and progressives' overall weak position in the states. Once again, state parties will weigh their dilemmas and try to regain their footing. Platforms like Act Blue will help dispatch small dollar donations. New Era Colorado and the New Florida Majority and hundreds of other local groups scattered nationwide will round up staffers and volunteers and register voters. And people like Leslie Herod, in Denver's District 8, and Crystal Stephens, in outstate Missouri's District 18, will ask for help from people like us—we who cannot unsee what we have seen. Our lives are on the line, and the key to our long-term strength is to win close to home.

ACKNOWLEDGMENTS

The best part of working on this book, far and away, was talking with so many people who get up every morning and try to do the right thing. Many more people were generous with their time, expertise, and insights than I could possibly name in the text. An enormous thank you to everyone who made time to talk with me, especially because I was usually cold calling in the middle of an election season or legislative session, when you definitely had other things to do. I am grateful to everyone I met along the way. Special thanks to those who invited me along for a ride: John Cauthorn, who showed me how soy is harvested; Leslie Herod, who brought me to Larimer County; Lynda Stewart, who showed me the Mississippi; the New Florida Majority, who let me tag along during canvassing; the Public Leadership Institute, who invited me to their conference. And thanks to Alison Dreith, who accompanied me on my first journey down this rabbit hole.

This book would not exist without the local and statehouse reporters whose journalism laid the groundwork for me—and for many other writers and journalists. In particular, I learned from the *Denver Post* and the *Tampa Bay Times*, the *Miami Herald*'s Tallahassee bureau, and St. Louis Public Radio, especially its

Politically Speaking podcast (which I highly recommend to any political junkie).

I have been very lucky. Sarah Blustain at Type Investigations taught me how to report and write long-form stories, and I will always be grateful for her mentorship. Many thanks, too, to Esther Kaplan and everyone at Type Investigations, whose support set me on this path. I am very grateful to have my agent Molly Atlas in my corner. Her judgment is impeccable, and my trust in her is complete. A huge thanks to Bold Type Books editor Katy O'Donnell for believing in me and this book and providing the invaluable guidance that shaped it. Another huge thanks to my stalwart editor Remy Cawley, for generously making time to talk through ideas and problems, and for providing the insights and edits that sharpened the book so much. Pete Garceau designed a cover that I love. Glenn Novak's incisive copy-edits and notes saved me, as did Darren Ankrom's research ensuring that every detail was correct. Many thanks to Nora Knight for transcribing interviews for me. And thank you to Stephanie Summerhays, Brynn Warriner, and everyone working behind the scenes at Perseus Books Group.

I couldn't have pulled this off had Heather Samples and Meechal Hoffman of the Bernard L. Schwartz Communication Institute at Baruch College not been so supportive and flexible. Thank you. And many thanks to my BLSCI colleagues for their generosity of spirit, which kept me tethered to the world beyond my screen during many long days of writing.

There are no words to express my appreciation for Anya Yurchyshyn, Abby Rabinowitz, Rachel Riederer, Tana Wojczuk, and Jeannie Vanasco. Thank you for listening to me talk endlessly about word counts and state government, and for reading early drafts and knowing exactly what to say. Thank you, Rose Lichter-Marck, for taking photographs of me. I was so drawn to New Era Colorado because it was founded by friends, and friendship was key to its success. An eternal thank you to my friends—you know who you are—for all of the conversations that have made me who I am. Thank you for encouraging and challenging me, and for providing me a compass.

I owe a lot to my family. Thank you to my mother. I am lucky that I inherited from her a love of books and curiosity about people. And thank you to my father, who showed me how to file a Freedom of Information Act request when I was about twelve years old. Many thanks to my brother Matt, who read drafts, gave advice, and taught me a lot about local activism. And thanks to both Matt and Nina for putting me up in DC. My brother Dennis has helped me move, the real test of loyalty, more times than I can count. There is truly no way to adequately thank my incredible sister, Kaitlin, for everything that she does for me every time we talk. Finally, my favorite person to argue with, Milko Lima: te quiero porque tu boca sabe gritar rebeldía.

NOTES

INTRODUCTION

1. Steve Bousquet and Elizabeth Kohl, "As Students Watch, Lawmakers Debate Porn but Refuse to Take Up Assault Weapons Ban," *Miami Herald*, February 20, 2018.

2. Jana Kasperkevic, Oliver Laughland, and Jon Swaine, "US Justice Department Announces It Will End Use of Private Prisons," *Guardian*, August 18, 2016; David Gambacorta, "The Secret, Dangerous World of Private Prisons," *Philadelphia Inquirer*, August 17, 2017.

3. "State Legislatures Are Making Progress on Major Issues That Are Still Stuck in Congress," American Legislative Exchange Council, August 14, 2017, www.alec.org/public-affair/state-legislatures-making-progress-on-major-issues-that-are-still-stuck-in-congress/; Jennifer Hickey, "Republicans Build on Their Dominance in State Legislatures," Fox News, November 18, 2016, www.foxnews.com/politics/2016/11/18/republicans-build-on-their-dominance-in-state-legislatures.html; "State Government Trifectas," Ballotpedia, accessed April 8, 2019, https://ballotpedia.org/State_government_trifectas.

4. Nick Rathod, "Democrats Take Opposition Fight to the States," interview by Linda Wertheimer, *Weekend Edition Saturday*, NPR, December 24, 2016, www.npr.org/2016/12/24/506817049/democrats-take-opposition-fight-to-the-states.

5. Mallory Daily, Jo Mannies, and Jason Rosenbaum, "Missouri General Assembly Votes to Expand Legal Use of Deadly Force Known as Stand Your Ground," St. Louis Public Radio, NPR, May 13, 2016, http://news.stlpublicradio.org/post/missouri-general-assembly-votes-expand-legal-use-deadly-force-known-stand-your-ground#stream/0; Amber Phillips, "Missouri and Why Voter ID Laws Might Be Here to Stay," *Washington Post*, May 16, 2016.

6. Miranda Blue, "GOP Lawmaker Calls Pregnancy God's 'Silver Lining' for Rape," Rightwingwatch.org, May 4, 2016, www.rightwingwatch.org/post/gop-lawmaker-calls-pregnancy-gods-silver-lining-for-rape/; Claire Lampen, "Pregnancy Is the "Silver Lining" of Rape, according to Missouri Republican Tila Hubrecht," Yahoo.com, May 5, 2016, www.yahoo.com/news/pregnancy-silver-lining-rape-according-143500095.html; Anna Merlen, "Surprise: Missouri Republican Who Called Pregnancy a 'Silver Lining of Rape' Isn't Sorry," Jezebel.com, May 6, 2016, https://theslot.jezebel.com/surprise-missouri-republican-who-called-pregnancy-a-si-1775208313.

7. Isaac Arnsdorf and Kenneth Vogel, "Clinton Fundraising Leaves Little for the State Parties," Politico, May 2, 2016, www.politico.com/story/2016/04/clinton-fundraising-leaves-little-for-state-parties-222670.

8. Chris Hopson, "I Believe in States' Rights. Do You?," *Harvard Political Review*, January 28, 2018, http://harvardpolitics.com/united-states/i-believe-in-states-rights-do-you/.

9. American Federation of Labor and Congress of Industrial Organizations, a progressive union.

10. Clare Malone, "The Young Left's Anti-Capitalism Manifesto," FiveThirtyEight.com, January 22, 2019, https://fivethirtyeight.com/features/the-young-lefts-anti-capitalist-manifesto/.

11. Lee Epstein and Thomas G. Walker, *Constitutional Law for a Changing America: A Short Course* (Thousand Oaks, CA: CQ Press, 2017).

12. Mathew Ingram, "Fake News, Clickbait Still Going Well after Facebook Algorithm Change," *Columbia Journalism Review*, March 29, 2018, www.cjr.org/the_new_gatekeepers/fake-news-clickbait-facebook-algorithm.php.

13. Julia Horowitz and Chris Isidore, "Foxconn Got a Really Good Deal from Wisconsin. And It's Getting Better," *CNN Money*, CNN.com, December 28, 2017, https://money.cnn.com/2017/12/28/news/companies/foxconn-wisconsin-incentive-package/index.html; Robert Samuels, "Walker's Anti-union Law Has Labor Reeling in Wisconsin," *Washington Post*, February 22, 2015.

14. Gregory J. Martin and Josh McCrain, "Local News and National Politics," Stanford Graduate School of Business, Working Paper 3681, Political Economy, April 19, 2018, www.gsb.stanford.edu/faculty-research/working-papers/local-news-national-politics; Mark Jurkowitz, "5 Key Takeaways from Our Census of Statehouse Reporters," Pew Research Center, July 10, 2014, www.pewresearch.org/fact-tank/2014/07/10/5-key-takeaways-from-our-census-of-statehouse-reporters/.

15. Nancy MacLean, *Democracy in Chains: The Deep History of the Radical Right's Stealth Plan for America* (New York: Viking, 2017), xxii.

16. Adam Liptak, "In Health Case, Appeals to a Justice's Idea of Liberty," *New York Times*, March 30, 2012; Ilya Shapiro, "Justice Kennedy: The Once and Future Swing Vote," Cato Institute, November 13, 2016, www.cato.org/publications/commentary/justice-kennedy-once-future-swing-vote; Mike DeBonis and Sean Sullivan, "With Little Fanfare, Trump and McConnell Reshape the Nation's Circuit Courts," *Washington Post*, August 14, 2018.

17. Nicole DuPuis, Trevor Langan, Christina McFarland, Angelina Panettieri, and Brooks Rainwater, *City Rights in an Era of Preemption: A State-by-State Analysis; 2018 Update*, National League of Cities, 2018, www.nlc.org/sites

/default/files/2017-03/NLC-SML%20Preemption%20Report%202017-pages.pdf; Lori Riverstone-Newell, "The Rise of State Preemption Laws in Response to Local Policy Innovation," *Publius: The Journal of Federalism* 47, no. 3 (July 2017): 403–425, https://academic.oup.com/publius/article/47/3/403/3852645; MacLean, *Democracy in Chains*, 1; Sean Darling-Hammond, "The Electoral College Is Even More Biased Than You Think. But Democrats Can Beat It," *Nation*, January 19, 2018.

18. "2018 Legislator Compensation Information," National Conference of State Legislatures, April 16, 2018, www.ncsl.org/research/about-state-legislatures/legislator-compensation-2018.aspx; Kirby Wilson, "Why Doesn't Florida's Legislature Look Anything Like Florida's Workforce?," *Tampa Bay Times*, February 14, 2018, www.tampabay.com/projects/2018/data/paychecks-balances-florida-legislature-jobs/.

CHAPTER ONE

1. "Americans for Prosperity," Americans for Prosperity, accessed March 7, 2019, https://americansforprosperity.org/.

2. Gordon Lafer, *The One Percent Solution: How Corporations Are Remaking America One State at a Time* (Ithaca, NY: Cornell University Press, 2017), 26; *The State Legislators Guide to Repealing Obamacare*, American Legislative Exchange Council, November 8, 2011, www.alec.org/publication/the-state-legislators-guide-to-repealing-obamacare/; David Daley, "How Republicans Rigged Congress—New Documents Reveal an Untold Story," Salon, February 26, 2018, www.salon.com/2018/02/06/how-the-republicans-rigged-congress-and-poisoned-our-politics/.

3. Rosalind Helderman, "Cuccinelli Sues Federal Government to Stop Health-Care Reform Law," *Washington Post*, March 24, 2010; Adam Liptak, "Supreme Court Upholds Healthcare Law, 5-4, in Victory for Obama," *New York Times*, June 28, 2012; Rachel Garfield, Anthony Damico, and Kendral Orgera, "The Coverage Gap: Uninsured Poor Adults in States That Did Not Expand Medicaid," Henry J. Kaiser Family Foundation, June 12, 2018, www.kff.org/medicaid/issue-brief/the-coverage-gap-uninsured-poor-adults-in-states-that-do-not-expand-medicaid/.

4. Robert Mutch, *Campaign Finance: What Everyone Needs to Know* (New York: Oxford University Press, 2016), 108–117; "Giving USA 2018: Americans Gave $410.02 Billion to Charity in 2017, Crossing the $400 Billion Mark for the First Time," Giving USA, June 13, 2018, https://givingusa.org/giving-usa-2018-americans-gave-410-02-billion-to-charity-in-2017-crossing-the-400-billion-mark-for-the-first-time/.

5. "Average Grant Sizes Increased in 2016, Foundation Source Finds," *Philanthropy News Digest*, July 29, 2017, https://philanthropynewsdigest.org/news/average-grant-sizes-increased-in-2016-foundation-source-finds.

6. Foundation Directory Online by Candid (accessed May 8, 2018, in person at the Foundation Center New York), https://fconline.foundationcenter.org/. Data was generated through the author's proprietary search of the database and is held in the author's possession.

7. Alexander Hertel-Fernandez, "Explaining Liberal Policy Woes in the States," *PS: Political Science and Politics* 49, no. 3 (July 2016): 461–465.

8. Nancy MacLean, *Democracy in Chains: The Deep History of the Radical Right's Stealth Plan for America* (New York: Viking, 2017), 24.

9. Karen Paget, "State of the Debate: Lessons from Right-Wing Philanthropy," *American Prospect*, September–October 1998.

10. "The Powell Memorandum," Powell Memorandum: Attack on American Free Enterprise System, Powell Archives, Washington and Lee University School of Law, accessed March 10, 2018, https://scholarlycommons.law.wlu.edu/powellmemo/1/.

11. MacLean, *Democracy in Chains*, xxvii.

12. MacLean, *Democracy in Chains*, 141; Jane Mayer, *Dark Money: The Hidden History of the Billionaires behind the Rise of the Radical Right* (New York: Doubleday, 2016), 74.

13. Linda Greenhouse and Reva Siegal, "Before (and After) Roe v. Wade: New Questions about the Backlash," *Yale Law Journal* 120, no. 8 (June 2011): 2028–2087.

14. Jane McAlevey, *No Shortcuts: Organizing for Power in the New Gilded Age* (New York: Oxford University Press, 2016).

15. Paget, "State of the Debate."

16. Joey Garrison and Maria Giordano, "Koch Brothers Group to Keep Pressure on Common Core," *Tennessean*, August 13, 2014; "Common Core is Common Sense for Business," US Chamber of Commerce, October 20, 2014, www.uschamber.com/above-the-fold/common-core-common-sense-business.

17. David Callahan, *The Givers: Money, Power, and Philanthropy in a New Gilded Age* (New York: Knopf, 2017).

18. Hertel-Fernandez, "Explaining Liberal Policy Woes in the States."

19. Alexander Hertel-Fernandez, "Explaining Liberal Policy Woes in the States," *PS: Political Science and Politics* 49, no. 3 (July 2016): 464.

CHAPTER TWO

1. Martin Luther King Jr., *Letter from the Birmingham Jail* (San Francisco: Harper, 1994).

2. Will Schmitt, "Analysis: Missouri Redistricting Favors Republicans but Falls Short of Gerrymandering," *Springfield (MO) News-Leader*, June 25, 2017.

3. Chris Wilson, "Advanced Polling Techniques: Road to the Right Message," in *Winning Elections: Political Campaign Management, Strategy and Tactics*, ed. Ron Faucheux (Lanham, MD: Rowman & Littlefield, 2003), 171.

4. Jeff Stein, "'Without My Country, the Union Means Nothing': How Pro-Trump Voters Back Labor," *Washington Post*, August 10, 2018, https://www.washingtonpost.com/business/economy/missouris-rejection-of-right-to-work-shines-light-on-pro-union-pro-trump-supporters/2018/08/10/6aaa3aae-9c03-11e8-b60b-1c897f17e185_story.html?utm_term=.540c391addfb.

5. Adam Winkler, *Gunfight: The Battle over the Right to Bear Arms in America* (New York: W. W. Norton, 2011), 143.

6. Winkler, *Gunfight*, 210.

7. Winkler, *Gunfight*, 253.

8. Kristen Goss, *Disarmed: The Missing Movement for Gun Control in America* (Princeton, NJ: Princeton University Press, 2006), 21, 29.

9. Goss, *Disarmed*, 160.

10. William T. Horner, *Show-Down in the Show Me State: The Fight over Conceal-and-Carry Gun Laws in Missouri* (Columbia: University of Missouri Press, 2005), 16.

11. Horner, *Show-Down in the Show Me State*, 95.

12. Goss, *Disarmed*, 101.

13. Dennis Hevesi, "Constance E. Cook, at 89; Wrote N.Y. State Abortion Law," *New York Times*, January 25, 2009.

14. Kristin Luker, *Abortion and the Politics of Motherhood* (Berkeley: University of California Press, 1984), 31; Patricia Miller, *Good Catholics: The Battle over Abortion in the Catholic Church* (Berkeley: University of California Press, 2014), 135.

15. Miller, *Good Catholics*, 44.

16. Miller, *Good Catholics*, 74.

17. Cynthia Gorney, *Articles of Faith: A Frontline History of the Abortion Wars* (New York: Simon & Schuster, 1998), 278.

18. Miller, *Good Catholics*, 85.

19. Mary Ziegler, *After Roe: The Lost History of the Abortion Debate* (Cambridge, MA: Harvard University Press, 2015), 107.

20. Meaghan Winter, "Roe v. Wade Was Lost in 1992," Slate, March 27, 2016, www.slate.com/articles/double_x/cover_story/2016/03/how_the_undue_burden_concept_eroded_roe_v_wade.html.

21. Seth Gitell, "Making Sense of McCain-Feingold," *Atlantic*, July/August 2003, www.theatlantic.com/magazine/archive/2003/07/making-sense-of-mccain-feingold-and-campaign-finance-reform/302758/.

22. "American Civil Liberties of Missouri," ProPublica Nonprofit Explorer, https://projects.propublica.org/nonprofits/organizations/320295491; "American Civil Liberties of Missouri Nonprofit Foundation," ProPublica Nonprofit Explorer, https://projects.propublica.org/nonprofits/organizations/436070952; "American Civil Liberties Union of Arkansas," ProPublica Nonprofit Explorer, https://projects.propublica.org/nonprofits/organizations/710467186; "American Civil Liberties Union Foundation Incorporated," ProPublica Nonprofit Explorer, https://projects.propublica.org/nonprofits/organizations/710473676; "American Civil Liberties Union Foundation Inc," ProPublica Nonprofit Explorer, https://projects.propublica.org/nonprofits/organizations/136213516/201842749349301309/IRS990.

CHAPTER THREE

1. Matt Bai, *The Argument: Inside the Battle to Remake Democratic Politics* (New York: Penguin, 2007).

2. John Miller, "America's Best Governor," *National Review*, September 2, 2002, 17.

3. Adam Schrager and Rob Witmer, *The Blueprint: How the Democrats Won Colorado* (Golden, CO: Speaker's Corner Books, 2010).

4. Schrager and Witmer, *Blueprint*.

5. Paul Sullivan, "How Top Philanthropists Wield Power through Their Donations," *New York Times*, April 17, 2017; Joshua Green, "America's Gay Corporate Warrior Wants to Bring Full Equality to Red States," *Bloomberg Businessweek*, April 24, 2015; David Callahan, *Fortunes of Change: The Rise of the Liberal Rich and the Remaking of America* (Hoboken, NJ: John Wiley & Sons, 2010), 146.

6. Thomas E. Cronin and Robert D. Loevy, *Colorado Politics and Policy: Governing a Purple State* (Lincoln: University of Nebraska Press, 2011).

7. Schrager and Witmer, *Blueprint*, 77.

8. Schrager and Witmer, *Blueprint*, 101.

9. Michael Scherer, "Inside Obama's Idea Factory in Washington," *Time*, November 21, 2008; Callahan, *Fortunes of Change*, 147.

10. Katrina vanden Heuvel, "Building a Progressive Majority," *Nation*, December 7, 2003, www.thenation.com/article/building-progressive-majority/.

11. Paul Farhi, "Democratic Spending Is a Team Effort," *Washington Post*, March 24, 2004, A01.

12. Bai, *Argument*, 25.

13. Bai, *Argument*, 63.

14. Thomas Edsall, "Rich Liberals Vow to Fund Think Tanks," *Washington Post*, August 7, 2005, A01.

15. Callahan, *Fortunes of Change*, 155.

16. Joseph McAuley, "The Legacy of Louis Brandeis, 100 Years after His Historical Nomination," Americamagazine.org, January 27, 2016.

17. "Youth Voting," Center for Information & Research on Civic Learning and Engagement, Tufts University, accessed March 7, 2019, https://civicyouth.org/quick-facts/youth-voting/.

18. Michael Roberts, "CU Boulder's Plan to Neuter Student Government Hits a Bump," *Westworld*, April 10, 2018.

19. Lee Drutnam, "Political Divisions in 2016 and Beyond: Tensions between and within the Two Parties," Democracy Fund Voter Study Group, June 2017, www.voterstudygroup.org/publications/2016-elections/political-divisions-in-2016-and-beyond.

20. Sarah Burris, "Naked Vote, New Era's Political Partying," Spark Action, August 27, 2008, https://sparkaction.org/content/naked-vote-new-eras-political-partying.

21. Burris, "Naked Vote."

22. Burris, "Naked Vote."

CHAPTER FOUR

1. Richard Luscombe, "Obama and Clinton Join Forces to Try to Swing the Sunshine State," *Guardian* online, October 20, 2008, www.theguardian.com/world/2008/oct/21/obama-clinton-florida-democrat-election.

2. Arian Campo-Flores and Paul Overberg, "White Retiree Influx Helps Keep Florida in Play for Donald Trump," *Wall Street Journal*, August 29, 2016, www.wsj.com/articles/white-retiree-influx-helps-keep-florida-in-play-for-donald-trump-1472431335.

3. Jonathan Martin, "In Florida, Not All Politics Are Local as Trump Shapes Governor's Race," *New York Times*, July 30, 2018.

4. Susanna Kim, "2010 Had Record 2.9 Million Foreclosures," ABC News, January 2011, https://abcnews.go.com/Business/2010-record-29-million-foreclosures/story?id=12602271; Todd Wright, "Upside Down, Inside Out," NBC, NBCMiami.com, accessed July 20, 2018, www.nbcmiami.com/news/local/Upside-Down-and-Inside-Out-84030882.html; Bureau of Labor and Statistics, US Department of Labor, "Regional and State Unemployment—2010 Annual Averages," BLS press release, February 25, 2011; Li Yanmei, "Geography of Opportunity and Residential Mortgage Foreclosure," *Journal of Urban and Regional Analysis* 3, no. 2 (July 1, 2011).

5. Louis Jacobson, "Looking Back at Howard Dean's 50-State Strategy," *Governing*, May 6, 2013.

6. Alexander Brittel, "Foreclosures Put Spotlight on Sink," Real Deal Miami, accessed July 21, 2018, https://therealdeal.com/miami/2009/05/29/foreclosures-put-spotlight-on-sink-alex-sink-bill-mccollum-governor-race/.

7. Jake Sherman, "CRS Report: Acorn Didn't Break Law," Politico.com, December 22, 2009, www.politico.com/story/2009/12/crs-report-acorn-didnt-break-law-030919; John Atlas, "ACORN Closes Its Last Door, Filing for Bankruptcy," Huffington Post, accessed July 26, 2018, www.huffingtonpost.com/john-atlas/acorn-closes-its-last-doo_b_778047.html.

8. Tom Hamburger and Peter Wallsten, *One Party Country: The Republican Plan for Dominance in the 21st Century* (Hoboken, NJ: John Wiley & Sons, 2006), e-book version.

9. David Colburn, *From Yellow Dog Democrats to Red State Republicans* (Gainesville: University Press of Florida, 2013).

10. Hamburger and Wallsten, *One Party Country*.

11. Colburn, *From Yellow Dog Democrats*.

12. Gray Rohrer, "Number of Women, Hispanics Lags in Tallahassee," *Orlando Sentinel*, May 13, 2016.

13. Hamburger and Wallsten, *One Party Country*.

14. David Colburn, "Role of the Florida Cabinet Has Evolved throughout History," *Gainesville Sun*, March 1, 2015, www.gainesville.com/article/LK/20150301/News/604152884/GS/; Spencer Woodman, "Florida Has Not Held an Employer Responsible for Violating the Minimum Wage since 2011," *Nation*, July 11, 2016.

15. Spencer Woodman, "Remember How Jeb Bush Dismantled Florida's Department of Labor?," In These Times, February 19, 2018, http://inthesetimes.com/working/entry/18899/how_jeb_bush_dismantled_floridas_labor_department.

16. David Daley, *Ratf**ked: The True Story behind the Secret Plan to Steal America's Democracy* (New York: Liveright, 2016).

17. Kenneth Vogel, "Karl Rove and the Modern Money Machine," Politico, July/August 2014; Stephanie Mencimer, "The Man behind Citizens United Is Just Getting Started," *Mother Jones*, May/June 2011.

18. Kurt Eichenwald, "HCA Is Said to Reach Deal on Settlement of Fraud Case," *New York Times*, December 18, 2002; Marc Caputo, "Columbia/HCA Legacy Follows Rick Scott to Governor's Mansion," *Miami Herald*, October 24, 2018.

19. Jim Ruttenberg, "Health Critic Brings a Past and a Wallet," *New York Times*, April 1, 2009; Jerry Markon, "Conservative PR Firm That Repped Swift Boat Vets Now Helping Fight Sotomayor," *Washington Post*, June 13, 2009; John Kennedy, "Smith & Ballard Powerhouse Lobbying Firm Breaks Up, Replaced by Ballard Partners," *Palm Beach Post*, June 10, 2011; Steve Bousquet and Marc Caputo, "McCollum Has Long List of Funding Allies," *Bradenton Herald*, August 17, 2010.

20. NBC, "22-Mile-Long Oily Plume Mapped near BP Well Site," NBC.com, August 19, 2010, www.nbcnews.com/id/38770508/ns/disaster_in_the_gulf/t/-mile-long-oily-plume-mapped-near-bp-well-site/#.W66NXxNKjxp.

21. Bryony Jones, "BP Profits Hit $5.3 Billion, Year on from Oil Spill," CNN.com, July 26, 2011, http://edition.cnn.com/2011/BUSINESS/07/26/bp.profits.dudley/index.html; Hugo Martin and Ronald D. White, "Spill May Cost Gulf Coast $22.7 Billion in Tourism, Study Estimates," *Los Angeles Times*, July 23, 2010.

22. Jill Treanor and Julia Kollewe, "Robo-signing Eviction Scandal Rattles Wall Street," *Guardian*, October 13, 2010.

23. Nathaniel Rich, "Losing Earth: The Decade We Almost Stopped Climate Change," *New York Times*, August 1, 2018; Nina Banerjee, Lisa Song, and David Hasemyer, "Exxon: The Road Not Taken," Inside Climate News, September 16, 2015, https://insideclimatenews.org/content/Exxon-The-Road-Not-Taken.

24. Cristina Silva, "Rick Scott Says 700,000 Illegal Immigrants Take Jobs," Politifact.com, August 18, 2010, www.politifact.com/florida/statements/2010/aug/18/rick-scott/rick-scott-says-illegal-immigrants-taking-jobs/; Marc Caputo, "Trump Hires Pollster and Former Scott Advisor Tony Fabrizio," Politico, May 16, 2016, www.politico.com/states/florida/story/2016/05/trump-hires-top-pollster-and-former-scott-adviser-tony-fabrizio-101771; Jules Darmanin, "Marine Le Pen Worked with Trump's Campaign Pollster in the Closing Days of the French Election," BuzzFeed News, January 15, 2018, www.buzzfeednews.com/article/julesdarmanin/trump-pollster-marine-le-pen#.ohVKdjLMX; Lloyd Dunkelberger, "McCollum Draws on Political Experience," *Sarasota Herald-Tribune*, August 15, 2010.

25. Lloyd Dunkelberger, "Capital Comment: Can Scott Unite Florida GOP?," *Sarasota Herald-Tribune*, August 29, 2010, www.heraldtribune.com/news/20100829/capital-comment-can-scott-unite-florida-gop.

26. Robert Trigaux, "Why Do Florida Metro Areas Dominate the Nation for Fraud Complaints?," *Tampa Bay Times*, March 6, 2015; Jay Weaver, "South Florida Still No. 1 for Healthcare Fraud, following Massive Takedown across the Nation," *Miami Herald*, June 28, 2018; Tim Padgett, "Is Florida Ready for Governor Rick Scott?," Time.com, December 23, 2010, http://content.time.com/time/politics/article/0,8599,2039510,00.html; Scott Powers, "Scott, Crist, Raised Most of Their Cash through PACs," *Orlando Sentinel*, February 1, 2015.

27. Anthony Man and Scott Wyman, "Gloves Come off Again as Alex Sink and Rick Scott Face Off in Debate," *Sun Sentinel*, October 20, 2010, www.sun-sentinel.com/news/fl-xpm-2010-10-20-fl-governor-debate-nova-20101020-story.html.

28. Jeff Ostrowski, "Attorney Who Sued Bank of America Says Sink Had Nothing to Do with Securities Fraud," *Palm Beach Post*, October 6, 2010; Aaron Scharockman, "Alex Sink Faces Her Own Fraud Charges at CNN / St. Petersburg Times Gubernatorial Debate," Politifact.com, October 26, 2010, www.politifact

.com/florida/statements/2010/oct/26/rick-scott/alex-sink-faces-her-own-fraud-charges-cnnst-peters/.

29. John Koenig, "Taking Stock after a Sleepy Session," *Florida Trend* 31, no. 3 (July 1988): 15; John C. Van Gieson, "Businesses Battling Workplace Bills; New Rules Would Pinch Wallets," *Orlando Sentinel*, April 23, 1989, D1.

30. William Branigin, "Obama Reflects on 'Shellacking' in Midterms," *Washington Post*, November 3, 2010.

31. Steve Bousquet, "Alex Sink Regrets Defeat to Rick Scott in 2010, Thinks about 2014 Rematch," *Tampa Bay Times*, February 20, 2012.

CHAPTER FIVE

1. Danielle Kurtzleben, "Planned Parenthood Investigations Find No Fetal Tissue Sales," NPR, January 28, 2016.

2. "Missouri Clinic to Keep Abortion License during Court Battle," Associated Press, December 28, 2015.

3. Meaghan Winter, "Why National Pro-choice Groups Are Giving Up in the Very States That Need Them Most," Splinter, October 12, 2016, https://splinternews.com/why-national-pro-choice-groups-are-giving-up-in-the-ver-1793862750.

4. "District of Columbia v. Heller," Oyez, https://www.oyez.org/cases/2007/07-290; Marc Joseph Stern, "The Supreme Court Is Preparing to Make Every State's Gun Laws Look Like Texas," Slate, January 22, 2019, https://slate.com/news-and-politics/2019/01/supreme-court-new-york-gun-case-heller.html.

5. Eric Wemple, "NPR Issues Large Correction about Gun Control Activist," *Washington Post*, June 23, 2016; Bruce Horovitz, "Gun Control Group: 'Skip Starbucks Saturday,'" *USA Today*, August 21, 2013.

6. Wemple, "NPR Issues Large Correction."

7. Cheng Cheng and Mark Hoekstra, "Does Strengthening Self-Defense Law Deter Crime or Escalate Violence? Evidence from Castle Doctrine," *Journal of Human Resources* 48, no. 3 (2013): 821–859; Mallory Daily, Jo Mannies, and Jason Rosenbaum, "Missouri General Assembly Votes to Expand Legal Use of Deadly Force Known as Stand Your Ground," St. Louis Public Radio, NPR, May 13, 2016, http://news.stlpublicradio.org/post/missouri-general-assembly-votes-expand-legal-use-deadly-force-known-stand-your-ground#stream/0.

8. Sam Dotson, letter to the editor, *St. Louis Post-Dispatch*, September 23, 2016.

9. Jason Hancock, "Republican Donor David Humphreys Spending Big to Oust Missouri Republicans," *Kansas City Star*, July 4, 2016.

10. Shelia Solon, interviewed by Brian Ellison and Matt Hodapp, *Statehouse Blend*, KCUR, August 28, 2016.

11. Darin Straus, "Missouri's $10M Man," Politico, August 14, 2017, https://www.politico.com/tipsheets/morning-score/2017/08/14/missouris-10-million-man-221850; Fang Lee, "King Rex," Politico, July/August 2014; Alan Greenblatt, "Rex Sinquefield," *Governing*, June 2015.

12. Paul Kiel, "The Payday Playbook: How Lenders Fight to Stay Legal," ProPublica, August 2, 2013, www.propublica.org/article/how-high-cost-lenders-fight-to-stay-legal.

13. Kevin McDermott, "Progressive Donor George Soros Bigfoots into Missouri Ballot Fight over Redistricting, Ethics," *St. Louis Post-Dispatch*, January 29, 2018.

14. Koran Addo, "Bill Protecting Women against Discrimination for Having an Abortion Passes in St. Louis City Hall," *St. Louis Post-Dispatch*, February 11, 2017.

15. "Police Arrest 70 at First Day of Kavanaugh Hearings," *Washington Post*, September 4, 2018, video.

CHAPTER SIX

1. John Daley, "9 Numbers to Know about the Colorado Impact of the Affordable Care Act," Colorado Public Radio, March 8, 2017, www.cpr.org/news/story/9-numbers-to-know-about-the-colorado-impact-of-the-affordable-care-act.

2. "Gun Rights Supporters Rally at State Capitol," CBS Denver, January 19, 2013, https://denver.cbslocal.com/2013/01/19/gun-rights-supporters-rally-at-state-capitol/.

3. "Colorado Governor Signs Landmark Gun Bills," Associated Press, March 19, 2013, www.denverpost.com/2013/03/19/colorado-governor-signs-landmark-gun-bills/.

4. Jack Healy, "Colorado Lawmakers Ousted in Recall Vote over Gun Law," *New York Times*, September 11, 2013.

5. Margot Sanger-Katz, "Overdose Deaths Reached Record: 72,000 Last Year," *New York Times*, August 16, 2018, A1.

6. Liz Farmer, "Taxpayers Have Their Own Bill of Rights, but Who Benefits?," *Governing*, October 2017.

7. John Frank, "Koch Political Group AFP Wants Lawmakers to Sign TABOR Pledge," *Denver Post*, January 6, 2016; "Policy Basics: Taxpayers Bill of Rights," Center on Budget and Policy Priorities, last modified June 26, 2017, www.cbpp.org/research/state-budget-and-tax/policy-basics-taxpayer-bill-of-rights-tabor.

8. "State Map of Laws and Policies," Human Rights Campaign, accessed November 19, 2018, www.hrc.org/state-maps/housing.

9. Esteban Hernandez, "Colorado's Young Voters Are Expected to Turn Out and Focus on Issues," *Denverite*, June 4, 2018, https://denverite.com/2018/06/04/colorado-young-voters/; https://denverite.com/2018/06/04/colorado-young-voters/; Lizzy Stephan, e-mail to author, February 6, 2019.

10. Kate Brumbeck, "Lawsuit Challenging Georgia Election Process Filed by Stacey Abrams–Backed Group," PBS.org, November 27, 2018, www.pbs.org/newshour/politics/lawsuit-challenging-georgia-election-process-filed-by-stacey-abrams-backed-group.

11. Matt Ferner, "This Is How to Fight Big Energy Companies in Your Local Community," Huffington Post, September 4, 2013, www.huffingtonpost.com/2013/09/04/this-is-how-to-take-on-bi_n_3867003.html; "Boulder Municipalization (2B and 2C)," *Boulder Weekly*, November 1, 2011, www.boulderweekly.com/news/boulder-municipalization-2b-and-2c/.

12. "CFPB Sues Nation's Largest Student Loan Company Navient for Failing Borrowers at Every Stage of Repayment," Consumer Financial Protection Bureau online, January 18, 2017, www.consumerfinance.gov/about-us/newsroom/cfpb-sues-nations-largest-student-loan-company-navient-failing-borrowers-every-stage-repayment/.

13. "Report: Colorado Suicide Rate Climbs," *Denver Post*, May 3, 2016, www.denverpost.com/2016/05/03/report-colorado-suicide-rate-climbs/.

14. Andrew Kennedy, "Supervised Drug Injection Facilities Face Uphill Fight at Colorado Statehouse," *Denverite*, January 22, 2018, www.denverite.com/2018/01/22/safe-injection-law-colorado/; Jennifer Ng, Christy Sutherland, and Michael R. Kolber, "Does Evidence Support Supervised Injection Sites?," *Canadian Family Physician* 63, no. 11 (November 2017): 866.

15. Lynn Bartels, "Colorado's Neville Family Growing into a Political Dynasty," *Denver Post*, December 28, 2013.

16. Glenn Thrush and Stacy Cowly, "Mulvaney Downgrades Student Loan Unit in Consumer Bureau Reshuffle," *New York Times*, May 9, 2018.

17. Sandra Fish, "Super PAC Money Dominated 2018 Election and Democrats Controlled the Cash Race," *Colorado Sun*, December 10, 2018, www.coloradosun.com/2018/12/10/campaign-finance-2018-colorado-super-pac/.

CHAPTER SEVEN

1. Amy Sherman, "Charlie Crist Says Rick Scott Cut K–12 by $1.3 Billion in His First Year and Higher Ed by $300 Million in His Second," Politifact.com, November 11, 2013, https://www.politifact.com/florida/statements/2013/nov/11/charlie-crist/charlie-crist-says-rick-scott-cut-k-12-13-billion-/; Noreen Marcus, "In Florida, Medicaid Is a Matter of Life and Death," *U.S. News & World Report*, August 14, 2017, www.usnews.com/news/best-states/articles/2017-08-14/in-florida-medicaid-is-a-matter-of-life-and-death; Christine Sexton, "Florida Uninsured Rate Tops National Average," *News Service of Florida*, September 12, 2018; Carl Hiaasen, "The Fight over Enterprise Florida Is a Power Play—and Millions Are at Stake," *Miami Herald*, February 18, 2017, www.miamiherald.com/opinion/opn-columns-blogs/carl-hiaasen/article133580844.html; John Kennedy, "Scott Touts More Jobs, but Analysis Shows Pay Is Subpar," *Florida Times Union*, August 4, 2018; Robert Trigaux, "United Way: 44 Percent of Florida Households, Mostly Working Poor, Struggle to Meet Basic Needs," *Tampa Bay Times*, February 22, 2017.

2. Dan Kam, "After 700M in Water District Cuts, Florida Governor Wants $2.4M More," *Palm Beach Post*, December 6, 2011.

3. Gabrielle Russon, "Florida Tourism: 116.5M Visitors Set Record Despite Hurricane Irma," *Orlando Sentinel*, March, 20, 2018, www.orlandosentinel.com/business/tourism/os-bz-florida-vacation-2017-tourism-116-million-20180320-story.html; Katie Sanders and Amy Sherman, "Will Weatherford Says 1,000 People a Day Move to Florida Because of Freedom," Politifact.com, April 2, 2013, www.politifact.com/florida/statements/2013/apr/02/will-weatherford/will-weatherford-says-1000-people-day-move-florida/; John Kennedy, "Florida's Job Growth Brisk, but Relatively Low Wages," *Gainesville Sun*, August 4, 2018; Leanna

Garfield, "The Largest Mall in the US Is Coming to Miami, and It Will Have a Massive Indoor Water Park and Ice Rink," *Business Insider*, May 25, 2018, www.businessinsider.com/largest-mall-us-american-dream-miami-2018-5.

4. "Florida Governor Rick Scott Inaugural Address," State of Florida website, accessed February 6, 2019, www.flgov.com/florida-governor-rick-scott-inaugural-address-2/.

5. Hope Kudo, "Stealing in the Shadows," *Harvard Political Review*, September 8, 2018, http://harvardpolitics.com/united-states/stealing-in-the-shadows-state-level-political-corruption/; Jeremy Wallace, "Here's How Much Florida Paid Pitbull to Promote Its 'Sexy Beaches,'" *Miami Herald*, December 15, 2016; Mary Ellen Klas, "Sen. Frank Artiles Updates His Report to Reflect Nearly $2,000 in Travel, Food, Expenses from FPL," *Miami Herald*, March 17, 2017, http://miamiherald.typepad.com/nakedpolitics/2017/03/sen-frank-artiles-updates-his-report-to-reflect-nearly-2000-in-travel-food-and-expenses-from-fpl.html.

6. Abby Rabinowitz and Amanda Simson, "The Dirty Secret of the World's Plan to Avert Climate Disaster," *Wired*, December 10, 2017, www.wired.com/story/the-dirty-secret-of-the-worlds-plan-to-avert-climate-disaster/.

7. Olivia Milman, "How the Trump Administration Is Rolling Back Plans for Clean Power," *Guardian* online, August 21, 2018, www.theguardian.com/environment/2018/aug/21/epa-clean-power-plan-rollback-affordable-energy-rule.

8. Alan Stonecipher, Brad Ashwell, and Ben Wilcox, *Power Play Redux: Political Influence of Florida's Top Energy Corporations* (Tallahassee: Integrity Florida, 2018); Mary Ellen Klas, "FPL Drafted Portions of Bill That Puts Tough Requirements on Rooftop Solar Companies," *Miami Herald*, April 5, 2017, https://www.miamiherald.com/news/politics-government/state-politics/article142904899.html.

9. Eric Barton, "In Sunshine State, Big Energy Blocks Solar Power," Florida Center for Investigative Reporting, April 3, 2015, https://fcir.org/2015/04/03/in-sunshine-state-big-energy-blocks-solar-power/.

10. "Editorial: Scott's Terrible Choice for Public Service Commission," *Tampa Bay Times*, October 5, 2017; Mary Ellen Klas, "Gov. Rick Scott Appoints Lawmaker to Public Service Commission," *Miami Herald*, September 18, 2014, https://www.miamiherald.com/news/politics-government/state-politics/article2154097.html; Ivan Penn, "Florida Regulators Approve Plan to Gut Energy Efficiency Goals, End Solar Power Rebates," *Tampa Bay Times*, November 25, 2014; "Renewable Energy," Next Era Energy, accessed March 19, 2019, http://www.nexteraenergy.com/sustainability/environment/renewable-energy.html.

11. Everglades Foundation, *2016 Impact Report*, www.evergladesfoundation.org/wp-content/uploads/sites/2/2018/07/EF-Annual-Report-2016_Final-Rev_Lores-Single.pdf.

12. Everglades Foundation, "Eric Eikenberg Applauds Governor Rick Scott's Everglades Budget Proposal," January 27, 2015, https://www.evergladesfoundation.org/eric-eikenberg-applauds-governor-rick-scotts-everglades-budget-proposal/.

13. "Special Interests behind Anti-solar Ballot Initiative Consumers for Smart Solar," Energy and Policy Institute, press release, November 16, 2015, www.energyandpolicy.org/special-interests-behind-anti-solar-ballot-initiative-consumers-for-smart-solar/.

14. Stonecipher, Ashwell, and Wilcox, *Power Play Redux*.

15. Tim Dickinson, "The Koch Brothers' Dirty War on Solar Power," *Rolling Stone*, February 11, 2016, www.rollingstone.com/politics/politics-news/the-koch-brothers-dirty-war-on-solar-power-193325/.

16. Mary Ellen Klas, "Insider Reveals Deceptive Strategy behind Florida's Solar Amendment," *Miami Herald*, October 18, 2016, www.miamiherald.com/news/politics-government/election/article109017387.html.

17. Chris Marr, "Miami Beach Minimum Wage Lawsuit Heads to Florida High Court," *Bloomberg News*, August 29, 2018, www.bna.com/miami-beach-minimum-n73014482107/; Ina Paiva Cordle, "Proposed Miami-Dade Ordinance Would Require Sick Leave for Employees," *Miami Herald*, October 18, 2012; Bryce Covert, "Florida's Governor Signs Business-Backed Bill Banning Paid Sick Leave," Think Progress, June 17, 2013, https://thinkprogress.org/floridas-governor-signs-business-backed-bill-banning-paid-sick-leave-f24780b4d21b/.

18. "Our Grants," Ford Foundation, "Past Grants," no. 17320, Organize Florida Education Fund, 2017, https://www.fordfoundation.org/work/our-grants/.

19. Madison Pauly, "Thanks to Trump's Family Separations, Democrats Are in the Hot Seat for Taking Private Prison Cash," *Mother Jones*, June 30, 2018, www.motherjones.com/politics/2018/07/thanks-to-trumps-family-separations-democrats-are-in-the-hot-seat-for-taking-private-prison-cash/.

20. David Smiley and Alex Daugherty, "DeSantis Says Florida Shouldn't 'Monkey This Up' by Electing Gillum," *Miami Herald*, August 29, 2018, www.miamiherald.com/news/politics-government/state-politics/article217507400.html; Felicia Sonmez and Tim Craig, "White Supremacist Targets Florida's Andrew Gillum in Racist Robocall," *Washington Post*, October 23, 2018, www.washingtonpost.com/politics/white-supremacist-group-targets-floridas-andrew-gillum-in-new-racist-robocall/2018/10/23/; Eugene Scott, "'Racists Think He's a Racist': Gillum on White Supremacists' Support for DeSantis," *Washington Post*, October 25, 2018, www.washingtonpost.com/politics/2018/10/25/racists-think-hes-racist-gillum-white-supremacists-support-desantis/?utm_term=.476c8b2ddc07.

21. Madeline Berg, "Why Out-of-State Billionaires Have Gotten behind This Democrat in Florida," *Forbes* online, November 2, 2018, www.forbes.com/sites/maddieberg/2018/11/02/why-out-of-state-billionaires-have-gotten-behind-this-democrat-in-florida/#62f6d521c3b0.

22. Lawrence Mower, "Amendment 4 Will Likely Cost Millions to Carry Out. Here's Why," *Tampa Bay Times*, April 4, 2019, https://www.tampabay.com/florida-politics/2019/04/04/amendment-4-will-likely-cost-millions-to-carry-out-heres-why/.

INDEX

Meaghan Winter has written for many publications, including *New York Magazine*, *Bloomberg Businessweek*, *Cosmopolitan*, *Essence*, the *Believer*, Slate, and *The Best Magazine Writing*. She lives in New York City. This is her first book.